MUDDY

MUDDY

WHERE FAITH AND POLYGAMY COLLIDE

A HISTORICAL NOVEL

BOOK ONE

DEAN HUGHES

DESERET
BOOK

SALT LAKE CITY, UTAH

© 2019 Dean Hughes

All rights reserved. No part of this book may be reproduced in any form or by any means without permission in writing from the publisher, Deseret Book Company, at permissions@deseretbook.com or PO Box 30178, Salt Lake City, Utah 84130. This work is not an official publication of The Church of Jesus Christ of Latter-day Saints. The views expressed herein are the responsibility of the author and do not necessarily represent the position of the Church or of Deseret Book Company.

This is a work of fiction. Characters and events in this book are products of the author's imagination or are represented fictitiously.

Deseret Book is a registered trademark of Deseret Book Company.

Visit us at deseretbook.com

Library of Congress Cataloging-in-Publication Data
CIP data on file
ISBN 978-1-62972-585-7

Printed in the United States of America
Lake Book Manufacturing, Inc., Melrose Park, IL

10 9 8 7 6 5 4 3 2 1

For my granddaughter
Carrie Lenore Hughes

A NOTE TO THE READER

As you read this novel, you may wonder whether I have been accurate in portraying not only Brigham Young but also the Saints he led. We often speak in reverent tones about the people we call "the pioneers," but they were human, and Brigham Young was both a prophet and a man. I think it's important for us to remember that.

"Brother Brigham," as the Saints called him, served not only as President Young (1847–1877) but also as Governor Young during the early Utah period (1851–1858). But even when he no longer functioned in an official governmental capacity, he was director of more than a religious organization. He was the principal planner for the settlement of a large part of the western United States. When he asked people to settle a new region of the territory, he hoped they would catch the vision of living as a Zion people, but he also felt obligated to advise them about irrigation canals, choice of crops, provisions to take along, and many other practical matters.

In a sermon delivered in the Tabernacle on Sunday, December 11, 1864, President Young stated his view of temporal matters very simply: "In the mind of God there is no such a thing as dividing spiritual from temporal, or temporal from spiritual; for they are one in the Lord" (in *Journal of Discourses,* 11:18). I believe as Latter-day Saints we conceive of the spiritual and temporal worlds as two parts of a grand unity.

It might not be easy for current Church members to imagine a prophet so intimately involved in ordinary-life decisions, but there is no question that a strong leader was needed in these formative years, and the integration of Church matters and government matters was advantageous, even necessary.

Modern leaders still offer advice about temporal matters: we have been taught to plant gardens and raise our own food, store commodities for emergencies, stay out of debt, exercise our right to vote, and prepare ourselves for careers. But these are general principles. Brigham Young was much more specific. Early Church members believed in obedience, but this is the crucial point: then, as now, they also defended their right to think for themselves. President Young himself encouraged this, saying, "I am more afraid that this people have so much confidence in their leaders that they will not inquire for themselves of God whether they are led by Him" (in *Journal of Discourses,* 9:150).

This conflict between independence and obedience was especially important in choosing whether to enter plural marriage. Even to mention this subject probably causes some modern readers to say, "That's where I would have drawn the line. No one would have talked me into marrying a married man (or taking more than one wife)." In other words, in any age, people have had to struggle with religious conviction and deep-seated personal standards.

For current members to understand questions of obedience and agency in the nineteenth-century Church is a little like boarding a time machine and stepping out into a slightly different world. We think we know the people we call pioneers, but, in truth, we actually know more legend than reality.

A NOTE TO THE READER

Understanding polygamy is an even greater challenge. If we take with us our twenty-first-century attitudes about love and marriage (and, especially, physical intimacy), we cannot get beyond the revulsion we now experience when trying to imagine ourselves living what the early Saints called "the principle."

So this note is actually a bit of a warning. You are about to take that leap in time into a Latter-day Saint world that we think we ought to be able to understand, but one that operates on subtly different assumptions. We do understand our personal desires for independence, but we may not comprehend how far-reaching the authority of the prophet was at that time. And yet, the similarities between then and now are more important than the differences. In each age, we have to decide how deeply we are committed to obedience and what part of ourselves we cling to and hold as untouchable. Sometimes those decisions can feel a little muddy.

When it comes to polygamy, our life experience actually works against our understanding. We must be ready to grant the faith and religious devotion that lay behind the practice. We must cast away the shame many people today feel that our church once authorized and encouraged that kind of life. Importantly, we need to look to our own heritage. Like many modern Saints, I am the descendant of polygamous families. They made hard choices and lived a difficult law as best they could. It's time that we honor our heritage rather than duck our heads and change the subject.

That is what I have attempted to do on these pages.

—DEAN HUGHES

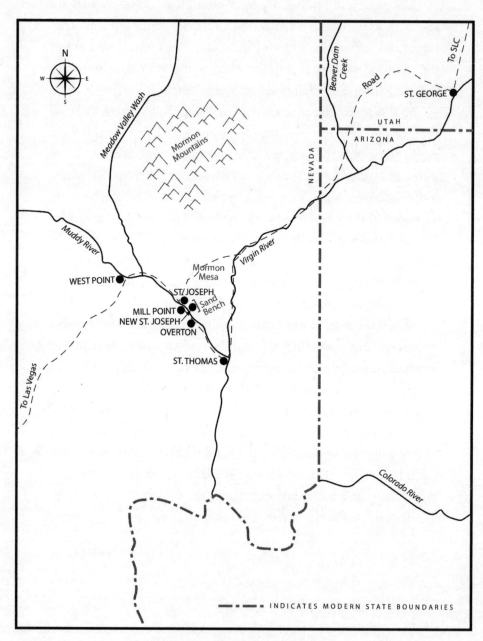

The Muddy River Settlements

CHAPTER I

Morgan Davis, sitting alongside his friend Eb Crawford, was waiting outside President Brigham Young's office. Morgan was nervous, but Eb was sitting back with his eyes closed, surely tired after their long ride that morning. Morgan wished he could be that calm, but he wasn't. He could hear his own heart pounding in his ears. He was fairly sure he knew what this was all about, so he had been practicing his response—silently repeating words that he had tried to memorize these last few days. He definitely didn't want to go on a mission, if that was what Brigham wanted. He didn't mind working hard—in fact, he liked to work—but his bishop had asked him to speak in church a few months back, and he had stood at the pulpit, soft in the legs, his knees shaking. He was sure he had made a fool of himself in front of his entire ward. He had known what he wanted to say, but his words had tumbled out in mumbled bursts, nothing making any sense even to him.

Since that day, Morgan had known that the last thing he wanted to do was to tramp off somewhere in the world to preach the gospel. It wasn't that he doubted the things he had been taught in church all his life; he just didn't trust his tongue—or his legs—to hold up when he had to face a crowd. So when his bishop had informed him that Brother Brigham wanted to meet with him in

Salt Lake City, Morgan had made up his mind instantly. He would have to say no and face the consequences. If President Young chose to kick him out of the Church, so be it. There was no way to get water to run uphill; he wasn't going to try to turn himself into something he wasn't.

The door swung open, and there was Brigham, stout as a bear. He slapped his hands together with considerable force, the sound echoing off the walls. "It's a cold day, boys," he said. "I think winter's coming early this year." He glanced from Morgan to Eb and then back again. "Who's first?"

Morgan had no idea. He took a quick look at Eb, but by then Brigham was saying, "Are you the Davis boy?"

"Yes, sir."

"I can see that. You have your mother's features. Come on in. It doesn't matter a whit which one of you goes first, but I'll make you the first to squirm." He broke into a baritone laugh and stepped to Morgan and Eb and gave them each a firm handshake. Then he turned and walked with heavy strides back into his office, stopping at a pedestal table in the center of the room. "Come on in. Sit down, Brother Davis," he was already saying by the time Morgan reached the door.

Morgan had wondered what sort of grand room this might be, located as it was between Brigham's two fine houses, joining them. But the office wasn't fancy: just the table and four chairs, a small oak desk by one wall, and a tall cabinet on the other side. There was a fireplace, but no fire, and a round floral painting above the mantel. Now that Morgan saw it, he thought the simplicity of the room made sense. Brother Brigham always preached that members of the Church should wear plain, homespun clothes. He especially hated to see women decorate themselves with ribbons and bows and "gew-gaws." Morgan thought the President would be wrong to take that attitude with the members and then perch himself on a golden throne.

But still, Brigham's suit of clothes appeared well tailored. He was wearing a dark knee-length frock coat over a tan waistcoat, and a broad necktie, tied in a bow and stuck through with a silver stickpin. He had also set his silk top hat on his writing desk. Morgan was suddenly self-conscious about his own clothes. He had dressed for riding a horse all day—in denim trousers and a heavy shirt—not for a church meeting.

President Young slid out one of the padded chairs and sat down, then motioned for Morgan to do the same. "So, is your harvest all in, Brother Davis?"

"Pretty much. We still have—"

"You work with your father on his farm, as I understand it."

"That's right. So far. I hope to have my own—"

"Did you ride down this morning?"

"Yes. We got up early, started out at four o'clock." Morgan had walked in with his church hat in his hand, and now he wasn't sure what to do with it. He thought of sliding his chair back a little and setting it on his lap, but that seemed awkward, so he reached over the arm of the chair and set it on the floor.

"Four o'clock. Oh, my. Well, don't try to make it back today. Come here and have supper with me tonight and I'll introduce you to my flock of pretty daughters. I'm sure they'd like to lay eyes on a brawny boy like you."

Morgan laughed and shook his head in denial, and at the same time made up his mind not to accept the invitation. He was nervous enough without having to meet a "flock" of daughters. Besides, if this conversation went the way he expected, he would much rather ride seventeen miles on horseback than spend the evening chatting with Brigham and his family. "We've gotta get back to—"

"I'm sorry I was a little late coming in just now. The folks in this Church have got it in their heads that I have to solve every problem, attend every meeting, perform every marriage. I'm surprised they manage to feed themselves or strap on their own boots."

Morgan smiled at Brigham's complaint and at the emphatic way he waved his thick finger in the air. But in spite of all his vigor and bluster, he looked older than Morgan remembered. He figured the prophet must be well over sixty now, and his hair and beard, reddish at one time, had grayed a good deal lately. More than that, the lines around his eyes had deepened—or maybe Morgan had simply not seen him this close up before.

President Young clapped his hands together again, blew on them. "It's cold in here. I should have had a fire laid. But the day before yesterday it was sixty degrees. That's November for you, I guess." Morgan was trying to think what to say when Brigham continued as though he hadn't changed the subject at all. "Do you know anything about the Muddy River Mission?"

"Yes, sir. You called Thomas Smith and Ewan Morrison, from Farmington, to serve down there. I think you wanted them to grow cotton."

"Well, yes. That's part of it. We sent down a company of settlers with Brother Smith a couple of years back—early '65—and we made him the president down there. Brother Morrison followed last year, and I guess you know, Thomas Smith got sick, so just recently, we told him to come home for a rest. He may not be able to go back. But the people we've called have managed to build up two little towns on the Muddy, just a few miles apart. Now we need more folks to strengthen those settlements and get a solid foothold established."

Morgan realized now what Brigham wanted of him. He tried to think how he felt about it. He was relieved that it wasn't a call to preach, but the reports from Brother Smith were that the Muddy, which was in the desert south of St. George, was as lonely and desolate as any spot in the territory.

President Young was now looking at Morgan as though he expected him to say something. But the only words Morgan came up with were, "I hear it's hot as blazes down there."

"Of course it is. That's the whole idea. It's not just cotton that does well there—all sorts of crops thrive in that warm weather. Every kind of grain, sugar cane, grapes, squash, melons—everything. The growing season lasts almost year round. They cut lucerne hay five or six times a year. But there's more to it than that. Did you get any sense from Brother Smith what we're trying to accomplish down there?" The President put his hands flat on the table and leaned closer, with his green eyes, still and confident, locked on Morgan.

"Well, I'm not sure. I guess we have a great need for cotton . . . and maybe . . ."

Brother Brigham's lips stretched, twitched, and he suddenly sat back. "It doesn't matter how much I preach to this people. Not one of you comprehends—not fully—what it means to be part of the kingdom of God."

Morgan didn't think he deserved that. He had long thought that President Young was too quick to tell the Saints that they didn't amount to much. Morgan didn't look away, but he also didn't say anything.

The President fiddled with his necktie that slouched below his beard. He took his time, as though he wanted Morgan to stew in his own discomfort. "Yes, we need to grow our own cotton. We can't keep shipping it in from across the country—or, worse yet, buy ready-made clothing from the East. I know you've heard me talk about self-sufficiency. Do you understand what I'm trying to say to the Saints?"

Morgan pretended the question wasn't meant to be answered.

"Son, listen to me. We cannot rely on Gentiles to ship their goods out here and take all the profits back to the States. We have to grow our own food, weave our own cloth, make our own clothing. We have to develop our own business enterprises. It's not just a matter of providing for ourselves. It's a matter of telling the government and all the Gentiles to mind their own business. And it's a matter of the Spirit. When we work together, build up a Zion society, we also build strength to survive the hardships that are ever mounting in these latter days. That's what I think of every day of my life—bringing the people together into a holy society in which all of us love the Lord and respect one another. Do you glimpse that idea at all?"

Morgan nodded. "I think so."

But that was apparently the wrong thing to say. Brigham tossed his head back and looked at the ceiling, as though baffled by Morgan's stupidity. Morgan felt ready to get up and tell the President that he didn't like being treated that way. He had no desire to go off to some dry-as-bones desert to farm cotton anyway.

But Brigham's tone changed, mellowed, when he said, "Some of these things we have to figure out a little at a time, and we have to keep growing in understanding. You'll understand in time, Brother Davis. It will be good for you to take on a stiff challenge and find out what you're made of. And I believe you'll be up to it."

The President seemed to think that Morgan had already accepted, and he hadn't. But again, he said nothing.

"Before I called Thomas Smith, I sent Anson Call down to the Colorado River, not far from where you'll be settling. We built a warehouse there, and we've tried to bring products from the East across the Isthmus of Panama, up the West Coast, and then up the Colorado on steamboats. But it's not working out the way I hoped. Since the War Between the States has ended, this new railroad across the country is coming fast, and it will be cheaper to bring products and new converts in on trains than by water. But the thing is, that was only one part of what we were trying to do. Yes, I want to fill up all of the territory with our people, but when we call our members to settle and build up a new area, we're building *people* more than towns. The Muddy Valley is a hard place to live, no doubt about it, but it builds character, and those who settle that country will pass their strength on to generations to come."

That was all well and good, but what Morgan really wanted was to farm land like his father's—and, if possible, live not very far from his family. He thought he could be a strong man—and pass on his strength—without going so far away.

"How old are you, Brother Davis?"

"Twenty-two."

"Well, you're young. You'll understand all this in time. Brother Morrison says you're a hardworking young man, moral, and clean living. Is that right?"

"I try to be."

"What does that mean?"

Morgan knew immediately that he should have said "yes" and nothing more. "Well, I've mostly given up chewing tobacco, but last year I drove a wagon back to Florence, Nebraska, on one of your down-and-back expeditions. The days were long and . . . I don't know . . . I went back to the stuff. My father thinks that's about the dirtiest habit there is, and I know he's right. So I've been trying to quit again."

"Well, son, I've had the same struggle with tobacco for years and years. So I won't say too much about that. Still, I want you to break the habit now. Can you do that?"

"Yes. I'm sure I can."

"But more important, are you willing to join this new company that's setting out in two weeks or so—and settle in that Muddy River country?"

"How long would I—"

"It's not that kind of mission. We want you to move there, settle in, maybe spend your whole life there."

Morgan felt sick. This sounded like a death sentence. But he didn't say no. Not yet. Still, he knew he was going to do that—as soon as he got his nerve up.

"You'll need a yoke of oxen—two yokes would be better—a sturdy wagon, and what household goods you can haul with you. Pots and pans and all that sort of thing. Is that something you can put together?"

"I guess I could. My father might have to help me with some of that."

"I know your father. He loves God, and he loves the kingdom. He'll sacrifice if he has to, but he'll make sure you have what you need."

Morgan nodded. He thought that was true, but he also knew it would not be easy. His father had a good team of oxen and some strong draft horses, but he couldn't spare any of them. Buying a new pair of oxen would be expensive, and two yokes impossible. Maybe that was something he could tell Brigham: that he just couldn't afford to go off on his own at this point in his life.

"I understand you're not married," the President continued. "You'll need to take care of that. I want you to take a wife with you, and I want you to raise a family. That's the point of this, to build up a population and make that desert blossom as a rose."

Morgan felt as though he were going to pass out and slip right off his chair. Get married in two weeks? He could only think to say, "I don't know who I'd marry, President. I don't think I could do that."

"Son, you're a big, strapping boy, a lot prettier than you need to be with those robin-egg eyes of yours. There's girls everywhere in this territory who would sign up to marry you on the spot. All you have to do is ask. Will you do that? And will you answer the Lord's call?"

What was Morgan supposed to say to that? He had lost his power of speech—and yet, he found himself nodding.

"You'll be traveling with a fine group of people—about fifty families, I hope. And most of them will be young, like yourself. I've already told some other men that they need to find themselves wives before they go, so you won't be the only one in that fix. But you'll all do it, and you'll bring new life to the settlers we've already sent to the Muddy. You'll start your families there, and your children will grow up in the desert chasing lizards and having a grand time. They'll think it's the only way to live."

"I guess that's right," was all Morgan could think to say.

"All right. If you're heading back today, think all the way about which of the young ladies up there in Farmington you might like to marry, and start asking tomorrow. Then bring the one you choose down here to the Endowment House and we'll seal you for time and all eternity. But don't choose some silly little thing who won't hold up in that desert heat. She needs to be as sturdy as you are and ready for some hard years."

Morgan nodded again. For now, he just wanted to get out of the office. Maybe in a day or two he could send a letter and say that he couldn't find a wife and had decided not to go. But he couldn't bring himself to say that to the President's face.

Brother Brigham looked down at a sheet of paper on his desk. "Was that Ebenezer Crawford out in the waiting room?"

"Yes."

"Send him in—but don't warn him." Brigham broke out into a full laugh, his big voice like the first crash of a thunderstorm.

Morgan forgot to shake hands. He grabbed his hat and walked from the office. As he stepped through the door, he cleared his voice, looked at the carpet, and said, "Go ahead, Eb. He wants to talk to you now." He didn't want Eb to quiz him. More than anything, he needed to sit down, and he needed to think what he had just committed himself to do.

• • •

By the time Eb stepped from the President's office, Morgan had composed—in his mind—a letter to President Young. He was sorry, he would tell him, but he hadn't been able to find a wife. And, with due respect to the President, he didn't think such an important decision should be reached on such short notice. He was happy to serve the Church, but unfortunately, he couldn't comply with this request.

Brother Brigham was the President of the Church, and Morgan honored that, but every man had agency, granted by the Lord, and Morgan was not going to give up his right to think for himself. When he set his mind to do something, he did it, but when someone else gave him orders, something in him simply rebelled.

But then Eb stepped out of the office, looking happy. President Young was with him, with his arm around his shoulders. Eb looked like a little boy by comparison, not only smaller but almost childish with his innocent, beardless face. "You look rather dumbfounded, Brother Davis," Brother Brigham said, and he laughed again. When he stepped closer, Morgan stood, and the President looked him in the face. "Don't worry, you'll manage this. I have great confidence in you. The Lord has whispered to me that you will be a great leader, a valued man not only in the Muddy River Valley but throughout the Church."

And then he did something Morgan hadn't expected. He took hold of both Morgan's shoulders and leaned in close. "I know I've asked a great deal of you two young men. I don't blame you for feeling a little knocked off your feet right now. I've had the same feeling at times in my life. I was called to teach the gospel in England when my family was deathly sick and living in utter squalor. I was filled with concern, even doubt, but the Lord blessed me, and He blessed my family. It's the way we build the kingdom, Brother Davis. We do hard things. God calls us to walk into the dark, unsure of what lies ahead, but when we do it, He offers His light, and we find our way."

He gave Morgan's shoulders a gentle shake and added, "So forgive me. If it were up to me, I would let you take your time and marry when you like. But know this: it's the Lord who called you, and I can't apologize for carrying out His will."

Morgan was nodding again, and this time he was pretty sure he wouldn't be writing Brother Brigham any letters. All the same, there was still the matter of finding a wife.

• • •

When Morgan and Eb started out for home, the cold was not so bad, but as evening came on, the temperature dropped again. They tied bandannas around their faces and pulled on their gloves. Their horses were anything but eager to face the north wind that was now blowing, but with urging, they continued at a hard walk.

Eb talked about the honor of receiving such a call, and he laughed about Brother Brigham's way of calling them. Morgan didn't say much. After a time, Eb asked him, "So what do you think? Can we live up to this?"

"I'll farm all he wants—*wherever* he wants," Morgan said, "but I'm thinking I'll have to head down there without a wife. How can I find a girl to marry me in the next few days?"

"What are you talking about, Morgan? The girls in Farmington have been trying to get your attention for as long as I can remember. I can name off half a dozen prospects right now." He laughed, his childlike voice muffled behind his bandanna. "Just don't try to take Mary Ann Bowen away from me. She'd probably choose you over me, any day."

"Not a chance. She's been sweet on you for as long as I can remember."

"Only because I spark her all the time. She told me once that she thought you were the handsomest fellow in town, and she just couldn't figure out why you avoided all the dances—or stayed on the sidelines if you did go."

"Because I can't dance," Morgan said.

"How do you know? You never try."

This was pointless. It was true that Eb was not very handsome. He had a round face and round eyes, more like a cherub's than a man's, but he had a big smile and a good word for everyone. He could always make girls laugh. When Morgan was alone with a young woman, he found himself desperate just to think of anything to say.

"What about Glory Winston?" Eb asked. "She's pretty as a picture. And a nice girl, too."

"A good breeze would blow her away. There's no way she would hold up in an adobe shack down in the desert."

"Adobe? Is that what the houses will be?"

"That's what I've heard," Morgan said. "I guess that's right."

This stopped Eb for a time, but finally he said, "Well, we can finish things off inside the houses, plaster the walls and everything. I'm sure we can make them nice enough. Mary Ann will have to roll up her shoulders and learn what she's capable of doing—but I have no doubt she can do it."

Morgan was not so sure. He listened to the subtle squeak of the leather saddles as the horses strode hard against the wind. He wondered how far the trip to the Muddy would be, how long it would take to get there with winter coming on, and how a delicate little girl like Mary Ann would hold up in conditions like that.

"I'll tell you who I'd ask if I was you," Eb said. "If I didn't have Mary Ann, I'd go for Betsy Crittenden. She'd keep you laughing your whole life, and she's good-looking, too."

"Eb, come on. She's the silliest thing I know. I can't abide her giggling."

"All right. Fine. But you must know someone who isn't too silly for you, or too skinny."

Morgan didn't answer. He had already let his mind run through all the single girls in their town—and a few other towns. He considered most of them spoiled. They hadn't had to work the way their mothers had, back when the first settlements had been established in the valley. And there weren't so many available young women as Brigham Young and Eb were claiming. Some of the best had accepted proposals from men who already had wives. A lot of girls preferred a man who had a farm built up and a good house, and maybe a high position in the Church.

Still, Morgan was gradually admitting to himself, there was someone he had thought about. Angeline Moore. He saw her at church sometimes, but he knew her mostly from his school days, when she was two grades ahead of him. He liked that she could not only ride a horse but saddle one by herself. And she knew how to work. She wasn't what he would call pretty, but she looked all right. She also had some muscles, and that would help plenty on this kind of mission. But he didn't know how he could just walk up to her and propose marriage.

He set the idea aside. She was not only older than he was, she surely had no interest in him. In school, she had disagreed with him one time and said so in front of the whole class. And that was how she was. A boy named Karl Sandstrom had teased her when she was about twelve or thirteen. She had told him to be quiet, but he hadn't let up, so she had hit him with her fist, right on the jaw, and he had dropped to the ground like a sack of barley. Old Karl had stayed flat on his back for a while, and then, when he'd finally managed to get to his feet, he had skulked away, holding his face and mumbling under his breath. All the boys had given the poor guy a hard time, but not one of them, from that time on, ever dared to cross Angeline.

Morgan and Eb didn't talk much after that. They pulled their hats down over their faces, and they kicked at their horses' flanks to encourage them to keep up the pace, but it was after midnight when they made it home, and they were almost frozen by then.

• • •

Morgan got up early the next morning in spite of the late night. The fact was, he hadn't slept much. He put on his heavy coat and headed outside to help his father, who was already out feeding his animals. Morgan found him in the chicken coop. He had filled the feeder trough and was checking under the hens for eggs. "Good morning," Morgan said as he stepped inside. His father had hung a tin lantern on a nail by the door. The holes in the metal were casting candlelight in odd patterns, like stars in a dark sky. Morgan could see only his father's back, hunched a little under his old blanket coat.

"Mornin'. So tell me about it. What did the President want?"

"He wants me to resettle down on the Muddy, where the Morrisons are."

Father turned around. Morgan watched for some sort of reaction, but his father only nodded. The two had worked together since Morgan was a boy, and that would be hard for both of them to give up. But Morgan also knew that Father would never think of turning down a call from the Lord—or of advising Morgan to do such a thing.

Morgan told him about the call, about raising cotton and establishing settlements, and about the requirement to take a wagon and a yoke of oxen, tools, and household goods.

"We'll make that happen somehow," Father said. "I'm proud you were chosen. But you're going to have to face some tears around here. Your mother is going be heartbroken, and your sisters will set up a howl that will fill the whole valley."

Morgan had thought about that. He had four sisters younger than himself, all still at home, and he knew they wouldn't like to see the family split up this way. Overnight, though, he had thought even more about his little brothers, Jacob and Sam. They were six and four, and they followed Morgan around like he was the lead wolf in a pack. Morgan wondered whether he could leave those two behind—or really, all six—without shedding a few tears of his own.

"Don't tell Mother this morning, all right?" Morgan told his father.

"Why not?"

The chicken coop was cramped and smelled sour. Morgan

wanted to get out. He stepped back out into the cold air, and his father came with him. "Just don't tell her quite yet," Morgan said. "I have a few things I've got to take care of, and then maybe we can call the whole family together. I can tell them all at the same time."

"Well, fine. But you figure out how to avoid all her questions this morning, and there's no waiting past tonight."

"All right."

Morgan took a step away, but stopped when his father said, "Brigham isn't sending you down there alone, is he?"

Morgan had been expecting that question. "No. He says I should find me a wife."

"That's what I figured. You got anyone in mind?"

"I guess I do. I've thought about it all night. But I doubt she'll accept my offer. I'll have to see what happens."

• • •

When Morgan knocked at Angeline Moore's house, Willy, her little brother, came to the door. Morgan hadn't thought about that happening. As soon as he asked whether Angeline was home, the freckle-faced boy grinned. "Why?" he said.

Morgan felt his face heat up. "I just need to talk to her for a minute."

"Well, you better take a look out in the barn, or at the hog pen. She's outside some'eres."

As cold as it was, Morgan wondered that she hadn't stayed in the house a little longer, but he was glad that he might find her by herself, without any sort of audience. It turned out that he was actually just a bit wrong about that. The audience turned out to be a pair of tall draft horses. Angeline was wearing a baggy pair of men's overalls, and she was pitching hay over a gate. When Morgan entered the barn, she reacted to the light from the door and turned to look at him. Her face showed a hint of surprise, but only for a moment. She seemed entirely calm when she said, "Well, if it isn't Morgan Davis—right here in my barn. Are you lost? I never seem to see you anymore."

Morgan tried to think of some quip, or any sort of thing to say, but nothing came to mind. He hated to think that he was blushing. But Angeline was smiling, and maybe blushing a little herself, and she actually looked quite nice—with something like mischief in her eyes. Her hair was tied up and tucked inside a floppy hat, with a few light brown strands falling out around her ears. She had thrown her coat off to one side, and she was wearing an old shirt that looked like something handed down from a big brother. Certainly it was warmer inside the barn than outside, but Morgan was surprised at her ability to withstand such weather. It seemed a good sign.

"I see you at church," Morgan finally thought to say.

"Oh, you do, do you? Well, you never manage so much as to say, 'Nice day, isn't it? How are you, Angeline?'"

"That's just how I am. I don't talk unless I have something to say."

She laughed. Her features had always seemed too masculine to Morgan, with her strong jaw and cheekbones, but her smile was mild and changed her looks entirely. Her figure was a little more solid than a lot of men liked, and she was tall, almost as tall as Morgan, who was six feet tall himself. But Morgan didn't mind her size. She always gave him the feeling that she could look after him as much as he would ever look after her.

"So what are you doing in my barn?" Angeline asked.

Morgan suddenly lost his nerve. He realized this whole thing had been a bad idea. "I just came by to say hello and . . . I don't know . . . see how you've been."

"So you can't speak to me at church because you don't have anything to say, and now you wander over here on a cold morning and ask about my health." She was still smiling. "Well, here's your answer: I'm fit as a fiddle. The only thing I ever do is work, but I don't really mind that, so I guess I'm pretty well off, all in all. What about you?"

"I'm kind of the same way. I work around our place, or I work a little on some other farms. And I do some building. Me and my father have built two rock houses this year—you know, for hire. It brings in a little extra income."

"Good for you." She set her pitchfork against the horse stall, crossed her arms, and waited. He knew she wanted him to tell her what he wanted.

"I rode my horse to Salt Lake and all the way back yesterday," he said. "It was one cold trip, I'll tell you. Me and Eb Crawford went together, and we just about froze coming back. My old horse was wobbling with every step by the time I put her in the barn."

"You better go take care of her, then."

"I already did."

Again she waited. He didn't know whether his words had been designed to fill up the quiet or whether he was getting around to something. He was still thinking of leaving, but then he added, "Me and Eb met with President Young. That's why we were down there. He called us on a mission—but not a preaching mission. He wants us to help settle that area down south of St. George on the Muddy River. He wants us to leave in a couple of weeks."

"Good for you. Sounds like an adventure."

"I guess. I don't want to go all that much, but you know, it's a call from God, I guess you'd say, and I didn't figure I could turn it down."

"So you and Eb are leaving town," Angeline said. "Did you come to tell me good-bye?"

He was about to say yes when the words, "Well, no," came out of his mouth. He took a deep breath. She was smiling only slightly now—and waiting—as though she suspected what he was up to. "The thing is, Brother Brigham wants us to get married before we go." He took one more breath, and he looked at her feet, not her eyes. "So I was just wondering if you'd like to marry me and go with me to . . . settle that area?"

Now it was Angeline's turn to take a breath. When he looked up, he saw that she had stopped smiling. She seemed to be think-ing, probably deciding to tell him no.

But then she said, "Well, all right. I guess I could do that."

They stared at each other for several seconds before Morgan managed to say, "Are you sure?"

"You heard me. I said yes."

Morgan nodded. He knew she was twenty-four, and maybe she was thinking she might as well take this offer since there might not be any more. But that smile was coming back, as though she felt good about the idea.

"Why me, Morgan?" she asked.

"You mean, why am I asking you?"

"Yes."

"Well . . . I guess I've had you in mind for a long time," Morgan said.

"So why didn't you ever bother to mention that to me?"

"I sort of thought, if I ever said anything, you'd tell me to take a hike."

Now she smiled fully, and she looked better than she ever had before. "I sort of knew you paid me some attention, Morgan. And I've had you in mind for a long time myself."

Morgan felt breath coming back into him.

"So when will this wedding take place?" she asked.

"It'll have to be next week, I guess."

"That should work out about right," Angeline said. "We've got our crops in, so we're not too busy right now."

"Well, good." Morgan thought about shaking her hand, but that seemed too strange. He even thought about kissing her. If she had stepped toward him, he might have done that. But she was staying put, and he didn't have the nerve to walk to her. "I'll tell you what. I'll stop back tonight, or maybe tomorrow, and we can pick a day to go down to the Endowment House."

"Good. Any day is all right with me."

"Should I ask your father?"

"You can if you want. He'll be glad to send me on my way, as old as I am."

"Is he around this morning?"

"No, he's not. Come over tonight. We'll pick a date for the wedding and you can talk to Father—and maybe the two of us can get to know each other just a little."

Morgan laughed. "I guess that would be good." He nodded. "All right, that's what we'll do. I'll see you later on."

He backed his way toward the door of the barn, nodding.

"I do have one question," Angeline said.

"All right."

"Are you thinking you want one wife, or do you want a whole raft of 'em?"

"I always figured on just one. Like my father."

"And not like *my* father, who decided two was better than one."

"Yes. Or no, not like him," Morgan said.

"All right. Stop by tonight."

Morgan put his hat on before he stepped outside. The last

glance he got of Angeline, she was standing with that pitchfork in her hands again but not doing anything with it yet. He figured she must be thinking about all the changes about to come in her life. That was exactly what Morgan thought about, too, as he walked home.

CHAPTER 2

Angeline continued to stand in the barn clutching her pitchfork and trying to think what she felt about all this. She liked Morgan, always had, and she had sensed that he liked her. She had even allowed herself to imagine that he would someday ask her to marry him. And yet, she had sternly rejected the idea, not wanting to build up hope. So many girls had talked about him, all through school, how handsome he was with his dark hair and his brilliant blue eyes. They even liked how shy he was. And every one of those girls was prettier than Angeline. She longed to have long eyelashes like Belinda James, or a sweet little face like Mary Ann Bowen.

Now Morgan had proposed to her, not to Belinda or Mary Ann, and Angeline wanted to believe that meant she was not so bad-looking, or that there was something about her that would attract a man like Morgan. She had always known that she was smarter than a lot of the girls—and boys—and she knew she could work hard, but it was impossible to imagine that such things mattered to a man who was looking for a wife. Her own father had married a pretty woman who had never dared to confront her husband and always submitted to his wishes. And then he had married another woman, younger and even prettier. Her "Aunt"

Faith—Father's second wife—was not only submissive, her head was empty as a cave. Faith's single desire was to gain the advantage over Angeline's mother, to extract "things"—a nicer house, furniture, a one-horse buggy—from their mutual husband, and to manipulate him into paying her more attention.

But Morgan had stood right there in the barn and asked Angeline to marry him, even though she had been wearing her father's hand-me-down overalls and her tattered hat. It seemed impossible that such a thing could actually have happened. She had known for many years that Morgan had noticed her at church, had nodded to her and muttered hello. She never saw him pay even that much notice to other girls. But she didn't know why. Even now, he hadn't said that he loved her, or even liked her. He had only told her that he had "had in her in mind." Maybe he just wanted someone who could work alongside him on a farm, or maybe he thought she could get by all right on a hard mission, but she wanted to believe that she had gotten into his mind in some way other than that.

Still, Angeline was practical. She forked some more hay and tossed it over the gate, telling herself that none of this mattered. He didn't have to be head-over-heels in love with her. He was going to take her away from this farm, this barn, this way of life that had become so meaningless to her. She was twenty-four years old, and she had begun to tell herself that she had to accept things as they were. Two other men had asked for her hand in marriage—or at least had talked to her father about such an arrangement. But they were both men with wives. She had been almost certain that they had looked at her big shoulders and her willingness to work and had thought how they could use her on their farms. She had turned them down even though she expected no other chances, and she had never regretted those decisions.

Now Morgan, the one man she had liked to think of marrying, had shown up out of nowhere and offered to take her away. Maybe he was only being realistic, like a man choosing a plow horse over a fast saddle horse, but she could live with that.

She only wished that he had shown some sign that he wanted to kiss her, or at least to touch her hand. What had come to her mind, almost the instant he had asked her, was the wedding night. She had assumed that she had missed her chance for such a night, and now it was suddenly looming right before her. Did he even want her that way? She wondered how awkward that night would be. But more than anything, she feared his seeing more of her. She knew she was manly enough in a dress on Sunday, but what would he think of her big arms and legs, her thick waist? Had he thought about that? Was he ready for what she really was rather than what he had somehow allowed her to become in his mind?

These thoughts also led to another: his strong body, his smooth skin, those blue eyes and bright teeth. She lost her breath as she thought about all that, and she put down her pitchfork. It was all a little too much to deal with, coming so suddenly, so unexpectedly. She had to finish her work quickly today, go in and have a bath, fix her hair as nicely as she could, and do something about her terrible fingernails. She wanted him to look at her differently tonight, to see her as not all that terrible to look at.

• • •

When Morgan left the barn and headed back to his place, everything was becoming real to him. He had actually asked and she had accepted. He had no idea whether she even liked him. The fact was, she didn't know him, and he didn't know her. He remembered the girl she had been, smarter than most and sure of herself, but he didn't know why he had always preferred her to the other girls. He had never liked giggling and silliness, and flirting had always annoyed him, so maybe he had liked her because she wasn't as frilly as other girls. But this morning she had seemed rather business-like, hardly thrilled at all. And she had always had strong opinions. What if they married and then he found out that she wanted to boss him around? He had never been pushy, never quick to tell anyone else what to think or what to do, but, above all, he didn't like *anyone* to boss him.

Morgan decided he'd made his choice, though, and now he had to make the best of things, no matter what. Angeline had actually looked pretty good with her floppy hat and wisps of hair around her face. And he had liked the way she had decided immediately, without a lot of humming and hawing. He could usually get along with just about anyone as long as he didn't have to talk too much, and at least she hadn't forced him to make a sales pitch.

As he walked along, however, another image began to assert itself. There would be a wedding—very soon—and there would be a wedding night. He had always wondered about that sort of thing, what it would be like. He knew that he would like to be close to a woman that way, but he wondered how a couple got started, what they did the first time they were together. He thought maybe a man was supposed to know how to lead out, what to do, but he knew nothing. His parents had never said a word to him about such things. His friends had told him some things they thought they knew, but that was nothing to rely on. And yet, he thought maybe he would like figuring everything out, and he really did feel something for Angeline. He liked the way she had smiled at him, even teased him in a sly way. He thought maybe they could be happy together.

After Morgan had come home from his meeting with Brigham

Young, he had prayed, kneeling by his bed, and asked whether Angeline was the right girl to ask to marry him. He hadn't heard any answers rumble through the ceiling, but he had felt calm about it. That seemed to mean something. He decided to rely on that and not worry too much; he would take things a day at a time—and keep praying.

So Morgan spent the day trying not to think too much. He had work to catch up on, after having been gone the day before. He stayed outside, avoiding his mother, since he knew she would want him to talk about his visit with President Young. It was at the dinner table that night that he broke the news about his leaving for the Muddy River Mission. His mother was a dainty woman, in a way, but she seemed to be held together by baling wire, pulled tight. She didn't try to talk him out of anything, but tears began to stream down her face. "It's a call directly from a prophet," she said, "and I could never be happy if you turned it down. But will we ever see you?"

"Oh, yes. I'm sure. It's a long trip, but I can make it back up here from time to time." He had been careful not to say "we," since he knew what the next question would be. He didn't want to answer that one until he had visited with Brother Moore that night.

After dinner, Mother asked the girls to clean up, and then she went off to her bedroom. She didn't cry out loud, but Morgan knew she was crying. He thought he understood that, but he wished that the whole thing didn't seem so tragic to her. What he didn't tell her was that he didn't want to go, that he didn't want to leave his family any more than she wanted him to leave. Images of a bleak desert kept coming to mind, farming in sand. He didn't like to picture that, and he didn't like to think that life as he knew it would suddenly disappear. But he had learned from his father—and actually from his mother, too—that a good man kept his word.

• • •

Later that evening, after dinner, Morgan walked to the Moore farm. Everyone there seemed ready for him: Brother and Sister Moore and the five children who were younger than Angeline all seemed a little more spruced up than they usually would be. Angeline was wearing the gray dress she wore to church on Sundays, but she seemed brighter than usual, her hair parted neatly in the middle and curls flowing over the back of her neck. Her lips seemed to have more color than usual, too, and he wondered whether she had put a little something on them. He had heard that some girls used juice from berries to make their lips more red, but that hardly seemed like something Angeline would do.

The important thing was, Angeline gave him a little smile that seemed to say, *Everything is new between us now.* He tried to say the same to her with a little nod of his head.

Morgan knew that Angeline also had an older brother or two, and at least one older sister he was aware of, all of whom were married. Besides that, Brother Moore had another wife, another home, and some younger children. Morgan suspected that was where he had been that morning, and that Angeline had gone to find him and request he come home that evening to meet with Morgan.

As it turned out, things went more easily than Morgan expected they would. Everyone greeted him and then cleared out, leaving Morgan alone with Brother Moore, who motioned toward the couch. Brother Moore sat on a chair facing him. He was a serious man with a natural downward bend at the corners of his mouth, and it was clear to Morgan where Angeline got her strong jaw. Brother Moore was wearing a brown suit of clothes, not his working shirt and trousers. Morgan had also chosen to wear his

Sunday clothes. It crossed his mind that they must look like two men ready to do business, and that struck him as slightly comical.

Morgan figured that he ought to comment on the weather or some such thing, but he couldn't think what to say except that it had been cold lately, and that was too obvious to mention. He paused long enough to see whether Brother Moore wanted to make an observation of his own, but when that didn't happen, Morgan got to the point. "Brother Moore, I talked to Angeline this morning. I told her I would like her to marry me. I've been called to—"

"Yes, she told us about all that."

"Well, I did want to make sure it was all right with you."

"Yes, yes, that's fine. I don't know you very well, but I know your father, and he's a good man. He and I have disagreed at times in our understanding of the scriptures, but I don't hold that against him. Angie tells me that you have worked alongside your father, learned his skills, and that you try to live the gospel, the same as he does."

"Yes, sir. I do." He certainly wasn't going to mention the chewing tobacco this time around.

"Well, we're happy for Angeline. She needs a husband. We wish you weren't taking her so far away, but the Lord calls us and we serve. That's the way of our people. Angeline's mother fussed a little this afternoon about never seeing her daughter again, and I suppose that could happen, but in this house we don't tell the Lord what we would prefer. When we receive a call, we embrace it with a full heart, full mind, full spirit."

Morgan had heard Brother Moore preach in Sunday meetings a few times. He had always seemed a little pompous, and he was strict in his interpretation of God's laws. Morgan hoped that Angeline wasn't quite so stern in that way. She didn't seem to be, but how could he tell? He actually knew next to nothing about her attitudes. The good thing was, she had been raised to honor God, the same as he had, and that was what she would teach their children.

"I doubt we'll be gone forever, Brother Moore. The Muddy is a long way, I know—around four hundred miles from here, as I understand it—but we'll certainly make it back at times. I'll want to see my family too."

"That's right. And be sure to tell Sister Moore that. She's been carrying on a little—the way women do."

"Yes, sir. My mother has shed some tears too."

"All I ask, Brother Davis, is that you do right by my daughter. Provide for her, help her raise a good family, and live the gospel."

"I promise that I'll do that."

There was silence in the room for a time after that. The fire in the fireplace had burned down to embers, and the glow didn't make for much light. Morgan tried not to look away, but he felt a little uneasy with Brother Moore in the dim light still studying his face, probably attempting to measure Morgan's sincerity.

"Let me give you one piece of advice, Morgan. Angie can be stubborn. She's got some of her own ideas, and she holds to them even when I've tried to teach her better. You may have to be strong with her at times. She could rule the roost if she thinks you're not man enough to show her who the leader is in your home. Don't argue with her. That doesn't work. But be the man of the house—a rooster, not a hen—and don't let her doubt for a minute who holds the priesthood and who doesn't."

Morgan actually didn't like the sound of that. He nodded to acknowledge he had listened, but he didn't make any promises this time.

Brother Moore seemed not to notice that Morgan hadn't exactly agreed. He stood up, shook Morgan's hand, and said, "I wish you well."

Both men nodded, and then Brother Moore walked from the little living room into the kitchen and left Morgan standing there.

Morgan waited, looked around a little. It occurred to him that Angeline had grown up without a lot of fancy decorations in her house. His own mother liked nice things: little ceramic knick-knacks, crocheted doilies, and pretty pictures on the walls. Maybe the Moores had had to divide up such things between two houses.

After a minute or so, Angeline came in. She was smiling again in that sly way of hers. "I told you he would be glad to get rid of me," she said.

"Well, he didn't say that. He did say that your mother's heart is breaking."

"Oh, she likes to cry. But her biggest worry is gone now. She thought I'd be an old maid and I would never get out of her hair."

The words seemed a little harsh to Morgan, and he wondered again what Angeline was really like, but he didn't say anything about that. He was still standing well away from her, and he had the feeling that it was time to show some sign that he was happy she had agreed to marry him. "Should we sit down for a few minutes?" he asked. "We have some things to talk about."

So they sat down on the sofa, leaving a little room between them. Morgan wasn't sure if he had left the gap or if she had. What he feared more than anything now was thinking of what he could say. But he knew one thing had to be settled. "My understanding is, I'm to join up with some of the other Saints who are called to the Muddy, and then we'll travel as a company. We're supposed to be there by midday a week from Friday. I was thinking maybe we could get our wagon all packed and ready, and then ride down to Salt Lake early Thursday morning. We could get married that afternoon in the Endowment House. That way we wouldn't have to travel clear back up here afterwards. We'd be ready to leave with the other missionaries that next day."

"That would be fine."

"Did you want your family to be there, or—"

"No. I don't think so. It's a lot of traipsing around for them. I could just say good-bye to them here before we head out."

"That's exactly what I was thinking." He looked away from her eyes. "We wouldn't have to stay in the wagon that night. We could get a room at a hotel."

"Can you afford that?"

"I have some money—from my wages last summer when me and my father built those houses."

"That's good. I have a few dollars, but that's about all. Mother said she could spare some of her pots and pans and things, and that should help us get started."

"My mother can probably do the same thing, and Father is helping me put an outfit together: a wagon and ox team. I don't have enough cash for all that, but he said he wanted to help as much as he could." He glanced into Angeline's eyes for a moment, then looked away again. "I just thought it would be better if it's just the two of us when we get to Salt Lake. And—you know—we could have that one night alone before we set out with a bunch of other people."

"That sounds just right to me," Angeline said, and she did something new. She touched his arm.

Morgan hoped that he wasn't blushing again, but he felt a little heat in his ears and down along his neck. Still, he looked at her directly. "I guess everything will work out just fine."

She nodded. "All right, then. Next Thursday."

He remembered she had said something that morning about

getting acquainted, but he wasn't sure what else there was to say at this point. "Right. I'll stop over a few times, so we can settle on what we need and we can get the wagon packed."

"All right." She sounded a little nervous, something he'd never seen from her before. She was leaning just a little toward him. He knew this was the time, but he was not sure how to make it happen. Still, they seemed to decide at the same time, and they leaned sideways and turned their heads toward one another. It was only a little kiss, just smacking lips, not even an embrace. But that was a start.

The truth was, Morgan had never kissed a girl—not for real. This kiss hadn't been much more than a peck on the cheek he might have given one of his sisters, but he was surprised how happy it made him feel, even excited.

• • •

The next week was busy. Father helped Morgan negotiate a good price—one hundred twenty dollars—for a fine yoke of red oxen. Morgan and his father also worked hard to repair an old wagon that had been sitting behind the barn. It was not a heavy wagon that could hold a lot of household items and farm tools, but one ox team couldn't pull a big load anyway. They would have to make do as best they could with what they could fit in—and hope, in time, to accumulate other things they might need.

Mother decided she could spare two oak chairs and a bedstead, and Angeline brought her one possession, inherited from her grandmother: a maplewood chest of drawers. Morgan didn't think they had room for the chest, but he packed it in somehow and still left a narrow opening in the middle of the wagon—enough for him and Angeline to share as a bed. He didn't want her sleeping out on the ground with winter coming on, and the truth was, he rather liked the idea of their spending their nights close and warm.

On the following Wednesday, some of the ward members held a little going-away party for Morgan and Angeline, and also for Eb and Mary Ann. There was dancing and a great deal of food, and finally each of the "settlers" was asked to say a few words. Eb talked longer than anyone, but each one said about the same thing: they would miss their friends in Farmington; they were a little apprehensive about locating in a desert so far away; they were committed to fulfill the mission they had been called to serve. Most everyone in the ward knew about the Muddy River Mission. Thomas Smith, when he had returned, had talked a lot about it. He had told stories about all the hardships and the terrible heat, but he had also reported good crops and long growing seasons. Morgan mentioned warm winters in his brief talk. It was what he wanted to concentrate on at the moment, and not on his sisters, all wiping their eyes, and his little brothers, who were looking inconsolable.

Then Morgan made the mistake of taking a good look at Jacob and Sam—and at his whole family—and, to his humiliation, his voice broke for a moment. He had thought of a few more things to say, but instead, he ended quickly by saying, "We'll make the trip back here sometime and see everyone. I promise you that." And then he sat down. Angeline took hold of his hand, but she didn't say anything. He was glad he could keep quiet for a time and get himself under control.

The next morning, early, Morgan led his oxen as they pulled the wagon to the Moore farm, and he tapped on the door. Angeline had clearly been waiting. She slipped out into the dark, taking his arm as they walked to the wagon. "I couldn't sleep," she said, and she laughed.

"I know. I couldn't either." There was enough moonlight, glowing through thin clouds, that Morgan could see that she had on a new dress, hooped the way church dresses usually were. The fabric was a pale blue, or maybe lavender, and over it she wore a lacy shawl. He realized this was her wedding gown, and this was their day. He took her hand and helped her into the wagon, and it occurred to him that he already had stronger feelings for her now than he had had the day he had proposed. They had worked together to pack the wagon and had talked rather easily. He had a couple of quilts ready, and he wrapped her in those. He would walk at first, leading the oxen, so he thought he would be warm enough in his frock coat and vest—his own wedding clothes. Once the sun was up, he would climb into the wagon and sit by his soon-to-be bride; the oxen could follow the trail all right, or he could command them by voice.

Eb and Mary Ann, in their wagon, met them down the road, and the two couples headed south together. It struck Morgan that he was, for the first time, independent from his father. If troubles came, he would have to work them out himself—or with Angeline. He rather liked the idea, even if he was a little frightened.

Ben and Buck, the new team of red oxen, weren't in any hurry. Morgan longed to move at the speed a horse could carry them, but he knew he had to get used to this pace. "This will be our rate of progress for a few weeks," he told Angeline, raising his voice to be heard over the thumping hooves of the oxen and the squeak and rattle of the wagon. "I hope you don't mind."

"It's sort of nice," she said. "It's relaxing—after all the hurrying we've been doing."

Morgan wanted to feel the same way, but he was nervous: about the wedding and everything else ahead of them, but mostly about the wedding night.

As it turned out, however, all went well that day and night. The sealing in the Endowment House touched something deep in Morgan's spirit, and he saw the same reaction in Angeline's eyes. Later, at the hotel, nothing was quite so awkward as he had expected. On the following morning, he and Angeline stayed in bed later than he ever had in his life. He had paid a man to board his oxen, with his wagon, in a barn overnight. It was strange not to have chores early, but it was also very pleasant.

He and Angeline waited for Eb and Mary Ann, who had stayed in the same hotel, and then they all four set out again, this time for the traveling company's meeting place, not far away, at the south end of State Street, on the edge of Salt Lake City. Morgan found himself rather bashful about saying much of anything to Eb and Mary Ann. Eb was glowing, but Mary Ann would not even look toward Morgan.

Only Angeline seemed her usual self. "Well, let's get on with it," she told everyone. "We have an adventure ahead of us." She had put on a simpler dress this morning, the kind women usually wore around the house. It was made from a print fabric, and it had a high neckline and long sleeves. Over it all was a cream-colored apron. She did have a dark cape, but it hardly seemed heavy enough for a December morning. Morgan wrapped the quilts around her again.

Mary Ann was laughing. "We're pioneers now," she said. "Nothing can stop us."

The plan was for the wagons—twenty or more—to assemble by noon, and then for the wagon train to depart soon after. More wagons would join up south of Salt Lake City—some in Provo and others in Nephi and Manti. Another wagon train would form a week or so later, some of the families having failed to prepare themselves as quickly as requested. All this information had been carried to Farmington in a letter from a brother named Jens Larsen, who would lead the party.

The newlyweds were among the first to arrive at the meeting place. They found three covered wagons stopped along the road. Morgan led his oxen up behind the wagons, each with its double yoke of oxen. Morgan found himself wishing he could have afforded two teams himself, but he and Eb had each had to settle for one. As soon as Morgan stopped his oxen, a young man in a blanket coat and a wide-brimmed hat walked toward him. "Hello, Brother," the man said. "I'm James Wilcox. Are you called to the Muddy River Mission, the same as us?"

"We are. I'm Morgan Davis. And that's my wife, Angeline, in the wagon." It was the first time he had said "my wife," and he found himself smiling at the thought.

"Where are you from?"

"Farmington."

"You haven't come all the way this morning, have you?" Brother Wilcox was a compact little man, and the truth was, he hardly looked old enough to leave his mother. He not only had no beard, but he seemed never to have shaved. He made Eb seem old by comparison. But he had a good smile, like a boy who had just won a game of marbles, and his strong handshake hinted that he had done some work in his life.

"No, no. We came down yesterday. We . . . ah . . ."

Angeline, who had climbed down from the wagon, said, "We just got married yesterday. And so did Eb and Mary Ann, the ones in the wagon behind us." By then, Eb was approaching. He shook hands with Brother Wilcox.

"Well, that's wonderful," Brother Wilcox said, his breath making a puff of steam in the cold air. "If you need any advice, you can talk to me and my wife. We've been married seven times longer than either of you."

It took Morgan a second to realize what he was saying. "So you just got married last week?" he asked.

"That's right."

By then everyone was gathering. Mary Ann walked up to her husband and took his arm. Sister Wilcox, a tiny, black-haired girl, was wearing a purple dress with a hooped skirt and a matching bonnet. Morgan wondered whether she thought she was going to church, not on a cold, dusty ride behind two pair of oxen. She smiled and said, in a sprightly voice, "I'm Lydia."

As it turned out, all five couples in the wagons that had arrived so far had been married in the last week—and all under similar circumstances. James Wilcox, Arthur Brooks, and Lyman Hunt were all from the Thirteenth Ward, in Salt Lake, and they had returned together recently from the Scandinavian Mission. "But me and Art can't speak to Lyman," Brother Wilcox said. "He speaks Swedish, and we both learned Danish."

Arthur Brooks, whom the others called "Art," seemed as tall as his two friends added together. He had a narrow face with a wide smile and a way of talking much louder than seemed necessary. His wife, Susan, was short enough to stand under his arm, and she too, in a shiny green dress, seemed ready to go dancing.

"Brigham told our three husbands to find a wife, quick," Sister Brooks said. "Is that what happened to you?"

"Exactly," Eb said.

"Brigham told the boys—or so Art claims—to choose the three prettiest girls in the valley, but I don't believe him. Not unless Art got third choice."

Everyone laughed at that, and the truth was, Morgan thought, there probably were a few girls around the valley who might shine a little brighter than these three. But they were all nice enough looking, and cheery, and they seemed excited to get started.

"There was no order to it," Art said. "We all got on our horses as fast as we could and raced home. I wanted to ask Susan before these other two louts got to her."

Susan tucked herself closer to Art and wrapped her arms around him. "He knew he had to ask me," she said. "I waited for him during his mission for almost three years."

"Morgan lives just down the road from me," Angeline told Susan, "and I'm not pretty enough to catch his eye. I think he just started down the road and stopped at the first farm he came to—like a traveling salesman."

"It's not true," Morgan said. He wanted to make a joke of some sort, but nothing came to mind.

Sister Hunt—Alice—said, "I'm just excited that we'll all be together. It's going to be hard, I think, but we can all help each other."

Morgan liked that. Alice seemed a little more serious than the others, and thoughtful. He saw some resoluteness and confidence in her gray eyes. She was dressed plainly, with a dark shawl over her linsey-woolsey dress, and her bonnet was a little slouchy from wear.

Eb, sounding enthusiastic as always, was the first to agree with Sister Hunt. "They say it's hotter than hades down there, and everything that grows has thorns on it. It's a far cry from this valley, but we'll get through just fine."

There was a lot of nodding and agreement. Morgan did like this new group of fellow travelers, but he knew Eb and his optimism. Morgan had to wonder how far *talk* would carry him—all of them—once the heat came on strong, and once they realized how far they were from everything and everyone they had known all their lives.

• • •

The talk continued for a time, and then two more wagons arrived, each pulled by two teams of mules. The drivers, one a woman, stopped in the front of the line, not the back. The man, who walked back to the others, was much older than Morgan, and he had a look of authority about him. "Could I get all your names?" he asked, and didn't bother to go around shaking everyone's hand. He had a pencil in one hand and a logbook in the other. "I'm Jens Larsen. Brother Brigham asked me to lead this party—at least the ones leaving today. I won't be your leader when we get to the Muddy. There are other men called to that work, but I hope to offer some direction as we travel south."

The mood changed quickly as Brother Larsen brought his businesslike tone to the gathering. But Morgan liked that. He thought they needed a practical leader, someone with some experience. Morgan had noticed that Brother Larsen had several children, some of them almost grown, and they had filled up two wagons.

Brother Larsen listened to the names and wrote them down, asking each time for the correct spelling. He was not a short man, but he was a little stooped in the shoulders. When he came to Lyman Hunt, he raised his head and rubbed his fingers over his long beard, which was mottled gray and white. Brother Hunt had a good beard himself, not very long, but thick and reddish. He seemed a little older than James or Art. His ruddy face appeared to have seen some seasons of working in the sun. "Lyman Hunt and my wife, Alice," Brother Hunt said. "And tell me, Brother, I think I hear a bit of an accent in your voice. Do you spell your last name with an 'e' or an 'o'?"

"With an 'e.'"

"Danish?"

"No. Norwegian."

The returned missionaries all laughed. "One more language, and we still can't speak to each other."

Brother Wilcox explained about their missions, and Brother Larsen seemed to relax a little more, even smile. "Well, we can try to talk in English. I speak a little of that, and I believe you do too."

"You must have come to America when you were quite young."

"Oh, yuh. I did. And I come to the Church many years ago. I met my wife—my first one—in Kirtland, Ohio." He hesitated, and then he added, "She's stayin' here for right now, until we get established down south. It's my second wife, Glory, who is goin' along with us. And six of our children. You'll meet them soon enough— or hear them. They're wild as coyotes, the whole bunch of 'em. I have older children, married now, and they won't be coming, but if I had my way, I'd leave this little herd home and bring my grandchildren along."

Morgan liked the man. He had some humor in him after all. That had to be good.

More people kept coming after that, and lots of introductions had to be made. That was fine, but Morgan soon realized it took too much chitchat to get acquainted with everyone. So, after a time, he and Angeline stayed at their own wagon. More than anything, now, Morgan wanted to get on the road.

• • •

As the time for departure had drawn close, Angeline had gotten up into the wagon, but delays continued. She watched Brother Jensen move up and down the stretching wagon train as he continued to check on everyone. Angeline had always liked to get in and do her work and not be held up by others. She wondered whether every day along the way would be full of such delays. Most of the people she had met were young, just as Brigham had told Morgan they would be, but some of the couples had been married ten years or more and had young children. There were even some couples closer to the age of Brother Jensen. What she also noticed was that some of the men had two wives, or, in one case, three, going along. Others had made the same arrangement as Brother Jensen: to take one wife and leave another one or two at home for now.

Morgan had decided during the long wait to pull out the ox-bows and lift the yoke off Ben and Buck. He had let them graze alongside the road, and after a time they had settled on the ground, but now Morgan got them up and hitched them to the wagon again. Other animals—draft horses, mules, and milk cows—were neighing, braying, and lowing; chickens, in crates, were cackling. All this only added to the sense that the train needed to get going soon. Some of the settlers had brought sheep, and others, beef cattle. Before the wagons set out, Brother Larsen sent the loose animals ahead with two men herding them.

Angeline knew that she had never been a patient person. She had started the day in a sweet, happy mood, but she was wondering about herself now. She had always had plenty of independence at home. Her father had expected a great deal from her, but once he had learned that she was dependable, he had left certain chores to her and hadn't supervised her. She had always gotten up early, sometimes fixing herself a quick breakfast and then heading outside before the younger children got up. She had liked the solitude of the dark farm, the barn, the sheds and corrals. She didn't know how to get along with so many people, apparently all living quite close to one another, and some maybe needing her help. She sensed already that she was not just stronger than Mary Ann but stronger than these new women she had met, maybe even stronger than some of the men. She knew what she had heard in church all her life—that she should care for others, support them, "lift up the arms that hang down." She had done some of that, but the truth was, mostly she liked to do things by herself and for herself, and she thought others ought to be just as independent.

Morgan had walked back along the wagon train. He was gone for ten minutes or so, but when he returned, he said, "We're almost ready to go."

"Where were you?" she asked.

"I was helping a fellow named Callahan, back about ten wagons behind us. He had a wheel that was about to come off. I swear, the poor guy hardly knows what he's doing. He's been a schoolteacher and never farmed a day in his life. I have no idea how someone like that ended up with this company."

"You can help him, Morgan. You're the kind of man most of these people will need—not just when we get there, but along the way."

"Well, I guess there's a few things I can help with. I'll do what I can, anyway."

Angeline didn't say it, but she was thinking, He's a better person than I am. I need to be more like him now.

CHAPTER 3

The wagon train finally got under way—almost two hours later than planned—and Morgan hoped to get a few miles down the road before the early nightfall. At least the weather had warmed the last few days and was actually quite pleasant for December. There had been little snow so far that fall, so the road was dry, and the dust from the wagons up front roiled through the air. Angeline was in the wagon, and she had wrapped her shawl across her face to protect her nose and eyes from the dirt.

Morgan set out walking at first, leading the oxen. The road had become rutted over the years, so the wagon jostled more than was comfortable, jumping from one groove into another or bumping over embedded rocks. Morgan tried to avoid the ruts, but that only took the wheels into the dried bunchgrass on either side and made for a harder pull.

The oxen seemed more content to trudge in the ruts, and they followed the wagon ahead of them without much guidance, so Morgan finally climbed onto the wagon and sat next to Angeline. He snapped his whip over the backs of the oxen from time to time, not touching them, but letting them hear the crack and know to keep up their pace. "Ol' Ben and Buck have had life a little too easy these last couple of weeks," Morgan told Angeline. "They aren't pulling very hard. I won't tell them how far it is to the Muddy or they might resign their jobs before the day is over."

Angeline pulled the shawl away from her mouth. She laughed softly. "I think we'll be tired too. We didn't get much sleep last night."

Morgan was surprised she would mention that. He was still warmed from the night before, still basking in the pleasure of their closeness, but that seemed something too private to talk about out here in the world of people and oxen and jolting wagons. So he only said, "I'm fine. I'm not tired."

She laughed again and covered her mouth, but after a few moments, she said through the shawl, "It was nice, wasn't it?"

He tried to sound neutral, not dreamy, the way she had sounded. "Yes, it was."

She quieted for a time after that, and Morgan was relieved. He didn't want to make her feel bad, but it seemed to him that some things could be talked about, and others were better just to do and not discuss.

But then Angeline said, "To tell the truth, I was kind of scared when we got to the hotel. What I know about . . . life . . . I've learned on the farm. Rams and stallions are quick and rough. It always made me cringe when I saw it." The wagon lurched to one side, and Morgan was glad to shout at his oxen. He really didn't want her to describe something like that. "But the thing is," Angeline added, "I suspected it wouldn't be that way with someone you loved. And I was right."

Morgan barked "giddyup," and he snapped the whip. "I hate to fall too far behind," he told Angeline. "Most everyone has double teams. Ben and Buck will have to work hard to stay up."

Morgan was almost sure he had let Angeline know that he wanted to change the subject, but she took hold of his arm and nestled closer to him. "You were wonderful, Morgan. So sweet and gentle. I always thought the first night would be nice if a husband was that way, but it was nicer than I ever imagined."

Morgan had no idea what to do now. He stared at the red haunches of the oxen and didn't so much as glance at Angeline.

"I'll tell you something else I didn't know," she went on. "I never thought much about kissing. All I'd known were little smacks, and that was that. But kissing turns out to be one of the best parts. I mean kissing the way we did last night—and this morning."

It was what Morgan had discovered too, but he couldn't say it to her. He just couldn't.

"You don't want to talk about this, do you?" Angeline said, and she laughed again.

"Well . . . I . . . guess I'd rather not."

"It embarrasses you, doesn't it?"

"I don't know. Not really. I just . . ." But he didn't know how to explain. He coughed and pretended that a swirl of dust had cut off his sentence.

"You know what you are, Morgan? You're bashful. Maybe I should be. But I feel so close to you today, and it's the closeness I love even more than—you know—what we did. Don't you feel close to me now?"

"I do. I've been thinking that all day. I thought it would take more time than this."

"But you don't want to talk about it."

"Well . . . not much."

Angeline pulled the shawl away from her face again, leaned toward him, and kissed his cheek—just a little peck. "All right. I won't say anything else." She sat up a little straighter and pulled away just a bit. Now Morgan was afraid he had offended her, and he really didn't want that. He was trying to think what to say so she wouldn't be upset, but before he could come up with the words, she said, "But I do need to ask you one thing—just so I'll know."

"That's fine. Ask me."

"Are we going to sleep in the wagon together?"

"Yes. It's a tight space between all the furniture, but I think we can manage. Some people have tents, but we were already too loaded up, and canvas is heavy."

"But stay with me in the wagon, all right? Even if it's crowded, I don't want you out on the ground somewhere—and me all alone."

"No. We'll figure something out," he said, and then he laughed. "Even if we have to throw out that chest of drawers you brought."

She ignored that. "Morgan, don't you know what I want you to say?"

"I guess I don't."

"I want you to say that you hope to hold me close all night—every night. I want you to say that you want every night to be like last night, even in a crowded little wagon."

Morgan finally looked at Angeline. He even smiled. "That's what I was hoping too," he said.

She grasped his arm again, and this time she said, "I always thought I loved you. For years and years I thought I did. But now I *know* it. I had no idea I could be this happy. A month ago I had my mind made up that I would never marry, and now look at us, off on an adventure together. This is our honeymoon."

Morgan was feeling some of the same things, although he hadn't put quite so many words to his thoughts. The truth was, he still had no desire to start a farm in a desert. But he was happy. He was pleased he had married a woman who was ready to face such challenges and take a positive view of them. And even though he didn't want to talk about it, he was already thinking about camping that night . . . even on the hard floor of a crowded wagon.

• • •

Before the company had set out that day, Brother Larsen had called all the pioneers together. He had talked of hardship and warned them of a difficult trip ahead. He had also described some of the challenges in the Muddy River Valley: burning summers, snakes and scorpions, Indian beggars, and alkaline soil. Most of the settlers were young, and they had told Brother Larsen they were ready for whatever came. But during the next few days Morgan could tell that reality was asserting itself for pretty much everyone.

The weather turned sharply colder, and these inexperienced travelers seemed, at least to Morgan, to have more than their share of mishaps. After the last families joined the party in Manti, the wagons headed into the mountains toward Fillmore and Corn Creek, and then began a long, steep climb through Baker Canyon to Dog Valley. It was on this climb that draft animals began to tire. In a muddy gulley, two wagons slid sideways and tipped over. Wagon tongues broke, and iron tires loosened and came off wheels. The settlers started unloading items they had deemed crucial in the beginning. Morgan even talked Angeline into giving up a heavy iron fireplace crane and kettle, much to her disappointment.

And then, in Wildcat Canyon, snow began to fall. The wagons had been averaging about fifteen miles a day at first, but slogging through the snow changed everything. Men pushed one wagon after another through drifts, and even though the snow wasn't deep yet, there were places where animals couldn't get their footing. Extra teams had to be added, borrowed from other wagons. Three or four teams became necessary in some spots, and that meant one wagon crossing at a time and lots of hitching and unhitching—all of which took time.

Morgan found himself busy every minute. He soon learned that he was better at repairing wagons than anyone in the company, and when it came to moving teams around, harnessing or yoking them, and then joining in the push from behind, he was absolutely essential. Brother Garrick Callahan told him, "Morgan, I don't think we would have made it over this pass without you. How do you know so much for such a young man?"

"I don't know. I grew up on a farm, that's all."

"So did most of these men."

"Well, I did make a long wagon trip, out and back to Nebraska. I guess I learned a few things from that."

Brother Callahan was leaning against his wagon now. He was covered in mud, having worked with Morgan on the wagon's splitting undercarriage. His old wagon had been having troubles since the first day the settlers had started out. Down in the filth, under the wagon, the two had talked. Brother Callahan was Irish by birth, but he had been in America much of his life. He had joined the Church and moved to Nauvoo only months before the Saints had been forced to leave. He was a hatter by trade, but he had become a schoolmaster in Salt Lake City. "I crossed the plains with my family," he told Morgan, "but what I know about mules or wagons or outdoor cooking could all fit on the end of my little finger. I have no idea why Brigham called me on this mission."

"We'll need teachers, that's for sure. My wife and I hope to start a family of our own, and I do hope they can learn something besides raising cotton."

"Well, I guess we will have a school. And I would like to teach again, if that's what the leaders want me to do."

"Some of us may even want a fancy hat someday—to keep off the sun. You just might open a shop in a few years, once we become civilized again."

"Well, that would be fine. I would like that."

Brother Callahan was built like a tree stump, short and thick. Behind his heavy cheeks and his full beard were innocent, wide eyes, and his voice was soft as feathers. Morgan suspected he might be a good teacher, but he wondered how he would manage the kind of life they were heading toward.

By the time the missionaries reached Beaver Pass in the southern part of Utah Territory, the snow had let up—but there were still drifts to push through. When Angeline joined the men in pushing and muddied her boots and skirt, Morgan told her, "That's all right, Angeline. We'll manage. You stay with the wagon and keep yourself clean and warm."

But the truth was, he was proud of her when she paid no attention to him. She was one of the few women who worked so hard. When evening came and the camp had to be set up, she was also quick to help with everything: lifting the heavy yoke off the oxen's necks, feeding them, and then getting a fire going for supper. Brother Larsen told Morgan one night, "That wife of yours, she can work like a man. You got yourself a fine mate when you talked her into marryin' yuh."

Morgan grinned. He didn't say much, but he liked to think that Angeline would be able to work alongside him when they had to break ground for a farm and build a place to live.

• • •

The descent from the pass was not as bad as the climb on the other side had been, except that warmer air was melting the snow, turning the road into a muddy sludge. And then rain began to fall. It came hard and was whipped into sheets by a south wind. Morgan told Angeline to move back into the wagon, but she wasn't about to do that. She held up a quilt to block the rain from striking directly into their faces, but it was no use. Their clothes were soon soaked through, and the canvas wagon cover began to drip and then dribble in streams onto all the furniture and bedclothes in the back.

Angeline had felt moments of discouragement all along the way, but she had held up in the face of the cold, and she never worried about getting dirty or eating less than she might have liked. But she couldn't think what it would be like to sleep in wet quilts, wet clothes. Every morning the company gathered and prayed for a good day, good conditions, and safe travel, and every day things went wrong. If it wasn't snowdrifts, it was lost animals in the morning, or children falling and hurting themselves. One boy had fallen under a wagon, and a wheel had broken his arm. He had screamed as Sister Ballif, a midwife—with the help of some men—had set the arm and splinted it, and then the boy had whimpered for hours after. He was just a little fellow of six or so, and his cries had hurt Angeline. Another child, an older girl, had caught her skirt in her family's fire. She had escaped without serious burns, but Angeline could only think how many dangers they faced—and would always face. She heard coyotes at night, and that didn't scare her, but she did think about the Indian tribes in the area, mostly Pah Utes. Everyone said that they rarely bothered wagon trains, but they would sometimes raid single wagons.

"The Lord doesn't want this to be easy, does he?" Angeline muttered to Morgan between gusts of rain-filled wind.

He answered about what she expected: "It's always hard to travel this way. We've had it sort of easy so far."

There were times when Morgan's confidence and stoicism were a strength to Angeline, but she didn't like his composure right now. These blasts of rain in her face, and the water drenching her skirt and underclothes, simply made her angry. God could have guided this storm around his missionaries if He'd had a mind to. *Hard* was one thing, but this was cruel.

"I'm pretty sure we're close to the Beaver settlement now," Morgan told her. "We'll stop before long."

"And what good does that do us? Nothing is going to dry out tonight."

"We'll figure something out."

She had never been angry with Morgan—at least not since they were children—but she was angry now. She had always hated the way her father, who pretended to be so pious, would lose his control, cursing and swearing and blaming everyone but himself for things he didn't like. She didn't want Morgan to be like that, but at the moment she wanted to hear just a little passion from him, some sign of the resentment she was feeling.

"What worries me more than anything right now," Morgan shouted above the wind, "is poor ol' Ben and Buck. They can't pull through all this muck and mire much longer."

And that was too much. "I swear, you love those old oxen more than you love me," she yelled back at him.

Morgan looked over at Angeline and smiled, and then he said, "Not really. But maybe almost as much."

Morgan surely thought he was being funny, but it was the wrong time to joke with her. She turned away from him, held the quilt in front of herself, and didn't try to guard him. She reveled in her anger. She had never understood people who took everything as it came, without so much as a complaint. Maybe that was what Morgan was going to be like. She really knew very little about him, she admitted to herself. If he always took things in stride, maybe he would gradually make her crazy.

But Morgan had been right about one thing. The little town of Beaver was close, and the wagon train soon stopped among a little scattering of log and adobe homes. Angeline was relieved not to be pushing into the wind any longer, but she couldn't think what was next. There was no way to dry anything, and the rain was still falling hard. The afternoon sun was angling low, and night would only bring on freezing temperatures.

Brother Larsen directed the men to pull their outfits into the yard around the tithing office. By the time Morgan stopped his wagon, some men were already gathering wood. It took some time to get the kindling to ignite, but a small bonfire did sputter into bigger flames. The men kept adding fuel, and everyone gathered around for heat.

By then, locals were coming out of their homes, and they began to gather the travelers in. Morgan and Angeline followed an older man, Brother Sneddon, and then watched as his two-room house filled up with nine more people from the wagons. A strong fire was burning in the fireplace, and Angeline hurried to it when she got inside, but very soon she told herself to let the children and smaller women have their chance to draw near. She was already feeling ashamed of herself for all her self-pity and murmuring. She especially felt bad when Morgan carried a few things inside and then went back out in the rain to take care of the oxen. Ben and

Buck really had pulled hard, and she knew it took a good man to protect his animals before looking after himself.

Sister Sneddon fussed over everyone. She found clothes or blankets to cover people and told them to take off their wet things. So the men moved to the other room, and everyone skinned off their soaking clothes. Angeline, by then, saw that some of the women and girls were shaking all over, penetrated much more than she had been by the cold. Sister Sneddon helped dry them with whatever rags she could find, and then helped them cover up and get back to the fire. The men gradually returned to the main room, wrapped in strange garbs: coats, shawls, quilts, and Brother Sneddon's old trousers. By then, people began to laugh at each other.

When Morgan came back, he went to the bedroom and came back "dressed" in what looked like a robe. It was a bedsheet, draped over his shoulder and tucked in tight around his waist. He looked like a Roman emperor, Angeline thought, and now she really did laugh.

"We have plenty of food," Sister Sneddon was saying, "but it's not yet cooked. So you'll have to give me a little room around the fire. I'll make a big stew, and that should fill you and warm you."

The warmth was good, and later, the stew tasted wonderful. But best was the blessing that Brother Sneddon said over the meal. He thanked the Lord for guiding these good brothers and sisters to his home on a lonely winter night. And he thanked the Lord for never forgetting His chosen people.

Angeline said a prayer of her own that night and asked for forgiveness.

The company stayed another day in Beaver, and they brought in all their wet bedding to dry. They slept on floors—hard-packed dirt floors, but that didn't seem bad at all, in a cozy room.

• • •

During the following week, as the wagon train descended out of the mountains and dropped toward St. George, the weather changed dramatically. The days became much warmer, and the country took on more of a desert look. Ridges striped in red and orange and brown rimmed the valleys, along with buff-red cliffs. The landscape was now full of Joshua trees, cactus, and rabbit brush instead of cedar trees. Morgan found the scenery beautiful, in its way, but strange. He had lived among mountains most of his life, and however dry the northern Utah valleys could be at times, the soil there, once it was turned over, was rich and black. All this red—with distant purple hills, and long, black ridges cutting across the valley—was foreign to him, frightening in a way, as though God had not had people in mind when He had created such a place. Morgan watched lizards scramble away from wagon wheels and jackrabbits bounce through the sagebrush; he even spotted a huge tortoise sunning itself on a hillside. Certain animals belonged here, it seemed, but how could people who were descended from European ancestors adapt to such dryness, such drabness, such prickly plant life?

• • •

They camped outside Washington one night, near St. George, and Angeline invited Eb and Mary Ann, along with the Wilcoxes, Hunts, and Brookses, to bring what they planned to cook that night so all could share the same fire. They sat together on boxes and chairs that Morgan pulled from the wagon, and they ate beans and bacon, jerky, dried fruit, and fried potatoes. Their provisions were gradually running low after four weeks on the road, but the plan was to purchase more of what they needed in St. George.

Everyone talked about the hard days behind them. No one seemed to see the experience as an adventure now. Mary Ann sat as close to the fire as she could while she ate her food—and she didn't eat very much. "I hope it's warmer tonight," she said. "I've never warmed up since that day in the rain."

"She just about froze to death in the mountains, even before the rain," Eb added.

"Me and Morgan snuggle up close at night," Angeline said, "and we've managed all right. But out in that rain, I don't think I was ever so cold in my life."

"Poor Mary Ann needs a little more meat on her bones," Eb said. "She gets chilled all the way through and can't ever get warm enough to be comfortable."

Mary Ann looked up from the fire, and Angeline saw something that looked like fear in her eyes. "I guess, before long, I'll be complaining that I'm too hot," she said. "You know what they said about the heat down on the Muddy."

"I'm trying to take one day at a time," Alice Hunt said, her voice almost solemn. "I had no idea how hard it would be to get where we're going."

"We should have known," Art Brooks said. He stretched his long legs toward the fire. "I mean, it *is* winter. But all I heard about was the heat down south. No one ever said anything about those high passes."

"It's still better to come in winter," James Wilcox said. "We'll get to the Muddy before the heat sets in." But he too sounded subdued. He was leaning over, his elbows on his knees, his face glowing from the firelight. Angeline thought he looked older than he had a month ago; his cheeks were red and chapped, and his eyes had lost some of their innocence.

It was quiet for a time after that, and then little Lydia said, "When James asked me to marry him, that's about all I thought about. I didn't even know it was hot where we're going." She had long since given up her fancy dress, traded it for wool and a heavy cape.

"I know what you're saying," James said, and he sounded a little defensive. "That's how it was for me, too. Brother Brigham talked about accepting a call from God and being a pioneer. He even said it was desert country, but that didn't seem all that much to worry about. It was Brother Larsen who finally talked about the heat and the snakes and all those things."

"But it's the way life is," Angeline said. She had scooted her chair closer to Mary Ann's, and she wrapped her arm around the girl's shoulders. "There's lots of things we'd never do if we really understood what we were getting ourselves into. Think what the first pioneers thought when they got to the Salt Lake Valley. And now, look what we've done with it. We've built up cities. That's just what we'll do again." She decided not to admit how discouraged and cranky she had been coming into Beaver. Everyone seemed to need a lift tonight.

"That's what Eb tells me," Mary Ann said, "and I know that's right. I really do." But her voice broke, and Angeline could see tears glistening on her cheek, reflecting the light of the fire.

"She's been a little sick the last few days," Eb said. "That hasn't helped her."

"We'll get each other through, Mary Ann," Susan said. She was snuggled against Art, and he was holding his long arms around her. "If you don't feel well, try to rest all you can."

But clearly, Mary Ann couldn't speak now. She lowered her

head, and Angeline knew she didn't want everyone to see that she was crying.

The couples sang some songs after that: favorite hymns, even "Come, Come, Ye Saints," and various songs they had learned growing up. The music seemed to be good for everyone, and the mood was more cheerful as they began heading back to their wagons. Eb and Mary Ann left the fire first, but before long Eb came back, and he told Morgan and Angeline, "I wrapped her up in all our quilts. But I'm not sure what to do. I think, more than anything, she's homesick. She keeps talking about her mother and her sisters and saying that she'll never see 'em again."

"We all feel some of that," Morgan said. "This country just doesn't look right to me. And from what they tell us, this is still pretty green compared to what we'll see farther on south."

"I know," Eb said. "I've been thinking about all that. I don't know how Mary Ann will react when she gets there."

"Those who settled down there earlier must be managing all right," Morgan said. "I just keep telling myself that, and asking the Lord not to let me think too many fearful thoughts."

"I think we're all praying that way," Eb said. "But Mary Ann's lost control of her feelings these last couple of weeks. She's usually quick to laugh and tease, and she loves to dance. I think she's feeling like we're leaving all joy behind forever. It won't be that way, will it?"

"Not at all," Angeline said. "We'll have dances. We'll have our church meetings. We'll have a town in time, as good as Farmington."

"That's what I've been telling her. I'm just having trouble convincing myself that it's true." He looked at the fire for a time, and then he said, "But I can't think that way. I've gotta be strong for the both of us."

Eb said good night after that and returned to his wagon. Angeline picked up a stick and stirred the coals. Flames jumped up. "Talk to me for a minute, Morgan," she said. "You've been running around helping people all day, and I've hardly seen you."

"Sorry about that."

"No. I don't mean it that way. I'm glad that people depend on you so much." She reached over and put her hand on Morgan's arm. "There's just something I want to ask you about."

Morgan waited.

"Today, after the wagons stopped, I walked by the Shupes' wagon. Brother Shupe was telling Polly what was wrong with her—something about the way she was trying to build a fire. He sounded gruff as a bear, and she was hanging her head like a little girl."

"She is a little girl."

"I know. A few days ago I asked her how old she was. She said sixteen. But I'm not so sure she's even that old. She looks younger."

Morgan nodded. "She does."

"Do you think he talks that way to his first wife?"

"Maybe not quite so much, but he gets angry with just about everyone. I've heard the way he yells at Polly."

"Why do these men take on extra wives and then treat them like that?" Angeline asked.

"That's like asking why some men treat their children right and others beat them for almost no reason. I have no idea what gets into a man like that."

Angeline knew that some husbands were harsh with their wives. But she had expected better of this group. "Then why did they send him on a mission?" she asked. "Someone ought to call him home and take his priesthood away."

Morgan was nodding again. "I don't disagree with that. If a

man's going to take a second wife, someone should find out how he treats his first one—and his children. But some men put on a good show—a holy face and all that—when they're around Church leaders. I guess they think God won't notice how they act the rest of the time."

The evening was quiet. It was the wrong season for crickets, and the breeze, for once, had died away. The only sound was the soft rumble of a few people talking at their own fires. Somewhere, too, well up the way, a little group was singing, "Zion Stands with Hills Surrounded."

"The worst thing about Wilfred Shupe," Angeline said, "is that he thinks he's better than the rest of us. If he's not bragging, he's complaining, and if he's not complaining, he's telling people that they ought to be more like him."

Morgan laughed. "That's about right. But we don't have many like him. Most of our people are getting along just fine."

"That's not my point, Morgan. You always tell me that you don't know how to talk to people. But the best conversation is the one that starts with, 'Can I give you a hand?' And you have that conversation all the time."

"Don't make me out to be better than I am, Angie."

Angeline had never liked the name "Angie" when her father had used it, but with Morgan it seemed to come from a place of affection, and she liked that he had begun to call her that. She also had come to know that Morgan hated to be praised. So she let that go. What she did ask was, "What's life going to be like for us, Morgan?"

"I don't know. We'll farm. We'll have children. We'll accept the callings we receive in the Church. We'll live right, or at least the best we can. And we'll grow old and take pleasure in our grandchildren. That's the only life I know how to live."

"Do you want lots of children?"

"Of course I do. And remember, I grew up on a farm too. I know where they come from."

Angeline laughed. "I have a feeling you like that part—making babies."

"Haven't made any yet. But you're right. So far, I like my part of the job."

Angeline could see that he had embarrassed himself, his face turning red in the firelight, but she was glad he would finally joke with her that way. "Here's what I'm thinking about," she said. "And I guess hearing Brother Shupe act that way put the idea into my head. You told me on the day you proposed to me that you didn't want to marry anyone else. But what if, someday, the Brethren asked you to take more wives? Would you do it?"

"No, no. I was scared to death to ask you to marry me. I don't think I could ever go through that again. I'll stick with the one I've got."

"I'm serious, Morgan. Maybe you don't *plan* to have more wives, but you don't turn down callings when they come. And that's just what might happen."

"I don't see that as very likely down here in the desert. There won't be any extra women. And here's the thing. What would you say if a leader asked me to do something like that? I wouldn't make the decision by myself. We'd make it together."

"There's never a time I'll want to share you, Morgan. You might as well know that right now."

"Well, I've told you already. I don't want more wives."

Angeline felt relieved to hear him sound so definite. She hoped nothing would change his opinion, ever.

"We both feel the same way," Morgan said. "So that's settled."

"I suppose. But I have to be careful. I don't want to tell the Lord I won't do whatever He asks of me."

"I don't see it quite that way. I think we can follow our own inspiration on some things. I'm satisfied to live the way my mother and father do. No one's going to make me live in some way that I don't like."

Angeline wasn't sure she felt right about that. She had told herself for a long time that she was way too independent and self-willed. She didn't want to prod Morgan toward her own spirit of rebellion. But she also knew what she had imagined all the years she was growing up. "More than anything," she said, "I want my husband to love his children and make them feel loved. My father did more preaching than loving. If Mother or any of his children didn't respond just the way he expected, he let us know that his love could be withdrawn." She hesitated, thought about that, and then added, "No. That's not it. It wasn't that he withdrew his love. It was more that he had no love in him."

Angeline felt tears spill onto her cheeks. Morgan reached for her, but Angeline held back. She looked him in the face, close. "Those are terrible things to say about my own father. Maybe, in time, I'll forgive him, and maybe I'll realize I'm wrong. But here's what I have to say to you. More than anything else in my life, I want a husband who loves me and loves my children, and who isn't afraid to let us know that he does."

Morgan nodded. "I understand," he said. And then he did take her in his arms. "I love you more than anyone—even Ben and Buck."

She pulled back and shook her finger at him. "Is that the best you can do?"

"No. I just get embarrassed to say such things." He took her in his arms again. "When Brother Brigham asked me to find a wife,

I told him I didn't know who I could ask. That wasn't really true, though I hadn't admitted it to myself. I've known since I was a boy that you were the one I wanted. But I didn't know until after we got married that I loved you. When you were younger, I used to think some of the other girls were prettier than you. But the last little while, when we're riding along in the wagon, I'll glance over and think, *Why did I never notice how beautiful she is?*"

"Now you're getting carried away. I want love, not lies. If there's one thing I'm not, it's beautiful."

"You better check your mirror again. Or use my eyes for your mirror. You're perfect. I love your eyes, for one thing, and you have about forty different smiles—each one meaning something different—and every one of them says something to me. Twenty times a day, I think to myself, *She's the prettiest woman I've ever seen.*"

"Now, let's see," Angeline said. "Don't you always tell me that you aren't very good with words? You're a poet, if you ask me." And then they kissed, there by the fire, and he held her in his arms for a long time.

Angeline had never expected to be this happy.

Later, Angeline snuggled close to Morgan in the wagon, with heavy quilts both under and over them. She loved the feel of his hard muscles and his warm body. After all his sweet words tonight, and the sweetness they had shared when they first got under these quilts, she was basking in the glow of it all. She had liked Morgan from the time he had been that rough-and-ready younger boy at school—liked his quiet, good-natured manner and the athletic way he played at games with the boys. But she had never dared to dream that he would be so kind to her, so soft. Even more, she expected that he would always be that way. It wasn't something he was putting on just because they were newlyweds. She was scared, if the truth were known—scared about living in the desert and intimidated by the rough country they were traveling through. But Morgan made her believe everything would be all right. And she was deeply thankful for what he had said tonight. He wanted only her, not a collection of wives. Whatever else she had to face, she would do it. Morgan made her feel certain that she could.

CHAPTER 4

On the morning after their arrival in St. George, the settlers in Jens Larsen's company were waiting for Apostle Erastus Snow, who had sent word that he wanted to meet with them. Elder Snow had been assigned by Brigham Young to direct the Cotton Mission and the expanding settlements in the entire region, including those in the Muddy River Valley.

Morgan had always heard that January days in St. George were much warmer than in Salt Lake City, but this day, so far, was gloomy and cool. Morgan hoped for better weather soon—he knew how discouraged some of the company had become. He was especially worried about Mary Ann. Morgan had stopped to see the Crawfords after breakfast that morning, and he had found Mary Ann still bundled up in quilts in the back of the wagon. "I don't know if it's a cold she's got, or something worse," Eb told Morgan. "But it won't go away."

"We'll be heading into warmer country when we leave here," Morgan told him. "Maybe that will help her." But as he walked back to his own wagon, what lingered in his mind was the concern he had seen in Eb's face. He had known Eb all his life, and never had he known him to look so somber.

Apostle Snow was supposed to speak to the assembled Saints at

8:00 a.m., and everyone had cleared their breakfasts and gathered inside the circle of their wagons for the meeting, but at 8:30 he still hadn't appeared. One of the local leaders whispered to Morgan, "This doesn't surprise any of us down here. We call him 'the late Erastus Snow.' But don't worry, he'll get here, and he'll give a fine speech."

That certainly turned out to be true. Only a few minutes later, the Apostle drove up in a little buggy, climbed down, and doffed his wide-brimmed hat to the missionaries. They were camped on the edge of town on a stretch of red sand. Some had pulled chairs from their wagons, but most remained standing. Morgan and Angeline, both tall, stayed toward the back of the crowd, but Apostle Snow's voice carried well. He was a clean-shaven man, with graying hair, but Morgan didn't think he was more than fifty years old. He had the look of a scholar more than the colonizer and practical leader everyone knew him to be. Still, there was an earnestness in his strong, even voice.

He greeted everyone, and then he told them he was pleased they had accepted such an important missionary call to support the continued settlement of the Muddy. "We need more Saints there," he said. "It may be arid, and the temperatures are excessive at times, but we must go forward and fill the whole territory with our people. This is the kingdom of God, and we don't want it taken over by others."

Apostle Snow's pronunciation had echoes of his Vermont upbringing, somewhat like Brigham Young's, but the styles of the two men were quite the opposite. Brigham ranted at times, cajoled, laughed, criticized. Erastus chose his words carefully and thoughtfully.

"I am not certain what you have been told about the Muddy Valley. Sometimes, in encouraging settlement, not every detail of information is passed along to prospective settlers. You may not comprehend just how remote, how empty, how desolate the land south of here is. If you have grown up in verdant valleys with rich soil and pleasant mountain streams, you may conclude that you have been sent to some forbidding region of the underworld. But don't judge too quickly. The land along the Muddy produces well—even if it appears too alkaline and too sandy. It's a matter of applying new farming techniques, learning from those who have gone before you, and adjusting, not despairing."

Morgan tried to take the words as encouraging, but he didn't find it exactly inspiring to think of relearning his farming methods. Even more, he detected that Elder Snow was warning the settlers against disappointment. It sounded like he knew from experience that others had become disillusioned after settling there.

Apostle Snow's dark suit of clothes was faded, his knee-length frock coat rumpled. Morgan had noticed the same appearance on the other local people. The women wore homespun dresses, with cloth wraps, not lacy shawls. Men's trousers were baggy and patched, and their boots were scuffed, not seeming ever to have been blackened.

Angeline had told Morgan, after seeing some of the local children, "They don't look healthy. For all the sun they're supposed to have down here, they look pale. Blue, almost. Do you think they don't get enough to eat?"

Morgan had wondered the same thing, but he didn't know the answer. He had watched children as they played, and they seemed to lack the spark, the fun, of children in northern Utah. Many of the children were barefoot, and their clothes were tattered, patched and repatched. Even the warning Erastus Snow was offering didn't bother Morgan as much as seeing what this Cotton Mission was apparently doing to people.

"I could talk to you about self-sufficiency and our need for cotton," Apostle Snow was saying, "but that is not my thesis today. I want you to think of Adam. When the Lord asked Adam why he offered sacrifice, his reply was, 'I know not, save the Lord commanded me.' That is what *you* must say. If you are planning to take a look at the Muddy Valley for the purpose of deciding whether you want to stay or not . . . stop right here, turn around, and travel back where you came from. You must make up your minds, if you haven't already, that you will give your life to this mission.

"You are going to create a Zion city in the desert, and that can only happen when you unite, when you support one another. You will prosper together, and when you do, you must treat each other as brothers and sisters, the Lord's chosen, all equal in his sight."

Elder Snow hesitated, nodded, as if he wanted his words to penetrate the minds of all those gathered before him. This was all quite similar to what President Young and Brother Larsen had said, but to Morgan, it sounded new. It sounded like forever. Still, there was something powerful in the Apostle's confidence and trust. Morgan wanted to live up to that trust. He wanted to be a stalwart—a man of his word.

Erastus Snow seemed to be studying the people standing around him, as if to judge whether they were agreeing with him. "But don't be frightened," he said gently. "You can do this. All of you can. And let me add this." Now he raised his voice again. "Those of you who left part of your family behind, I call upon you to make plans, as soon as possible, to send for the others or go after them. You cannot divide your hearts and minds. You must gather your entire families and teach them to embrace your mission with the same commitment you possess."

Morgan knew that most of the polygamists in the group had

left one wife or more back at their homes in Utah. One of those men had explained to Morgan that it was a practical way to make the transition, but Morgan wondered what they would do now, after hearing an Apostle's opinion.

"Brothers and sisters," Elder Snow continued. He took one step closer to his audience. His hands began to rise, as if on their own, until they were higher than his shoulders, and then he turned those hands into fists as he said, "These are the last days. Do you understand that? Do you feel it in your very souls, know it by the power of the Spirit? Those of you who haven't entered into the law of celestial marriage, and tell yourselves you are perfectly happy with one wife, you must know that in the final days, as Isaiah prophesied, seven women will take hold of one man and say, 'We will eat our own food and provide our own clothes; only let us be called by your name.' That time is nigh upon us, and you must be ready to fulfill the ancient prophecies, embrace the *fulness* of the restored gospel."

This made no sense to Morgan. Apostle Snow had four wives, not seven, and Morgan didn't think there would be six single women grabbing at his coattails in the middle of a barren desert. He had no idea why the Apostle would make a point of this right now.

"And one last thing. You will meet up with Indians who look bedraggled and beaten down—dirty, naked, emaciated. You women will fear them at first, but there's an easy answer. When they beg, give them what food you can. Do as President Young has taught us. Don't shoot them with bullets but with biscuits. You can befriend them with kindness and, in time, convert them to the gospel of Jesus Christ. They will understand those doctrines when they hear them. They are, after all, from the house of Israel, descended from Joseph."

All this was a lot to think about. But when Erastus Snow ended his speech, Angeline clearly had one part of it on her mind. She whispered in Morgan's ear, "Was he saying that you *must* take more wives?"

"I don't know, Angie. I think he's talking about the very last days—and we aren't quite there yet."

"But he said we are."

Morgan thought of telling her that the numbers didn't add up. Where were these seven women for each man going to come from? But he knew better than to get into all that. "We talked all about this," he said. "And we settled the matter. I don't want another wife." And then he smiled. "When six more women grab onto me, I'll run like Joseph did, from Potiphar's wife."

"I'll shoot them," Angeline said. "And not with biscuits."

• • •

Angeline felt a change that night. People in the company seemed more subdued, as though the reality of what they were doing had finally set in. They continued to express their commitment to go forward, but she heard more nervousness in their voices.

After Apostle Snow had wished the Saints well and departed, Brother Larsen had offered one more recommendation: "I know that some of you lightened your wagons when we got bogged down in the snow up there on Beaver Pass, but I would ask all of you now to take another look at what you brought along. We'll be traveling through heavy sand much of the way from here, and the strain on your oxen and mules can kill them off. I know some of you brought china dishes, pretty pictures, and such things. And I understand why you want to keep all that. But it won't be worth it if you end up out in the desert with a dead ox and no way to finish your journey."

That night Angeline gave some of her clothing away to local people—who needed such things more than she did anyway—but it was abandoning her maplewood chest of drawers that broke her heart. Morgan had told her from the beginning that it was too heavy, and she had talked him out of leaving it behind. "We can come back and get it someday, when we don't have so much to carry along," Morgan had told her, but she hadn't listened. Now she told herself that she was moving to a place where furniture wouldn't have the same meaning. She stopped a man who rode past the camp in a farm wagon. She asked him if he would like to have the chest. He ducked his head and said, "Shore. But I ain't got a penny or even a sack of flour I could offer yuh for it."

"That's all right," she said. "Wait here a moment." Then she walked back to her wagon and helped Morgan carry the chest to the farmer, who had tears in his eyes when he thanked her.

"I'm sorry," Morgan told Angeline as the wagon rolled away.

"It's all right," she said. "All the sisters are making the same kind of choices today. We've changed a lot in the last month."

Angeline tried to think what had happened to her since the wagon train had set out from Salt Lake City. The mountains had been a test, but it wasn't the hardship that made the difference. Most of what had always seemed important was being stripped away, and she knew she would have to cling only to essential things—probably for the rest of her life. She felt sadness at the loss, but she also felt purified, as though all the fluff of life was being pulled from her, like dandelion dander in a hard wind.

Angeline tried not to think any more about the chest. She decided to get all that off her mind by paying a visit to Mary Ann.

But the poor girl was in no mood to talk, and Angeline came away worried.

As Angeline walked past a wagon on the way back to her own, she heard a woman inside the canvas cover say, "But you didn't say that to me. You said we'd go there and see how things worked out."

Angeline knew the wagon, knew the voice. It was Almira Donaldson, another of the new brides. She had told Angeline only a few days before that she had turned seventeen just recently and had never been away from home before. She had tried to laugh, but Angeline had sensed her homesickness. Her husband, Charlton, was a big, good-looking fellow who never seemed to worry about much of anything, but now he was saying, "I know I said that. That's how I figgered it. An' I guess I still figger it that way. If you ain't happy down 'ere, we'll go back."

"But you heard what Apostle Snow said. We'll go to hell if we do that."

Angeline stopped walking. She knew she was eavesdropping, but she wanted to know what Charlton would say.

"That's not 'xactly what he was sayin'," Charlton said. "I mean, I know he wants us to stay. But he can't make us do it if it just ain't the right thing for us."

"It *is* what he said. If we're not going to stay, we ought to leave right now. That's what he told us, and I think that's what we ought to do."

Charlton didn't answer for a time, and still Angeline waited. She could picture Almira, probably sitting on the floor of the wagon. She was an attractive girl who had started the trip with blonde ringlets, but she wore her hair braided now and pinned up, and her fair skin had turned red and chapped. "We kin say our own prayers," Charlton finally said. "The Lord kin tell us what's right, and when He does, that's what we'll do."

"Let's pray now and find out if we should go back."

"Well, shore. We kin do that. But we kin maybe go see what it's all about down there—and then keep on prayin'."

"I just want to go home now," Almira said, her voice tightening, and then she began to sob.

Angeline felt guilty by then. Surely Almira would have been humiliated to know she had been heard. So Angeline walked on, and that night she prayed for the Donaldsons. But she wasn't sure exactly what to say. It did seem right that people receive their own answers, and it also seemed right to carry out the callings the Lord had seen fit to bestow upon them. Surely, others in the company were facing the same questions.

The following morning, Angeline was happy to see the Donaldsons pull their wagon into line with all the others. What she didn't know was whether they had received the answer they sought, or whether they had merely been reluctant to go against the advice of an Apostle. Or maybe they didn't want to leave the company when all others were continuing to push ahead.

The day was warm, at least compared to the weather they had faced in the mountains, and there was something about moving forward that fit Angeline's needs. She had never liked to think too much about whether she was happy or not. She found it better to take one day at a time. She preferred being busy, but this rather uneventful day was pleasant. Morgan stayed with her in the wagon most of the time, and they chatted about the terrain— the strangeness of all the colors, the drab grays and browns of mesquite and dry cheat grass set off against the reds of the rock formations: rust and brick and vermilion. Morgan said at one point, "I think the look of this land can get into your blood at some point. There's something sort of rough and ready about it. I would've had a good time as a boy out here, chasing horny toads and catching snakes."

"I don't like snakes," Angeline said, "and I don't like sand in my shoes. But I can see myself perched out on one of those giant boulders, or maybe on top of a high ridge, just trying to see as far as I can see. I always climbed in the foothills above our place just so I could see the Great Salt Lake shimmering in the sunset."

"I liked that too. But I never sat very long. That's a little too dreamy for me. I'd rather wade in a creek and try to catch trout with my hands."

"I've done that."

"Well, we grew up a lot the same way," Morgan said. "We'll always have that inside us, no matter where we live."

There were times when Angeline wanted to stop the wagon and pull Morgan into the back. He *could* talk, no matter what he had always told her. And he could feel. She had come to believe that God had told her to love him, even when she was just a girl.

The wagons crossed the Santa Clara River early in the afternoon and then rolled on to Camp Springs, just two miles beyond. Angeline wondered why they were stopping so early, and Morgan went looking for Brother Larsen to ask him the same thing. When he came back, he said, "These springs are the last water for twenty-five miles, 'til we reach Beaver Dam Creek. So tomorrow's going to be a long day for our animals, and we have some steep hills to cross. We'll fill up our water barrels before we head out, and we'll have to let our oxen rest now and again all along the way. We're just lucky the weather's as nice as it is. Brother Larsen said that when folks travel this same road in summer, they have to rest in the day and push ahead at night."

Angeline was happy for the early stop. She wanted to bathe in those springs and get some of the accumulated dirt off her and her clothes. So she organized a little group of her friends who sought out a remote enough spot and spent an hour not only washing but splashing and romping in the cold water. And then, that evening, the two fiddlers in their group played while the emigrants danced. Brother Gerard and Brother Rintlesbacher only knew three or four songs, but they played them over and over, and Brother Garr Michaels called out the dance steps. They danced quadrilles and reels, and they laughed more than Angeline had heard them laugh before. She had a feeling that after Erastus Snow's sober warnings, people wanted to think of their mission as something more than a burden to be borne.

The next day was long, with some big hills to climb and descend, and gradually winter was feeling more like a warm northern Utah spring. People went without water all day and saved their supply for their animals. There was no dancing that night, as almost everyone turned in early. But the following day was easier, as the wagons traveled along the Virgin River, where there was not only water but dry grass for fodder and willow trees for shade.

In the next few days the road gradually fit the warnings the travelers had heard: more and more sand, deep in places. What Angeline was not ready for were the monstrous cliffs on either side of the river valley and the narrow passage that forced the wagons to wind from side to side and cross the river over and over. The spring runoff had not yet begun, so the river wasn't high and swift, but the sands in the riverbed were treacherous. Brother Larsen had warned the wagon drivers: "Don't let your animals stop in the river. They'll want to drink the water, but you can't let them have their own heads. Take them in hand as you enter the river and do what you have to do to keep them tromping on through. It's not just that they'll bog down. There's quicksand in this river, and if animals dawdle at all, they will sink. Your wagons will go down too. And sisters, if you didn't lighten your wagons in St. George, you'll want to do it now."

Angeline couldn't think of anything else to give up, but the first time they forded the river, she wished she had. Morgan led Ben and Buck across, pulling hard and shouting at them. Angeline stayed in the wagon, but Morgan told her to crack the whip over the oxen's backs, and that was something she knew how to do. Even at that, and even in this low-water season, the river sloshed into the wagon and at times pulled it sideways. She was relieved when the oxen kept going and lumbered up onto the opposite bank. At that point, she got out and led the oxen forward, and Morgan stayed behind to help others get across.

Everything went well at first, but early in the afternoon, shortly after making another crossing, Morgan came running to Angeline. "I need Ben and Buck," he was shouting. "Brother Baker's oxen are sinking in the sand."

Angeline helped Morgan unhitch the oxen as quickly as they could. Then Angeline led the animals and Morgan got between them and used their yoke to push them faster, yelling at them all the while. At the river, men were waiting. Brother Larsen was standing at the bank, and Brother and Sister Baker, a diminutive pair, were standing next to him. Sister Baker was holding her hands to her face, and Angeline could see her little body shake as she cried. Brother Baker kept calling out, "We'll get you, Whitey, don't bawl so. We'll pull you out now."

Whitey—and Whitey's partner, Red—were not consoled. They were bellowing plaintively in a sort of alternating rhythm. But they weren't struggling as they probably had at first. Their legs were clearly locked in the sand now, and water was flowing steadily against their sides. Angeline had no doubt that they were up to their hocks in the sand and could do nothing without help.

Art Brooks was standing in the water, wet up to his thighs. He had tied a rope around the big white ox's neck.

Several men helped Morgan and Angeline as they brought Ben and Buck into position. Art, by then, had walked to the bank with the end of the rope. Morgan tied the rope to the yoke, pulled the knot tight, and then urged the oxen forward. Angeline could see that he didn't want them to surge too hard, merely press steadily and gradually to pull Whitey loose.

The strain, however, was hard, and the ox's bawling became more desperate. The hollowness of the moaning was amplified by the narrow canyon and its bare rock walls.

But then, with a sudden gush of water and simultaneous lurch, Whitey bolted forward and, recognizing his new freedom, clambered ahead. The rope slackened, and the ox splashed his way onto the bank. Brother Baker wrapped his arms around Whitey's neck and stopped him from striking out for higher ground. "You're all right now," he kept telling the ox as Brother Brooks untied the rope.

"Hurry, hurry," Sister Baker was pleading. "Get Red out too."

Men were already seeing to that. Two men moved Whitey out of the way as Art plunged back into the water. He towered over the red ox, and Angeline could see that it had sunk deeper, the water rushing higher, even washing over its back.

Morgan worked his oxen again, stepped them ahead far enough to tighten the rope, and gradually he raised his voice, commanded them to pull harder. But Red had gone silent, maybe out of fear, maybe out of resignation.

Morgan seemed to sense that something more was needed. He slapped both his oxen across the haunches and shouted with force,

"Giddyup, you two. *Now! Giddyup.*" The oxen lurched against their yoke, but at the same moment Angeline heard a cracking sound. She hadn't known it was possible, but she understood immediately what had happened. Red's neck had snapped.

The ox slumped. All was silent for a few moments, except for Sister Baker's sobs.

Morgan backed up his own oxen, and Red dropped deeper into the water. Then Brother Larsen walked into the water far enough to hand a rifle to Art Brooks, who took it, seemed to steel himself for a moment, and then pointed the barrel at the back of the ox's head—the only part still showing above the water. Again he hesitated, as though he didn't want to do it, but finally he pulled the trigger, and blood gushed into the water and streamed away.

• • •

Once the rest of the company had crossed the river, Brother Larsen told the wagon drivers to stop at a site nearby where the canyon widened a little. "Set up camp. Get some rest," he yelled repeatedly as he walked past the wagons. "We'll have a meeting at four this afternoon, before you eat your dinners."

Morgan knew, of course, why they needed to meet. One ox could not pull a wagon across some of the land that lay in front of them, and somehow a way would have to be found to help the Bakers.

But it was only when the company gathered along the riverbank at four o'clock that the full weight of the situation became clear. Brother Larsen stood with his back to the willow trees along the river, deep in the corridor of cliffs. He did not have a loud voice, but he didn't need one now, with sounds carrying easily in the narrow canyon.

"As you know," Brother Larsen said, "we lost an ox this afternoon. It's not too surprising, really. We've put these animals
through some hard tests, and these crossings have turned out to
be the biggest ones yet. We had expected, sooner or later, that an
accident like this would happen—or sickness or injuries or something of that sort would stop some of us. We can be grateful that
we haven't had too much serious trouble so far."

Morgan heard a man near him, Brother Carpenter, whisper to
his wife, "I wouldn't call this a ax-dent. Some people brings things
on theirselves."

"Here's what we have to decide. We could let the Bakers stay
here. We could finish out our trek and then send a wagon and
some extra teams back. But I don't think that's a good answer.
We could make sure they had enough food, and they could hold
out all right, but a lone pair camped up here invites an Indian
attack."

He waited, as though he hoped someone would tell him that
he was right, that the Bakers shouldn't be left alone, but no one
said anything.

"So I think someone needs to step forward and offer assistance. Many of you have double teams, and maybe someone feels
that you could let the Bakers borrow one of your teams until we
reach the Muddy—or at least get to the Mormon Mesa. We have
quite a few days of travel ahead of us still, and it's over some
rough terrain, but some are getting by with one team, and I think
we can get through all right that way. So tell me, is someone willing to make that offer to the Bakers—lend them one of your
teams?"

No one spoke, and Morgan thought he understood. Those
with double teams often had children and bigger wagons. They
probably doubted they could get by with a single yoke of oxen.

Brother Larsen let the silence continue for quite some time before he said, "Surely one of you could see your way to make a sacrifice. We're all brothers and sisters here."

But Brother Carpenter raised his voice and cut through the quiet. "Brother Larsen, I don't mind helpin' a man out. I done it all my life. But sometimes people make their own troubles, and then they have to live with what they done. Brigham Young himself told me to bring along two teams, so I did. It's kinda hard to see why them that done what they was told now hafta pay for them that paid no heed to good advice."

Morgan heard a little stir go through the group. He suspected that some people were telling others that they would have brought two teams if they had been able to afford them.

Someone said, "Brigham only said, take two teams if you can. It wasn't a command."

"I understand what you're saying, Brother Carpenter," Brother Larsen said, "but we all have to do what we can. It does no good to start speaking ill of one another."

"I ain't speakin' ill of no one. I'm jist sayin' that when a man takes a gamble, he has to plan out what he's gonna do if things don't work out."

Brother Larsen put his hands on his hips. He looked down at the ground. Morgan could see the difference in the man, the changes since they had left Salt Lake. His trousers were stained with red dirt, and his shirt was torn in one elbow. Even more, he looked tired, his eyes squinted and his skin dry and rough. After a time, he said, "George, you know how much teams cost these days. Some just didn't have the ready cash. That's all it is—not so much a choice as a necessity. Now, let me say again, we're all brothers and sisters. Is there someone who could spare a yoke of oxen for this last week?"

The silence set in again. And then a man on the other side of the crowd, John Dickson, said, "I hate to bring this up, but I feel like someone's got to say it." He cleared his throat, and he sounded apologetic as he said, "You told us when we set out not to let our animals stop in the water. Most of us did everything we could to follow that advice. But I saw what happened to those oxen that got mired in the sand. Brother Baker let 'em stop and drink. He did exactly what you told us not to do. I guess people make mistakes, and I can understand that, but now we're all being forced to pay for one man who didn't follow instructions. Maybe George is right. Maybe Brother Baker needs to learn to live with his own disobedience."

Brother and Sister Baker were standing not far from Morgan and Angeline, and Morgan saw Brother Baker hang his head, not reply. But Morgan couldn't let that happen. "I saw what happened too," Morgan said, his voice louder than he meant it to be. He softened his tone a little as he continued. "We all know how oxen are. They have a mind of their own. When Brother Baker's oxen stopped, he pulled on them and he prodded them with a stick. When I saw what was happening, I went out in the river and tried to help. But we were both just a little too late. And I take responsibility for that. I should have gone out to help right from the beginning." Morgan let that settle in, and then he added, "Some of us have been around animals a lot more than others. Brother Baker has never driven a team of oxen this far before, and surely not through rivers and quicksand. He's not a large man to pull on those big animals. But he tried his best."

It was a long speech for Morgan, and now he wanted to step back, become part of the crowd, and hope that someone was ready to offer a team.

But still, no one offered. And Brother Dickson said, "Think about that for just a minute, Morgan. You tell us he's not good with animals, and Brother Larsen wants us to give ours over to him? All I can think is that if we do that, the first time we cross the river again, I'll lose my oxen."

"I guess we'd have to stay with them and make sure that didn't happen," Brother Larsen said.

"That's right," Morgan said. "I let the Bakers down, not helping them any more than I did. We all need to work together at these crossings."

But still, no one offered.

Morgan knew that the Bakers were a little different from most folks, and maybe that was why others felt no attachment to them. Israel Baker had become a farmer in Utah, in the Salt Lake Valley, but he had told Morgan that it was not something he understood very well. He had been raised in New York state and had made a living as a painter and carpenter and general fix-it man. He seemed to have a knack for such things; he had helped Morgan repair more than one wagon. But he and Minnie stayed mostly to themselves, and sometimes Morgan wondered whether they spent night and day reading the scriptures. Israel could quote long passages from the Bible or the Book of Mormon, and he liked doing that. Along the trail, when Sunday meetings had been held, he seemed to seek out moments when he could recite from the book of Revelation or even from the book of Moses, a scripture most members didn't know. He loved anything that took a grand view of the universe and the purpose of man's existence. Morgan had sensed that his recitations irritated people, and maybe it was some of that now that was making him and his reticent but emotional wife less sympathetic than another couple might have been.

But Morgan liked the Bakers. Israel was practical in his way, but his vision of life was grandiose and idealistic. That struck

Morgan as rather interesting, and besides, the man had opened up to Morgan a little as they had worked on the wagons, and Morgan found he always liked people when he got to know them.

"Well, let me ask you this then," Brother Larsen was now saying. "Can you think of another way to solve this problem?"

Surely, Morgan thought, everyone must see what had to be done. He counted to ten and told himself he would not say anything unless no one else spoke before he finished his count. But at ten he kept going and pushed on to twenty, and finally he said, "Brother Larsen, I guess I don't see the problem." Everyone looked his way. "Apostle Snow told us we were going south to set up a Zion city, and if I understand that, it means we all work together. How about this: someone who has a double team could loan one yoke of oxen to the Bakers for a day, and then someone else could take a turn for another day. And some of us with only one team could help too. I could drive my wagon ahead a couple of miles and then go back with my oxen and bring the Bakers' wagon forward. They might be alone for a while, but not very long. It's just a matter of having a will and every one of us feeling like we haven't done our job until we all get where we're going."

To Morgan's surprise, Brother Dickson said, "Well, sure. I could let Israel take one of my teams for a day, and then a few days later, maybe for another day. And I could travel close to him and help at the rivers. I never meant to say that I wouldn't help at all."

"I can do that too," James Wilcox said. Morgan knew that James and Lydia had had a hard time giving up some of their possessions, and they probably felt they needed their two teams.

Brother Larsen was nodding. "All right, then. Let's take it one day at a time. Tomorrow, Brother Dickson will help the Bakers. We'll figure out the next day tomorrow night. You know, Brother

Davis is right. When we get to the Muddy, we'll all have to look out for each other. Sooner or later, we may all need help, and maybe it's Brother Baker who will fix your wagon or do something else for you. That's what Zion is supposed to be."

Morgan felt Angeline take hold of his arm and hug it tightly to her side. "I'm proud of you," she said.

CHAPTER 5

The weather continued warm for December, and water and feed for animals was always close by as the wagon train continued to follow the path of the Virgin River. But the bends in the river meant that the frequent crossings could not be avoided. Some were shallow and not a problem, but the threat of quicksand was always present, and crossing in places where the river ran deeper was usually an ordeal. The members of the company did step forward and help the Bakers, and more than a few told Morgan that he had said the right thing and brought people together. Morgan didn't mind that people said that to him, but he didn't like the attention. What he had always liked was to be a problem solver and a help to his father—or anyone in his town—but in school he had sat at the back of the room if the teacher would let him, and he had never raised his hand to say anything in class. Once, Mrs. Manning, his teacher at the town school, had told him, "You're smart as a whip, Morgan. Do you know that?"

"No, ma'am," he had replied.

"Well, you are, even if no one knows it. You sit there like a bump on a log, and I wish you would speak up more often. But I have to say, I like a quiet boy who has some brains in his head rather than one of these children who talk all day and never have anything to say."

Morgan had always remembered that. He didn't know how smart he was, but he knew he could read as well as anyone, and he liked doing arithmetic. And Mrs. Manning had given him a good reason to think before he said too much. Still, he had to admit to himself that speaking up for the Bakers had been satisfying. He didn't regret that he had said something at the right time.

• • •

Brother Larsen came by one morning and said, "We won't be as close to the river as we have been today, and we'll have a stretch of desert to cross. So fill your water barrels. Your water will have to hold out—and you'll need plenty for your oxen. We'll also have to let the animals rest for a couple of hours, around noon, but let's try to keep rolling as much as we can."

Morgan was nodding, agreeing, but Angeline was mostly dreading. She didn't mind a big push, but she hated days with little change. At least the river crossings changed the pace of things. "How many more days 'til we reach the Muddy?" she asked.

Brother Larsen had taken a few steps away, but now he turned back. It was early in the morning, but Jens looked weary already. Angeline had noticed the same look in everyone's eyes the last few days. They were no longer facing the cold and snow of the mountain passes, but animals often bogged down in places where sand had drifted into dunes. Oxen or mules sometimes needed extra help, so the men of the company waited at these spots and pushed the wagons through. Angeline helped too because she liked to be useful, but she was aware how battered her dress had become—the calico dress she had begun to wear as the weather had warmed.

Her only other dresses were the linsey-woolsey she had worn in the cold and the lavender wedding dress she planned to wear to church once she was in the valley. Too often she had stepped on her skirt or caught it under a wheel. She washed her clothes and mended them when she had a chance, but she wondered how long her dresses would last in the desert, where sand and dirt would grind them and sun and sweat would bleach away the colors.

Morgan had two pairs of trousers, but both were stained with red from the sand and soil. Angeline supposed the stains would only deepen with time, and she had no idea how to purchase new clothing, hundred of miles from any store that sold ready-made apparel or cloth to sew. She knew a little about spinning and weaving, but such equipment had been too heavy to bring along. Morgan told her that in time they would be able to transport the cotton they raised to the Salt Lake Valley and sell it there, and they could receive store goods in trade. But how long would it take to produce that first crop of cotton?

"We've got a few more days to go," Brother Larsen was saying. "Apostle Snow told me we can cut some miles off by crossing the Mormon Mesa and then dropping into St. Joseph—one of the settlements on the Muddy. The only trouble with that is, it'll take us a whole day to get the wagons onto the mesa. It's a hard climb."

"So is that the way we're going?" Morgan asked.

"I think so. We'll take a look at it when we get there, but if we stay on the river and avoid the mesa, it's maybe thirty miles longer. We have to decide what's harder on our animals—more of this sand, or making that big climb."

Morgan was nodding.

Angeline didn't know how Ben and Buck would hold up, but the shorter route sounded better to her. Still, she told herself that she could take hard days as well as anyone. She would put up with the conditions she faced, and she would help the other women do the same. Mary Ann was doing a little better in the warmer weather, and Angeline had decided that one of her responsibilities was to visit with her every day and lift her spirits as much as she could. It wasn't always her first impulse to look after people, but she wanted to be more that way. She liked the talk of Zion and what it meant. She wanted to be part of that.

The wagons set out soon after that. The sand was still heavy, and the draft animals trudged through it until about eleven o'clock. Brother Larsen stopped the wagon train near a cliff, where shade had allowed grass to grow, and he walked back to speak to everyone again. "Let's take two hours," he said. "Let the animals feed, and you get some rest yourselves."

As usual, Angeline said what she was thinking instead of simply accepting Brother Larsen's directions. "I'm not sure two hours is enough. Our oxen are giving out. We might have to start cutting back our hours of travel each day."

"Some are saying that," Jens said, "and others are telling me that we have to get this journey over with—and then the animals can get a longer rest."

"Won't we have to start plowing as soon as we get there?"

Brother Larsen stared back at her, as if to ask, *Do you think you know more about this than I do?* But what he actually said was, "We'll see how things go this afternoon. We'll have to decide each day what we can do."

Angeline liked Brother Larsen, but something in his tone of voice seemed to say that women weren't quite up to the task of pioneering and didn't understand the things that men did. Angeline believed, however, that she could tell when an ox was worn out; she didn't need a man to make that judgment for her.

Morgan obviously knew what she was thinking. He laughed as

Brother Larsen walked away, and he said to Angeline, "Remember, everyone's probably telling him what he ought to do. It's not easy to satisfy this many people."

"I know. And I also understand that ladies shouldn't have opinions. We should listen to our husbands and leaders. They always know best."

"That's exactly right," Morgan said. He was grinning.

Morgan unyoked Ben and Buck and led them into the shade, where they began to feed on the grass. "Angie," Morgan said, as he walked back to her, "I'm going to check on Brother Baker while you get something ready for us to eat. Don't let the oxen wander off."

So Morgan had to tell her what to do too. Was she so stupid she would let the oxen run wild?

There was nothing to eat but jerky and dry "crackers" anyway. If Morgan wanted some of that when he got back, he could pull it out of their food sacks himself. She was thirsty, but she didn't feel like eating. For the moment there was something else she wanted to take care of. Out in the desert there was usually not a good place to hide and relieve herself. At least she didn't have to worry about that in this spot. She had already spotted a thicket of mesquite for that purpose.

She made that little trip, and when she returned, she pulled a dipper from a hook and sank it deep into the water barrel that was strapped to the side of the wagon, and then took a long drink. She knew what Brother Larsen had told her about using water carefully, but she decided, with a bit of defiance in her mind, to fill the dipper and drink again. She was wiping her chin with her hand when she heard a gentle voice, soft as a girl's, say, "How are you today, Sister Davis?"

Angeline turned to see Joshua Shupe, one of Wilfred Shupe's

many children—a boy of ten or so. She felt "discovered," and she quickly set the dipper into the wagon. "Hello, Josh. I'm just fine."

"It's a warm day, isn't it?"

"Yes, well, we have to get used to that, don't we? It's going to be a lot hotter before long." She sounded as superior as the men, and she didn't like that in herself. She quickly added, "I'm about done in, though. Aren't you?"

"Yes'm."

She could see his eyes trained on the water barrel. But surely he had his own water. She had already taken too much for herself. "Be sure to drink a little extra today, Josh, no matter what Brother Larsen says. We're just as important as the animals. We need water too."

"I can't drink today."

"Can't drink? Why?"

"Father told me to fill the water barrel this morning, but I forgot. So he filled it, but then he said I had to learn. No water for me all day."

"But that won't do. You can't go all day without a drink."

Josh was looking at her now, not at the barrel, and she knew he wouldn't ask. What she also knew was that she had taken a very big drink and he had watched. It took her only a second or two to know she couldn't turn the boy away. She retrieved the dipper and reached into the barrel again. She gave Josh one drink, and then a second. She just hoped that their water would last now, and that Morgan wouldn't notice how much she had dipped out. As soon as Morgan returned, he would surely want to water Ben and Buck.

"Thank you so much," Josh said, and he let out a long sigh of relief.

"Come back again if you have to," Angeline said impulsively, but she told herself that Morgan would have done exactly the same thing.

Joshua left then, and in a few minutes Morgan returned. By then, Angeline had decided not to sit in the shade, as she had planned, but to pull out something for Morgan to eat. She still wasn't hungry herself. She thought of telling Morgan about Joshua, but she wasn't entirely sure she had done the right thing, so she made a quick decision to drink less herself that afternoon and just not say anything to Morgan.

Just as Morgan was sitting down in the shade of the cliff to eat his dry meal, Angeline saw Wilfred Shupe coming her way. He was gripping his fingers deeply into Josh's shoulder. Josh was fighting not to cry and doing a poor job of it. Shupe was a thin, stringy man. He moved in awkward bursts, never did anything smoothly. "Did you give water to this child?" he was demanding to know.

Angeline's temper fired instantly. "Yes, I did," she said, and she stepped toward Brother Shupe, not away. "I know you had plans to kill him off today, but that didn't strike me as a good idea."

Shupe stepped closer still. "Sister Davis, that is none of your business. I don't know what kind of lies this boy told you, but he was being punished for failing to carry out his chores. That's a father's duty, and I don't like to be countered by a silly, ignorant woman who knows nothing about the matter."

Morgan was on his feet by then, and in a second he was next to Angeline. "Watch what you call my wife, Shupe," he said. "You may talk to your own wife that way, but don't come down here yelling at Angeline."

Shupe turned toward Morgan. "What do you know about the way I talk to my wife?"

"I hear you. The whole camp hears you."

"And I'll thank you, and all the rest, to mind their own business. I have half a mind to knock you on your backside."

"You have half a mind, all right," Morgan barked at him, their noses not a foot apart now. "And I just hope you'll take a swing at me—because I'll knock you halfway into tomorrow." He had doubled both his fists and moved back just enough to take a good punch if it came to that. "And by the way, pull those dagger fingers of yours out of that boy's shoulder. You're doing damage to him."

Shupe seemed to recognize that Morgan was no one to take on. He let go of Joshua, and the boy seemed to shrink an inch or two. "Your wife had no business giving water to this boy. I told him he couldn't drink today. He didn't do his chores this morning."

Suddenly all the attention was on Angeline again. She was still angry, but she felt the accusation—not so much from Shupe as from Morgan. "The boy was thirsty," she said to Morgan. "That's no way to punish a child. It's a hot day. He can't go all day without water."

Morgan turned back toward Shupe. "She's right about that. Boys don't always do their chores the way they should, but you can't let them go dry out here in this desert."

"I wouldn't have. I was going to give him a drink when I was ready. But then he comes back with water dribbled all down his shirt and he tells me lies. I had to *make* him tell me where he got a drink."

Angeline could see Morgan soften, his hands relax. He didn't like to confront people, didn't like to disagree with a brother in the gospel. Still, he didn't take anything back. "If Angeline gave your boy a drink, she was trying to do the right thing. But maybe she should have talked to you before she did it."

"What?" Angeline demanded of Morgan. "Josh told me the truth—that his father was punishing him for not filling the water

barrel. What was I supposed to say to a man who would keep water away from a thirsty child? I'll interfere with that every day of
the week." She pointed a finger at Shupe. "I know how you treat
Polly. If you said the things to me that you say to her, I'd be the
one to knock you on your back. And don't think I can't do it."
But Angeline was twice as angry at Morgan as she was at Wilfred
Shupe. Morgan had been quick to protect her, but it hadn't taken
much to get him over to Shupe's side.

"All right, this is settled," Morgan said. "Don't insult my wife
again. But we won't interfere with your family life, either."

Angeline wanted to grab these two men by their shirts and
knock their heads together. Shupe was a tyrant and a cruel father,
but Morgan was way too quick to make peace with a man like
that. Shupe was mumbling something about having had a right to
be upset, and Morgan was saying that he was sure it was all just a
misunderstanding.

Fine. A misunderstanding. Angeline hoped Morgan would
"understand" when she didn't speak to him again, maybe forever.

• • •

Morgan knew Angeline was angry. He also thought she had
been right to give the boy a drink. And maybe he shouldn't have
backed down to Brother Shupe quite so easily. But Morgan had
talked to the company about cooperating, about building a Zion
city, as Apostle Snow had admonished them to do. He couldn't say
things like that and then make an enemy of Shupe, who would be
part of that city.

Two or three times that afternoon Morgan tried to talk to
Angie. Once, he even offered something of an apology, but she
wouldn't give him more than a one- or two-word reply, and he

could see that he wasn't going to talk her out of her resentment. Still, she had never been this angry with him before, and he really didn't like it. He had always had a notion about marriage, that everything had to be worked out quickly. His own father and mother had shown a little irritation with each other from time to time, but somehow they had always settled matters. He didn't know what discussions or negotiations might have happened when he wasn't around, but he couldn't remember his parents ever staying angry very long. So that was his hope, that Angie would soften soon, that they could talk things out, and all would be well again.

But it didn't happen, not that day. Angeline had told him once, "I don't get mad very often, but when I do, look out, because I don't calm down right away." So it seemed much wiser to let her have some time. He didn't want to hear her talk to him the way she had talked to Brother Shupe. Morgan was pretty sure she *could* knock a man on his behind, and although he didn't think she would try to do that to him, her face was stern enough that he wasn't at all sure he wanted to find out.

The worst was, her anger didn't give way that night. She said next to nothing all evening, and then she went to bed in the wagon before he did—with her back turned to him. And the next morning, it was more of the same. Another day passed, and she wasn't quite so stern, but when he tried to discuss the issue, she cut him off immediately, and she turned her back on him again that night.

The trouble was, the next day Brother Larsen, after looking things over and talking with many of the men, decided to make the big climb onto the Mormon Mesa. When the wagons approached the steep grade, everyone got out and had a look. It was not a long stretch, but it was narrow, with no room for error. The first part of the climb didn't look too bad, but Morgan could see that farther up, the incline became severe and then turned into cliffs at the top. The men would have to lead the animals on a trail around the cliffs, and the wagons would have to be hoisted to the top with ropes and chains. From what Apostle Snow had told Brother Larsen, three or four teams would be needed to get each wagon up the final grade to the cliffs, but even then, wheels had to be blocked each time draft animals had to take a rest. So it would be a long series of short pulls, and people would have to be ready to set boulders behind wheels after each move forward.

The wagon train crossed the river, and then everyone rested before starting the climb. It was also a time for planning. At the end of the day, all the teams and all the wagons had to make it onto the flat land at the top of the mesa. Mules and horses could pull together, but oxen could only be hitched with other teams of oxen, and no one team of animals could make the ascent more than three or four times. Morgan was called in, with others, to figure out a schedule and make assignments to pull off the big project.

Morgan was still trying to break the ice with Angeline, so as he was about to walk to the front of the wagon train for the meeting, he said, "Angie, I'm going now. It's going to be a rough day. You might want to take a little rest yourself."

"Oh, I must. Women get sooooo tired," Angeline said. "You men can figure everything out for all us delicate little women. We'll just fan ourselves and sigh at the sight of all that brute, masculine work."

This was the most she had said to him in the last two days, but, of course, her sarcasm only meant she was still upset. He thought he understood why she was angry, but he doubted it would do any good to apologize one more time. The worst thing was, he was going to need her today. All the women would have to work, and no one could work harder than Angeline.

So Morgan said nothing more. He attended the meeting, where

a schedule for the ascent was worked out. Brother Larsen asked Eb Crawford to jot down in a logbook the order for the wagons and teams. And then Brother Larsen made assignments. Morgan was taken by surprise when Brother Larsen mentioned his name first. "Brother Davis, I want you to run the operation from the base of the hill. Make sure the right teams are hooked up, and—at least at first—work your way up with each wagon, to make sure people understand what they're supposed to do. If teams aren't hitched right, or if blocks aren't set when they need to be, we can have some terrible accidents. People could get themselves killed."

He then assigned several men to climb the grade ahead of the teams to set up the chaining operation at the summit. They set out with a team of mules dragging the heavy chains.

Morgan was happy for his assignment. He trusted himself more than he did a lot of the men, and he always felt better when work rested on his own strong shoulders. But he almost wished that he could do all the jobs. It worried him that some of the men were not experienced enough, not strong enough, not as reliable as they needed to be. These were mostly young men, and not all of them had a knack for an operation of this kind.

Still, things started well. People had been warned of the difficulty, and everyone seemed concerned not to be the one to make a mistake. Teams were also fairly fresh at that point, and the first ascent went well. The six oxen had to strain, but Lyman Hunt, assigned to stay at the head of the teams, made good judgments about letting the oxen pause and rest before they were pushed too far. Men and a couple of older boys had worked their way up the trail and set big rocks where they could be reached easily. Travelers in previous companies had made the climb in recent years, and they had gathered rocks and left them near the road.

At the top of the hill, on this first ascent, those who had

followed the wagon then hiked the final stretch and led the three ox teams around the cliffs. When they reached the top, they joined with the crew that Brother Larsen was leading. They hitched up the oxen, and with men also pulling, lifted the first wagon over the top of the cliff. Those three ox teams were kept at the top to hoist the other wagons, but most of the men walked down to start the process with the next wagon.

All was well so far, but Morgan saw the problem ahead right from the beginning. It was not fiercely hot, but the temperature was rising enough that all the workers were sweating, and each climb would be more difficult than the one before. Animals would wear down, and so would men. Women and children were called on to walk, not ride in the wagons, but women would have to block wheels and maybe even help with the chaining at the top, if they could.

Maybe Angeline had noticed the need, or maybe she wanted to prove what she could do, but she hadn't waited to be asked. She helped the men hitch up the second set of oxen. And then she worked with the crew, pushing the wagon and then blocking the wheels when it was time. Morgan was proud to watch her join in. Even when the animals rested for a few minutes, she worked her way up the hill to make sure other rocks were ready, and she checked the wagon to make certain that nothing was shifting or falling out.

The next couple of hours continued to go well, but a wind came up as the afternoon heat came on. It was a dry, hot wind, strong enough to add to the struggle to mount the hill. Eventually, it came time to move Morgan and Angeline's wagon. By then, most of the wagons had made it over the summit, and fewer men and women were on the hillside. Morgan didn't know whether they had given out the way a few of the animals had. He could see that everyone was soaked in sweat, and clothing had sometimes taken a beating. More than one man had torn a shirt or the knees in his breeches, and Morgan had seen one woman catch her skirt in a wagon wheel. She screeched as her skirt tore from bottom to top. She managed to pull away without losing her skirt, but then she walked back down the road to make what repairs she could. Bonnets were important in the sun, but as they filled with sweat, they sagged in women's faces. Some men wrapped cloth around their hands as bloody blisters broke open from chaining and pushing wheels all day.

When Morgan walked ahead of Buck and Ben with two other yokes of oxen aiding in the pull, Angeline stepped up next to him. "You've been doing this all day," she said. "Let me take our wagon up."

So she was talking to him.

"All right. That would help, but stay at the top when you get there. You've been up and down this road more times than I have."

"No. I'll come back. Too many people have quit on us."

So when they got to the top, they both continued on, led the oxen over the brim of the hill, and then helped chain their own wagon up the cliff. Then they walked down together. Angeline still wasn't saying much, but she seemed quiet, not hostile. He wondered whether he would ever understand things of that sort. Marriage, he could see, was going to be more complicated than he had expected.

• • •

Angeline could see when they reached the base of the mountain again that only one more wagon needed to be pulled up. Horses and mules—four of each—were waiting to do the hard work. The Campbell family was waiting now, having worked much of the day, but they were ready to get their own wagon to the top. Brother and Sister Campbell were older than most of the party. Angeline thought maybe Elizabeth was in her midforties, and Matthew might have been fifty. They had six children. One of them, Katherine, was fourteen or fifteen. Earlier in the day Angeline had seen her on the hillside moving rocks off the road. She was a small girl, thin, and hadn't been able to help with the heavier work. Surely, by now, she was weary of waiting for her own wagon to be pulled to the top.

"How are you, Katherine?" Angeline asked.

"I'm fine," she answered, but she looked wistful. "I'll be glad when we get to the Muddy River." And then she added, without a smile, "I guess I will."

"We'll make the best of it, won't we?"

Katherine nodded. "We'll try. Papa says we have to do our best. But everyone says this good weather will end. They say you can put an egg on the sand and it will cook like it's hard boiled."

"I know. I've heard that too." Angeline looked more carefully at Katherine, saw how really downhearted she appeared. "Are you missing home?"

"Yes."

But she didn't explain. Angeline was sure that Katherine had left behind friends, family, maybe the house she had lived in all her life. "Where did you live?"

"Nephi. We had dances there . . . and parties. We won't have any of that now."

"Maybe we can. This company doesn't have many people your age, but there will be some in the settlements, I'm sure. You'll find new friends."

Again Katherine only nodded. She didn't look convinced.

But the wagon was moving ahead, and this time Angeline walked with Katherine, who was carrying a little wooden case. "Papa said to get all the weight out of the wagon that we could," she explained. "He wanted me to leave this behind, but it's all my ribbons and bows. It isn't heavy. I just wanted to keep a few things."

"I know what you mean. I had to give up my maplewood chest of drawers back in St. George."

"Was it something you loved?"

"Yes. My grandmother gave it to me."

Katherine nodded, and then she looked away. "Some things don't seem fair," she whispered, and Angeline heard her emotion.

"But *things* aren't so important, Katherine. Really."

"You can call me Kate," Katherine said, and then she added, only faintly, "Some things matter more than others."

Angeline wasn't about to preach to her about that. She wanted to tell Kate that Zion mattered. Her new husband was trying to teach her that, but she was too stubborn to learn. All day she had watched him work, heard him counsel men much older than himself, even heard patience in his voice no matter how tired he was. And what she felt was that she had been much too severe with him. After all, he had only wanted to keep peace with Brother Shupe.

Angeline knew that all too often she didn't stop herself from saying things she shouldn't say. She had been thinking about that for two days, but only now had she brought herself to admit it.

But now there were blocks to set and that last wagon to push and pull. Angeline was so tired she could hardly walk, but she rolled a big stone behind a wheel, and then she looked up at Kate. "I can't lift such big rocks," Kate said. "I tried this morning."

"That's the whole thing, Kate. Trying."

Angeline could see that the horses and mules were tired, and they didn't pull with as much stubbornness as the oxen. Morgan was having to stop them after only forty or fifty feet of progress. The ascent was taking longer than the others. Finally, Brother Larsen led another team of horses down and added them to the eight animals already hitched up.

Progress was better with the added team, but when it came time for chaining, Morgan told everyone, "We've got to be careful now. We brought this wagon up last because the tongue on it broke a few days back. We've patched it back together, but we're a little worried that it could come apart again. While the men up above are pulling the chain, we all need to push it as high as we can to relieve some of the strain on it. If I see the tongue giving way at all, we'll bring it back down and figure out what we can do."

Everyone agreed without saying much, and then the hard lift began. The wagon was old, and it squeaked and moaned, but it rolled ahead to the cliff. Morgan called to the men above to begin the lift, and all those on the ground helped until the wagon was too high to reach.

The wagon was only halfway up the cliff when Angeline heard a splitting noise. Morgan shouted, "Let it back down." But at that moment the tongue broke loose, and the wagon dropped to the ground. The people below scattered as the wagon hit and then slammed forward onto its wheels. Before anyone could get back to the wagon, it started to roll backward, down the narrow road.

Angeline hurried to catch up. She and a few others tried to hold it back, but there was no hope on the steep slope. The wagon rolled heavily down the mountainside, bumping and jostling, picking up speed. Near the bottom of the hill it finally angled off the road and hit a large rock. A wheel shattered, the spokes flying in all directions. The wagon flipped over, and boxes and barrels scattered across the ground. A trunk crashed onto its top and then bounced over, the lid flying open. And suddenly colorful things were flying about in the wind. A yellow dress was kiting across the terrain, catching in sagebrush, pulling loose, tumbling and spinning. White underthings were blowing into the mesquite brush, catching on the thorny limbs.

Angeline watched everything settle, and then she looked at Kate, who was trying to catch a few of her ribbons. She had dropped her box in all the confusion, and now the contents were also wafting away.

She grabbed a few ribbons nearby, but she didn't try to chase the ones that were blowing like bright birds, lifting and then darting about in the gusts of wind. For a long moment, Kate said nothing. She seemed to be deciding how she was going to react. Finally she said, "They're just things. You told me that."

She didn't sound convinced, exactly, but Angeline heard the sincerity in her attempt to believe what she was saying. Angeline grasped her, held her tight. "But such lovely things," she said. "I'm so sorry."

Morgan had approached them by then. Angeline saw how upset he was. "We shouldn't have let that happen," he said. "I shouldn't have relied on that tongue holding."

"We did our best," was all Angeline could think to say.

"I'm going down to save what I can," Morgan said. "I'll make trips all night if I have to. Everything the Campbells have was in that wagon."

"I'll go with you," Angeline said.

"No. You're exhausted. Stay here. I'll get some of the men to go with me."

Brother Campbell stepped over to them. "Just leave it. You can't carry all those things up here," he said.

"No. We can. We will," Morgan said. "And we'll get it all to the Muddy. One way or another."

"There's no way to do that, Morgan."

But Morgan turned and called up the mountain, where lots of the company were looking down from the top of the cliff, "All who want to walk down with me, let's salvage what we can."

By then Morgan was already striding out. Angeline caught up with him quickly. She was thinking about Zion. And when she looked up the hill, she saw that plenty of other people were making their way down around the cliff. Everyone wanted to help.

"I'm sorry," Angeline whispered to Morgan. He took hold of her hand.

CHAPTER 6

Bishop Ewan Morrison was talking to the newly arrived settlers, but Morgan's mind was on the land around him. He thought he had been warned, and he thought he had understood, but nothing he had seen in the desert country around St. George or traveling down the Virgin River had prepared him for what he was seeing now. He had never envisioned anything quite so desolate.

The wagon train was camped along the Muddy not far from a little settlement called St. Joseph—and now referred to as "New St. Joseph." There were stunted willows on the banks of the river, but Morgan saw nothing that he could call a tree. The murky water in the river was warm and tasted of minerals. The bluffs of the Mormon Mesa, a mile or two north, were mottled pink and tan, and in the distance beyond them were some blue-gray mountains, but there was little color in the broad valley. He saw scattered sagebrush and greasewood, more gray than green, and prickly pears and salt grass, and a few scrawny mesquite bushes, but the sand and rocks were a weak shade of pink, or even white where the alkaline dust, pale as table salt, gathered in patches. How could this be farm country? Where was there anything he could call "soil"?

"I know this land looks forbidding," Bishop Morrison was saying. He had gathered the settlers in a big half circle near their wagons. "But the ground is not as bad as it looks. Lucerne grows pritty much year roun', so that gives you hay to feed yer animals. Cotton comes up fast and produces well. But you'll also need to put in wheat and barley, maybe oats, and some corn, too—and you'll want to git gardens in the groun' soon as you can. In time, you may want to plant sorghum or maybe mulberry trees for silkworms. Some are growin' indigo, for dye, which makes a good cash crop you can sell up north. On top of all that, you can also start orchards and vineyards. Almost anythin' will grow here. There's no rain to speak of in the summer, so we dig canals, but once you git water on this land, it pays you back for the effort."

That did relieve Morgan's mind a little.

Ewan Morrison had recently become bishop of the little settlement called St. Thomas, about nine miles south of New St. Joseph. Morgan had learned that Thomas Smith had remained sick and would not be coming back from Salt Lake. That meant that Bishop Morrison was now the leader of the Muddy Mission. Morgan had known Brother Morrison from hauling loads of grain to his gristmill in Farmington. He was a man in his fifties with white hair and a streaked white-and-gray beard, and he spoke with a strong hint of his homeland, Scotland. Morgan knew he was a good man, wise and kind, and one who could repair almost anything, having been a carpenter and a wheelwright as a young man.

"But I'll tell you what," the bishop said. "This is still winter, and you can feel how warm it is. When summer comes—and it starts early—the sun will burn the hide right off ya. But I guess you've heard 'bout that. I only warn you not to get scared off when the heat gets bad. Just remember this weather, now, in early spring, and think about all the snow back where you came from."

"How soon will we get some land assigned to us?" Brother Larsen asked.

"Well, that depends on what you choose," the bishop said. "We established this little settlement, shaped like a fort, when we closed up old St. Joseph, about three miles north of here. But it always was a temporary site. We've surveyed a new site on this bench of land you can see just above us. We're workin' on a ditch to get water to it, and that's pritty close to being finished. You could camp here, where there's water not too far away, and then build on the bench in a month or two, or you could settle in St. Thomas, where I live, south of here."

"Could we start building houses up on the bench now?"

"Yes, you could. But you'd have to haul all yer water for brick-making and mortar. We've learned a good deal about adobe houses, and I'll get some men to show you the tricks. Mud houses don't look very pretty, but timber is sixty or seventy miles off from 'ere, and in the heat, adobe is better anyway. Some of us prefer to sleep outside in summer, but the women folk worry about tarantulas and snakes—and, I'll admit, there are rattlers around. So never sleep on the ground. And be careful about boots. Scorpions like to crawl into 'em if you leave 'em out."

Morgan wondered what Angeline was thinking. But she was smiling ever so slightly. She didn't look worried. Morgan watched Eb put his arm around Mary Ann, who was looking deathly white and maybe about to slump down. She had done somewhat better lately, but the talk of snakes and spiders appeared hard for her to hear. Morgan wondered whether Eb could convince her to stay.

"Sickness has been a problem for us too," the bishop continued, "especially in St. Thomas. Some people have come down with shakes and fevers from ague, but it's not like Nauvoo, where so many got sick from the bad air. You'll find some marshy land along the river, but we're dryin' that up, mostly by diggin' irrigation canals."

None of this sounded good, but still Morgan was thinking that if he could grow good crops, he would be all right. What he wanted now was to receive his plot of land and get started grubbing brush so he could get seeds into the ground.

"One other thing. We have Pah Ute Indyuns down here. You've never seen such poor people in all yer life. We had a bad inc'dent last year. We'd put our loose stock out on an island made by a split in the river, and the Indyuns ran off with the whole herd. We got some of the cattle back in time, but not many, and that loss has hurt us bad. But we met with the chief after that, and Jacob Hamblin—our missionary to the Lamanites down this way— worked out a peace treaty. I don't think we'll experience that kind of trouble agin. There's still a theft now and then, but you gotta know how poor and desperut this tribe is.

"Jacob Hamblin comes by and talks with the chief whenever there's trouble. He says we have to think of the Indyuns as our brothers in the house of Israel. Chief Thomas was baptized already. We hope they all will join sometime down the road. But fer now, they come around beggin' quite often. The best thing is, don't give 'em everythin' they ask for, but don't shun them either. Be friendly, and if you can spare somethin' when they're hungry, help 'em as much as you can. We hire Pah Utes to pick cotton or to help the women with their washin'. That works out fine. You gotta remember, the Indyuns were here long afore we came along, and we hafta make life better for'm, not worse."

Morgan told himself that he didn't have a thing to give away right now if Indians came begging, but he would try to keep the right attitude. He had never lived in a place where Indians were so close, but that morning he had seen a few from the tribe, almost naked. What bothered him most was seeing women carrying their babies, both mother and child not only dirty but thin, burnt deep from the sun, their faces full of weariness.

"All right now," the bishop said in conclusion, "you need to make a choice. The first settlement down here was St. Thomas, named for Thomas Smith. The second company called their place St. Joseph. But 'bout a year ago, I guess it was, President Young asked us to move close together. You all know about the war with Chief Black Hawk up north of here. Brigham felt like that trouble could spread. He said we ought to move into one town and make the place into a fort." Bishop Morrison shook his head and looked down for a moment. "But moving ever'one to one place was not so easy. People in both towns thought they had chosen the best place. We also had a little settlement close by here called Mill Point. It was a gristmill and jist a few houses. Apostle Snow finally told us to break up St. Joseph and either move to Mill Point or down to St. Thomas. Most settled here, close to Mill Point—at least for the short run. The place we've picked out for a permanent town is that area up above we call the sand bench." He pointed to higher ground between the river and Mormon Mesa. He brushed his fingers down over his beard, smoothing it. "If you want to know the whole truth, when we broke up St. Joseph, quite a few said they weren't movin' to either place. They jist left the mission and went home."

Bishop Morrison sounded careful, as though he didn't want to discourage anyone with his account. "Once we get water on the bench, some swear it will be the best place to settle. So I'm going to let you choose between St. Thomas and New St. Joseph, where it will be reestablished up there on the bench. I think you might want to stay together, but there's nothin' that says you have to. You can make yer own choices about that."

"What about the Upper Muddy?" Brother Carpenter asked.

Morgan understood the question. Soon after arriving the previous evening, Warren Foote, who had come to the Muddy back in 1866 and was now a counselor to Bishop Morrison, had visited the camp. He told Morgan and some of the other men that the best place to farm was in another valley, farther north. It was supposed to be a little greener, and it was easier to irrigate.

"Well," Brother Morrison said, "just recently some folks settled that upper valley and called the place West Point. Apostle Snow said it was all right for 'em to do that, but it goes against the whole plan of stayin' close together. What I would tell you is that when the prophet of God warns me and gives me advice, I'm goin' to listen, and my best advice is that you choose from these towns that aren't too far apart."

Morgan wondered. He felt uneasy about the way decisions were being made. It sounded strange for President Young to use fear of Indian trouble as the deciding factor when Bishop Morrison had just said that those problems had been settled. And why had Apostle Snow given permission to settle up north if that was against Brigham's counsel?

Morgan took another sweeping look around. As nearly as he could tell, the higher ground looked as desolate as the land by the river—the same pink sand spotted with tufts of brush and mesquite. And the sound of "sand bench" was anything but enticing. He doubted that St. Thomas, farther south, was much different. The idea of a greener spot not too many miles away sounded much more appealing.

"So hold a meetin' tonight," Bishop Morrison said. "Decide what you're goin' to do, and as soon as possible, we'll help you get settled somewhere."

• • •

As Angeline walked with Morgan back to their wagon, she asked him, "Did you get the feeling Bishop Morrison didn't really believe much in his own advice?"

"You mean Brigham's advice—about not settling in that upper valley?"

"Yes."

"I noticed it all right. But he cares more about obeying Brigham than he does about what kind of land we're going to farm."

"Don't you feel the same way?"

"I guess I ought to, but some people make it sound like Brother Brigham chats with the Lord two or three times a day and gets all the latest information on every subject, from farming to business to women's dress styles."

Angeline was taken by surprise. Morgan's sarcasm scared her a little. She gripped his arm tighter. "Of course the Lord has an opinion about everything. He *knows* everything." She laughed. She didn't want Morgan to think she was arguing with him. She still felt bad about the cranky way she had treated him after the incident with Wilfred Shupe.

"And the Lord doesn't want us to think for ourselves, I suppose," Morgan said.

"I didn't say that."

"Which boot do you tie up first in the morning? Left or right?"

Angeline tried to think how she did it. "I don't know. I don't remember." She was conscious that Lyman and Alice Hunt were walking not too far ahead of them. She tried to slow Morgan enough to be sure that no one else heard their conversation.

"Do you pray about which boot goes on first, or do you just put them on?"

"Morgan, that's not the point. What Bishop Morrison was saying—"

"That *is* the point. We have to work out our own salvation. We make choices. If there's better land not far away, can't I use my own good sense and farm that land—not grub away at this alkaline sand down here?"

"But what if that upper valley is a dangerous place and the Lord feels to warn you—and do it through a prophet of God? Shouldn't you be thankful for that?"

Morgan didn't answer for a time. He slowed even more, as though he also wanted no one to hear him. "Yes. I should be thankful. But back when I was a boy, Brigham told folks to grow sugar beets, and he built a sugar house out south of Salt Lake City. My father planted beets instead of grain on some of his land, but the whole thing turned out to be a bust. That factory never produced an ounce of sugar that anyone could use—mainly because no one knew how to make it right. But someone should have thought of that from the beginning. The whole thing didn't hurt my dad much, but some went into beets in a big way, and they lost lots of money. So who do you want to blame for that: God or Brigham?"

"Neither one. Brigham knows what he's trying to do: make us independent by providing for ourselves—and surely that's what God wants. So Brother Brigham tried something and it didn't work. That's how life is."

"That's what I'm saying too. I should be able to try what I think is best, not write a letter to the president every time I have a decision to make."

Angeline understood exactly what Morgan was saying, but she didn't want to be disrespectful toward Church leaders, and she thought Morgan was edging close to that. "So what are you saying?" she asked. "That you want to give West Point a try?"

The two had arrived at their wagon. Morgan stopped, took his hat off, and raised his head toward the pleasant sun. He kept his eyes closed as he said, "Maybe. I don't know. I just get mad when we're told to obey—like everything comes straight from heaven—and then, when things don't work out, we decide it wasn't God's idea after all." He hesitated and looked at Angeline again, and then added, "I said something like that to my father once, and that's the angriest I've ever seen him. He told me I better humble myself or I was going to get in a lot of trouble."

"Did you believe him?"

"Probably. I don't know. I question things, but in the end I usually do what I'm told."

Angeline saw all the complications in Morgan's words. He didn't like himself when he rebelled. But he also hated to turn his choices over to someone else. She had no idea how he would work that out. And what was worse, she knew that, at least in this regard, they were much alike.

• • •

That evening, at the company meeting, Morgan told himself he would not say a word. He didn't need to introduce his own confusion—or willfulness—to everyone else. As it turned out, however, many of the men—and maybe the women, although they didn't say much—had the same questions in mind. Finally, Daniel Pulsipher, usually a quiet man, but one who had helped to settle towns before, spoke up. "Listen, brothers and sisters, I think we're making too much of this. A while back Brigham was worried about Indians down here and told people to gather up. But if Brigham came down here now—and remember, he's never been here—he'd say, 'Sure, pick out good land and farm where you'll do the best.' He's practical about things like that."

"Maybe we should get a message to him—ask him what he thinks," Brother Larsen said.

"And how long will it take to get word?" Brother Dickson asked. "By the time we hear something, we could have a house built and crops laid in. Besides, the bishop said that Apostle Snow already gave permission for some folks to settle up there."

Morgan heard a general mumble of agreement. And suddenly he couldn't help saying, "I talked to Warren Foote, who's been here for a couple of years. He says this idea of getting enough water on the sand bench is never going to work. The canal they're digging will have to run for miles, through sand, and a lot of the water will seep out. He told me the canal will fill up with sand every time the wind blows—and it blows a lot down here. I think Brother Foote knows what he's talking about. Personally, I don't want to get involved in an operation that's bound to fail."

Morgan heard more assent this time, some men saying, "That's right. That's exactly right."

"All right, then," Brother Larsen said. "Let's send a couple of men up on the Upper Muddy, and maybe two more could take a look at St. Thomas. We can do that tomorrow and meet again the next day."

And then, to Morgan's surprise, Brother Pulsipher said, "I think we ought to send Morgan Davis up to West Point. He'll give us a good assessment."

Morgan didn't want that. He had said too much already. He didn't want the whole judgment on his shoulders. "I don't have a horse, brethren," Morgan said. "To get up there and back in a day, it will take a good saddle horse."

"You can take my horse," Brother Larsen said. "But I don't want you riding up there alone. Who could go with him?"

Of all people, it was George Carpenter, who had spoken out against helping the Bakers back on the Virgin River, who said, "I've got a big mule that goes right along. I could go with Brother Davis."

And so it was decided. The next morning, long before sunup, Morgan and George set out to follow the Muddy north to the upper valley. It was at least a ten-mile ride, from what the local settlers had said, so Morgan knew they had a long day ahead of them. George was not one to go out of his way to make friends, and he wasn't afraid to say what he thought, but in some ways he was the kind of man Morgan preferred. He didn't talk all that much along the way, and he kept his mule walking at a steady pace.

What Morgan saw as soon as they arrived was that grass grew better there, and even though there was not much that anyone would call green at this time of the year, there was a bit more vegetation. It wasn't what Morgan had been used to in Farmington, but it looked like a place he could plow and plant.

"We wouldn't hafta dig canals here," Brother Carpenter told Morgan. "We could dam off the river in a few places and jist let the water flood out on the land. All we'd hafta do is dig furrows so the water would make't to the end of our crops."

Morgan had noticed the same thing. "This is a better place to farm, no question," he said.

Before they headed back, they met with Alma Gibson, who was leader of the group that had located in the area. He was more than happy to welcome them, and he encouraged them to come north as soon as possible. The little settlement needed more people, partly for safety, but mostly to help build up a real town.

So Morgan and George rode back, and they told the company

at a meeting the next morning what they thought. The men who had gone to St. Thomas reported that it seemed a little better place than the sand bench, but it looked bleak and forlorn, and the people who lived there appeared worn down. "Them folks hardly have enough clothes to cover theirselves," Brother Cullimore reported. "From what they said, cotton grew real good the first year, but too many got wore down by the heat, and they pulled out. And it turned out, ever'one had to start putting in more grain, just so they could eat. That cut into the cotton crop last year. It's going to take ever'thin' we've got just to make a go of it anywhere around here. The way I look at it, we might as well pick the place that has a decent chance to turn out all right for us."

Lyman Hunt, who had traveled with Brother Cullimore, said, "One man told me that the salts and alkaline in the ground come to the top when you start irrigating. He said that's why second-year crops were worse than the first year. I'm thinking that land in the upper valley might not have so many minerals in it."

"I'll tell you something else," Art Brooks said. "These people at the fort treat us like they don't want us here. A brother told me that young couples like us won't last long. He said, 'The first hot day that comes along, all your pretty little wives will start crying, and you'll be gone.' I didn't want to argue with him, but I don't exactly feel good about living next door to a man like that."

Everyone agreed.

So that was that. Brother Larsen told everyone to rest a little from their travels and reorganize their wagons as much as they needed to. Within a few days they would pull out and head for West Point. They would tell the bishop and send word to Erastus Snow, but they wouldn't wait for permission. They needed to get established as quickly as they could.

MUDDY

. . .

Two days later the Larsen company set out, and they arrived on the Upper Muddy late that afternoon. The few families who were already settled there were happy to see new members arrive. A little town had been drawn up on paper, and the morning after arriving, the new settlers drew lots and received assigned town plots for houses and five-acre parcels of land to farm outside the settlement.

The next two weeks were filled with work, sunup until sundown. The days had started to lengthen, and most days were mild, so it was good weather to work in. Once Angeline learned about making adobes by mixing mud with grass cut from along the banks of the river, she took over that job. She mixed up batches, shaped the bricks, and set them out to dry, and then she worked in the garden as many hours as she could. And all the while, she cooked meals on an outdoor fire.

Morgan spent his days on their new land. He used his oxen to drag out clumps of brush, working the animals as many hours as he dared. Some Pah Ute men offered to dig up mesquite brush, and they accepted a cup of flour for each deep root they could present to Morgan. Once dried, according to the men who had settled there earlier, these roots made the best firewood for cooking, and paying the Indians was a good way to establish a working relationship with them.

Morgan and Angeline slept in the wagon box. For all Angeline's bravery, she wasn't about to sleep on the ground. She hadn't seen any rattlesnakes so far, but she wasn't about to lie down where one might slither into her bedding at night. And every morning Morgan watched her check both her boots before she put them on.

Each day, when Morgan let his oxen rest, he put in some work on the house, first digging out a trench for rock footings, and then using the adobe bricks as they dried. Angeline worked with him, and it didn't take long to have the walls halfway up. In time, they would have glass windows, if they could transport them somehow, but for now, they had to settle for mere openings that would let in some light—and, surely, plenty of insects. The roof was more of an issue, with no timber available. Mesquite limbs, with reeds and cat-tails from the riverbanks, had to be spread out across the opening and piled rather thick. The brother who showed Morgan how to lay the covering said, "Rain will drip through. I'll admit that. But when we get rain, we're usually more than happy to get wet. It feels pretty good."

Before the single-room house was truly completed, Morgan and Angeline moved in what furniture they had, and they began to sleep inside. Morgan carried in clay from along the river and tamped it down to make a fairly hard surface, but he hoped some-day to get hold of enough lumber to put in a puncheon floor. The bedstead was tied with ropes, and they piled on a few quilts as a mattress, with another quilt to cover them. The nights were actu-ally quite cold, so they were glad to be in out of the wagon box.

• • •

Angeline was proud of herself. She had never worked harder in her life, and she had never felt so valuable. Several times a day Morgan told her how much he appreciated all she was doing. "Most of these sisters we brought down here think that sweeping a floor and maybe milking a cow is about all the hard work they can do," he said. "But you get out there and slap those bricks to-gether and then unyoke the oxen while I sit down to eat. I've never known a woman as strong as you."

"That's what you get," Angeline said, "when you don't worry if a girl's pretty and check her muscles instead."

"I don't know what you're talking about, Angie. You're the prettiest woman in this whole valley."

"And you're in danger of the Lord's judgment, bearing false witness that way."

But she loved that he claimed to see her that way, however little beauty she actually possessed.

"Eb told me that Mary Ann is expecting," Morgan said, "so I don't blame her if she can't work very hard right now."

"They're all expecting."

"What?"

"All the new brides. Every one of them is expecting—except maybe Alice. She hasn't said." Angeline waited and watched to see whether he would give some hint that he was concerned about that.

"I guess we're just lucky so far. We got our house up first. Now maybe we can take more interest in getting you that way."

"I haven't seen any lack of interest from you, Morgan—no matter how hard you work all day."

He laughed. "Well, if you quit working quite so hard, maybe your time will come."

The truth was, Angeline had begun to wonder whether there could be something wrong with her. She had been married almost three months now, and that should have been plenty of time. She did feel a little lucky that it hadn't happened quite so soon as it had with the others, but it was time now. More than anything, she wanted to give Morgan that big family they had talked about.

What she also knew was that she had concentrated almost completely on herself and the work she and Morgan needed to do. She knew she needed to help some of the others who were still living in their wagons. So early the next morning she walked over to the Crawfords' house, on the other side of the little settlement they were establishing. She found Mary Ann still asleep in her wagon. But Eb was up, had built a fire, and was frying bacon and bread dough. "How's Mary Ann doing?" Angeline asked him.

He looked up from the frying pan, seemingly surprised to hear a voice. Then he looked down when he said, "Not well. Not well at all. She gets up for part of the day, but she can't hold her food down, and she's getting way too skinny."

"What can I do?"

"Nothing, really. I just hope she'll get over the sickness before long. Some people say it's worst in the beginning."

"Yes, but the heat is going to come on, and that will also take her strength away," Angeline said. "Right now, she needs to get inside where she can be a little more comfortable."

"That's easy to say, but I'm still getting my land cleared. I haven't found time to make adobes."

"I just happen to be the best brickmaker in this valley—maybe the whole world. I'll get started right now. I'll help you put up your walls, too. And Morgan knows how to put on a roof. I'll get him over here to help you."

"You can't take away that much time from your own—" Eb began to protest.

"What about your garden?"

"I tilled some ground right over there." He pointed to a little plot not far away. "But I haven't planted anything yet."

"We'll need to get some early vegetables planted soon. But let me worry about the bricks for now, and you finish clearing your land. When she's ready, maybe I can get Mary Ann up for a while each day, and she can help me plant some garden seeds. She'll start to feel better if she's doing a little more."

"That might be true, but I doubt you'll convince her. It's not just the sickness and the heat. She wants to go home, and that's about all she thinks about."

"I understand. But I don't think that's one of her options. Or is it?"

"Not for me, it isn't. Unless I have to take her home to save her life."

"Eb, the trip would be more likely to harm her than anything else."

"I know. I've tried to tell her that. But she's still a little girl, if you want to know the truth. She misses her friends and Saturday night dances. She got all excited when I asked her to marry me, but I don't think she had any idea what this mission would be like. And I didn't tell her—because I didn't really know myself."

"What's done is done, Eb. Now we have to get her through this."

So Angeline spent her day making adobe bricks. And after a while she got Mary Ann out of the wagon and had her come and watch. Before the day was over, Mary Ann even got her hands into the mud and shaped a few bricks on her own. She didn't last long—and she threw up the little bit she had eaten when she first got up—but when Eb came in to check on her, he whispered to Angeline that Mary Ann had a little more color in her face.

Angeline was pleased to hear that Mary Ann was a little better—since she had seemed anything but well. She left late that afternoon and made dinner for Morgan, but then she returned to Mary Ann again the next day. She mixed the mud, and she got Mary Ann up earlier than the day before, and Mary Ann did more to help. And all the while, Angeline talked—and tried to keep Mary Ann talking. She didn't say anything about Farmington or the trip to this valley; she talked about the town they were building.

"Morgan and I have been talking about it," she said. "We'll plant trees and make streets. This will be a real town someday, and we'll be proud that we were the ones who built it. We're pioneers, Mary Ann. Just think of the celebrations people will hold fifty years from now. They'll honor us and talk about the brave pioneers who first came to this desolate valley—and made it blossom as the rose."

"I'm sorry, Angeline, but I can't see that, ever. I'm afraid a rose would wither up and die here, never blossom."

"I say you're wrong about that. I'm going to get us some rose-bushes from somewhere. And other flowers. And we'll take care of them—water them and prune them. 'They even brought roses to our valley,' people will say. They'll probably have a parade, and you and I, we'll be going on ninety years old by then, and they'll ride us through town in a nice buggy, and all the children will say, 'Those two planted the first flowers down here, and look how beautiful everything is because of them.' We'll wave to this side. . . ." She leaned to the right and made a shaky wave, as though she were old and frail. And then she leaned to the left and waved with her other hand, which was covered with mud. "Come to think of it, I'll bet they build a couple of statues in the town square. 'Mary Ann Crawford and Angeline Davis,' the plaque will say. 'The famous rose ladies.'"

Mary Ann finally gave way. She actually laughed. Angeline felt as though the girl had made a little breakthrough. Mary Ann stayed up even longer that day and helped even more.

When the bricks were ready, Morgan and Eb and Angeline spent a couple of days building up the walls of the house. Mary Ann was not strong, but she helped as much as she could, and she cooked for everyone that day—something she hadn't done until now.

Mary Ann was visibly changed by then. "Thank you so much," she kept saying. "Tonight I'll sleep in a bed."

"I think her sickness has mostly passed now," Eb told Angeline. "I think she'll be all right."

But Angeline checked on her the next morning all the same. They sat in the little house with openings where windows would someday be, and where a door still had to be built. They each had a cup of tea, and Mary Ann said, "I never expected to live in such a grand palace. I'm not sure where our footman is. He should be along soon."

"It's so hard to get good help these days," Angeline said. "Our chambermaids have absconded with all our silver." She laughed, but then she spoke seriously. "Morgan says we can plaster the inside of our house as soon as some of the other work around here is finished. He wants to add some more rooms, too."

"Is he expecting a need for that?"

Angeline looked down. "Not yet," she said. "You keep telling me that I'm a hard worker, but I'm starting to worry that I'm not good at the one thing that matters most."

"It's all the hard work that's kept you from conceiving, Angeline. Don't worry. You need to rest now, and then something will happen."

"That's what Morgan says too. I hope you're right."

And then, suddenly, a figure appeared at the door opening. The light was behind him, but Angeline saw immediately that he was an Indian—a small man, bare-chested, with ragged hair. He said something Angeline didn't understand.

Mary Ann jumped up. For a moment she clasped her hands to her face, and then she blurted, "Go away. Go away!"

The Indian stood his ground. Angeline knew she would have to be the one to deal with this. She stepped toward the door. "What is it you want, my friend?" she asked.

"Bread." Or at least that was what she thought he said.

"We have almost nothing ourselves. We haven't even planted yet."

She could see him better now, having drawn closer to him. He was a sad little man with dirty hands and arms—dirt everywhere, really. His hair hung in clumps, and his face and lips seemed charred by the sun. A deerskin breechcloth was wrapped around his loins and then folded over a belt, so it hung down in front like an apron. He also wore leather leggings—but nothing else.

Angeline knew that she had said nothing he could understand, but maybe he would understand her friendship, in spite of her refusal, merely from the tone of her voice.

"Bread."

"Go away!" Mary Ann was saying again, but she was staying across the room.

"No bread. I'm very sorry," Angeline told him. She shook her head and held out her empty hands.

"Bread." He rubbed his bare, distended stomach as if to say that he was hungry. But he didn't sound threatening.

"No bread."

But now his voice tightened, got louder. "Jes. Bread." He stepped into the opening, almost into the room.

Mary Ann was whimpering now, and, for the first time, Angeline felt some fear herself. But she didn't back away. She looked into his eyes. "We have no bread here. I would give you some if we had any. Honestly, I would."

He stared at her for a long time, seemed to consider. Then he lowered one hand, flattened it, and for a moment Angeline expected him to strike her, but instead he held it out, cupped, as though on the top of a child's head, and then lowered it to three more levels. "Bread," he said, and now she heard a plaintive tone. His children were hungry. That was what he was saying.

Angeline nodded and said, "Follow me. This way."

The Indian stepped back. He seemed to understand. Angeline walked briskly toward her own home, across the opening in the center of the "fort." There were other women in some of the houses, but probably no men, since they would be working in their fields at this hour. Angeline didn't look back; she didn't want to give the impression that she was frightened. She could hear the man's bare feet padding in the dirt, knew that he was keeping up with her.

When she came to her house, she stepped inside. She didn't want him to come in, but she didn't want to order him out, the way Mary Ann had done. She was relieved when she glanced back to see that he had stayed at the door. She had only half a loaf of bread. She had very little flour left from the provisions they had brought, but she had baked bread in a pan over the fire in the adobe-lined fireplace. She picked up the loaf from the kitchen table, carried it to him, and said, "It's all we have. I'm sorry I don't have more." She motioned with her hand, made a sweeping motion to indicate how little she and Morgan possessed. "We're almost as poor as you are, sir."

He took the bread, nodding by way of thanks, but then he held out his hand and pulled his fingers toward him, clearly to ask for more.

"I tell you, it's all I have. There is no more."

He made a guttural noise and said something in his own language. Then he stepped inside, raising himself taller. She knew this was his way of making his demand more pressing—to scare her.

But Angeline could stand tall too. She stepped toward the man.

"You are unappreciative and rude. I'll have no more of it. Give me that bread back and get out of my house." When he didn't move, she stepped even closer and raised her voice to an angry pitch. "Get out of my house this minute, you ungrateful lout!"

He stepped back suddenly, retreating a few steps. And then he smiled. Angeline had no idea what that meant. But he nodded to her as if to say, *You win,* and he walked away, carrying the bread in one hand, his arm hanging down. Angeline stayed at the door, watching as he headed out across the emptiness beyond the settlement. She only wanted to be certain he wouldn't go back to Mary Ann's house, but that seemed not to be his intention. When she was finally sure of that, she sat down, and finally she let the fear run through her. Her whole body began to shake.

After a time, Mary Ann showed up at her door, still looking upset. "Are you all right?" she asked.

"Of course I'm all right," Angeline answered. But she didn't tell Mary Ann that she had been sitting at the table ever since the Pah Ute had left.

"Did you give him your bread?"

"It was only half a loaf. I gave him what I had."

"But won't he come back and beg again?"

"He has children, and they are hungry. I think it's what we should do—help as much as we can."

Mary Ann sat down across from Angeline. Tears spilled onto her cheeks. "I don't like any of this," she said. "I don't want to look at a filthy man like that, his body all uncovered."

Angeline touched her hand, waited for Mary Ann to look up at her. "Actually, I think they have the right idea. What in the world are we going to wear in the summer around here? I might strip down like those Indian women, bare from the waist up."

"Oh, Angie, don't say such a thing," Mary Ann protested. But then she smiled. "Can't you just see us running around like that?"

And now they both laughed. Angeline needed to do that as much as Mary Ann did.

CHAPTER 7

Morgan was satisfied with the progress he and Angie were making on their farm, but when he found time to raise his head and look about, he didn't like what he was seeing from most of the new settlers. Several times a day people came to his farm and asked him for advice about grubbing brush or building with adobe bricks. Most were still sleeping in their wagon boxes and seemed nowhere near ready to start plowing. Few had been able to bring plows. The tools and equipment people possessed had to be shared, so Morgan's plan was to open his own land first, and then he could prove his appreciation for the loan of a plow by tilling land for his friends. But he wondered why more of them didn't feel compelled to work longer and harder to get their own land ready. It was true that only a few of the women were able to help with strenuous kinds of work, and no woman was as skilled as Angie, but most of the men seemed to waste time.

Or maybe they just didn't know what to do. The older men were generally more experienced and managed a little better, but many of the younger ones had learned little about farming in their growing-up years. A couple of the returned missionaries had served in the South, and they knew something about raising cotton, but they didn't seem to be moving ahead any faster than the others.

Angeline kept telling Morgan she saw signs that not only the new brides but some of the young second wives were pregnant— and were struggling. He had watched his mother carry and then bear his younger sisters and brothers, but he couldn't remember her easing up at all from her usual routine. Not only were some of the young women sick, but their husbands seemed to feel a need to stay close to them and help with some of the women's chores. Eb did more cooking than Mary Ann these days, and that was true of James Wilcox, too. Alice Hunt had now admitted to Angeline that she was also expecting, but she wasn't one to complain, and she showed no signs of being sick. The problem was, Lyman could spend more time in a day getting ready to get ready than anyone Morgan had ever known. He wondered what would happen when the heat drove people inside during the middle of the day.

Morgan worried that if some of the men didn't get their farms cleared and plowed fairly soon, the scorching sun would wipe out the crops that were planted too late in the spring. That could mean too little food to go around, even if everyone shared.

All the West Point settlers lived close together in the settlement, and they farmed outside the centralized living areas. That made sense, but in the initial draw—slips of paper pulled from a hat—Morgan and Angeline had received a plot of farmland almost a mile from their house. The walk back and forth added to the time it took each day to get their work done, but what Morgan hated more was that he spent most of his time away from Angeline. He already missed those first weeks of their marriage when they had been almost always together.

Henry Cullimore and his wife, Flora, lived next door to Morgan and Angeline. Henry was probably not much more than thirty, but that was still older than many of the men. He was a bulky man with big arms and huge hands. He had worked as an overland hauler until lately, and even though he had farmed as a boy, he didn't seem to remember much about that. What he did know how to do was cuss. "Sorry you heard that," he would say to Morgan, or especially Angeline. "I drove mules for many years, and I learned mule talk. If you don't cuss at 'em, they don't think you mean what you say." Angeline told Morgan she didn't care what Henry said to his animals; what she didn't like was that he sometimes talked the same way to his three little sons.

"Do you ever get the feeling we—all of us—are not as good as we ought to be?" Morgan asked her.

"What do you mean?"

"We don't like to hear Henry talk like that, but when I get mad enough, I use words I've been taught not to say, same as him."

"I don't hear you do that—at least not very often," Angeline said.

"I call ol' Ben and Buck plenty of names when I'm out grubbing brush. I hear that sort of thing from the other brothers, too, and old Brother Shupe, he uses the Lord's name in vain just like it's a normal thing to do."

"Well, we all have things we can work on. Just about all men swear from time to time. Even my father, with all his preaching, would lose his temper and spout off with something that would shock my mother. It always made me laugh—just to know that he was human."

"But I'm not just talking about cussing. I'm talking about the quarreling and accusing I hear sometimes. Half the people in our company don't even like each other. How are we supposed to build Zion—and make sure we all prosper together—if we can't talk to each other without getting mad?"

Angeline was lying on their bed—something she almost never

did—but she had put in a hard day, and, after supper, Morgan had told her to take a rest. He was sitting on a chair nearby, trying to repair the handle of the plow he had been using. The old wood was splitting apart, so he was wrapping it with leather strips, which he intended to wet and then allow to dry and tighten.

Angeline seemed to consider for a time before she said, "What's even worse is what *I* think about other people. Half the women come across as weaklings to me. I don't know why they even came down here. I can't imagine that they'll stick it out. But I shouldn't be judging that way. I should be supporting them."

"You've kept Mary Ann going, Angie. You have a better heart than I do when it comes to things like that."

What Morgan knew was that he judged people much too harshly—more than Angeline did. His father had always reminded him that brothers and sisters in the gospel shouldn't talk—or think—ill of one another. But it wasn't something he had been able to overcome. He couldn't get the thought out of his head that to pioneer a valley like this, strong people were needed—like the pioneers who twenty years earlier had crossed the plains and settled the Great Salt Lake Valley. But then, maybe they hadn't been so wonderful as everyone said. Maybe they cussed and quarreled and judged each other too—though that wasn't what people said on the 24th of July each year. Morgan had believed since he was a little boy that the first pioneers had been pretty much perfect. He wasn't sure this company would ever rise to that level. For now, he decided, he just had to do better himself.

• • •

Angeline was working in her garden one morning about three weeks after they had arrived in West Point. Mornings were quite cool, but afternoons, most days, were comfortable. If she hadn't heard so much about the summer heat, she would have thought this a wonderful climate. Some of the seeds she had planted were starting to break ground as frail little sprouts. It was hard to believe that in February seeds could germinate, but radishes were peeking up, and so were onions and leeks. She was planting potatoes now from cuttings she and Morgan had brought along in their wagon.

As Angeline stood up straight and stretched her back, she looked out across the valley. She liked the look of the blunt bluffs off to the north, the changing shades of color as the sun got higher in the sky. What the valley lacked in green, it made up for in oranges and rusty reds and even violet-colored distant mountains. If she thought about it, she still preferred a place with trees and meadows and rushing canyon streams—but she tried not to look back to all that. This was her home now, and she would plant those flowers she had promised Mary Ann. She would watch this place grow, and someday she would take pride in what they had all done together. Morgan worried too much about righteousness. It was fine to preach and try to improve, but the fact was, the people she admired most got up each morning and did what they had to do without accusing themselves more than they needed to. And that was what she wanted to do.

She looked across the Cullimores' building lot to the south, where a house was finally taking shape. Beyond the town, she saw a plume of dust rising in the distance. She soon realized that it was a man in a one-horse buggy. This had to be someone from one of the other settlements, and she wondered what that would mean. She hoped that someone was bringing mail.

Angeline wanted to walk out and meet the man, but that was a waste of time, and Brother Larsen would probably be the person to meet with the visitor, whoever it was. Women weren't needed when men had business to transact. But still, she kept watching, and once the man drew close, she could see that it was Bishop Morrison. He entered the fort area on the other side of the Cullimore place, and then she couldn't see where he had gone.

Angeline had never liked to be left out of whatever was "going on," and she was anxious to walk to the center of the settlement and see what the bishop was doing, but she resisted the urge and went back to her hoeing. Still, she kept watching, and after ten minutes or so, she saw Art Brooks walking toward her. He called from some distance, "Angie, where's Morgan?"

"Out on our farm," she answered. "Do you need him?"

"Bishop Morrison is here. He wants to have us all come together for a meeting. Right now."

Art was still striding toward her. He looked a little more serious than usual.

"What's it all about?" Angeline asked.

"I don't know. He won't say until we're all together, but he says to drop whatever we're doing and come now. I'll walk out to your farm and bring Morgan back."

"No. Tell the others. I'll go get Morgan."

Art smiled. "My wife would never walk that far to get me. You're one in a million, Angie."

"I just have long legs—almost as long as yours," she said, and then she felt herself blush. She knew very well that a woman never should mention legs—hers, or anyone else's. All her life she had been proud not to be like other girls, but lately she had been wondering whether she didn't need to be more ladylike.

All the same, she used those long legs to stride out to Morgan. If she had had her way, she wouldn't have been wearing a dress that flounced when she walked. Men seemed to have all the advantages, including trousers.

• • •

It took the better part of an hour to gather everyone to the center of the fort—the place where, in time, a school would be built. Bishop Morrison asked everyone to assemble on one side of the square, and he stood before them. Just glancing about, Morgan could see that a few people—women and children—had not been reached or had chosen not to gather with the others, but he thought that every man was there.

Bishop Morrison looked serious, even nervous, and that worried Morgan. He only worried more when the bishop started with words that sounded hesitant and indirect. He stroked his beard, nodded, and then said, too solemnly, "You have done a great deal of work in the short time you've been here. I'm impressed with your industry. That'll help you all along the way, wherever you serve in this mission. I just hope you are committed for the long haul—to serve as you are required and to follow the guidance of our leaders."

Morgan noticed Angie glance his way. He saw concern in her face. She must have sensed what he did: the bishop was about to "require" something of them.

"Brothers and sisters, I hope you understan' that a mission like this is built mostly on trial and error—and adjustments, when change is necessary. A number of times we've seen a need to move our location and start over, and each time, it seems impossible, but with hard work—the kind of work you've done here—we go forward. Slowly but surely, we are findin' the right places, the right crops, and the right farming methods. In all that, it's still our attitude that makes the difference—a willin'ness to take advice, to help one another, and a will to make this desert blossom no matter how hard the work."

Bishop Morrison kept looking about, but his gaze seemed just above the heads of the crowd, as though he were thinking what to say but was a little fearful of looking people straight in the eye. Morgan thought he knew what was coming now, and he felt frustration, even some anger, arising inside him.

"I want you to listen to me," the bishop was saying. "You need to remember that you're called to a mission and that you've made promises. Don't decide anythin' in haste. Take the time to pray and consider and talk things over as a group."

Morgan felt like saying, *Quit beating around the bush. What do you want from us?*

"Yesterday, I heard from Apostle Snow. It took some time afore Erastus got word that you'd settled in the upper valley. Once he did, he sent a telegram to President Young, tellin' him of yer decision. Brother Brigham sent back a telegram right away. He doesn't want you stayin' here. What he said, to be exact, was that he doesn't want our settlements to be spread out. He wants all of you to move down to one of the two towns on the lower Muddy."

Someone in the crowd, a man with a deep voice, muttered more than spoke, "I won't do it. He can't make us do that."

Bishop Morrison surely heard the words, but he didn't acknowledge them. "The President did give you another choice. He said that if you aren't willin' to follow that counsel, you should break off your mission and head back to your homes in the north."

The bishop finally looked into the faces of the people, slowly scanning from one side to the other. "I didn't stop you when you chose to move up here, but that's because I'm a bishop, not a boss.

I knew that President Young had said, in times past, that he wanted us to stay close together, but I wasn't sure he would still feel that way. Now we have an answer. Remember that this counsel comes from the heart of a man who loves you."

It was George Carpenter who suddenly spoke in a raised voice. "So Brigham *is* the boss. Is that what you're tellin' us?"

"No, Brother. We have no bosses in the Lord's church. No one will force you to obey. I will say, however, that when you go against the direction of your leaders, you take the first step toward apostasy."

That hardly seemed the point. Morgan knew he was too upset to speak his mind, but somehow Bishop Morrison needed to understand what the past few weeks had cost all these people.

Daniel Pulsipher, who had been strong in his opinion that the company should settle here, spoke in a controlled voice, obviously trying to avoid the tone that Brother Carpenter had taken. "Bishop, has Brigham Young ever visited this area?"

"No. He hasn't had the chance. Apostle Snow has told me more than once that the President does want to make the trip down this way sometime soon."

"Well, let me just tell you what I worry about. He doesn't know the Indians around here. He knows about Indian attacks up north, and he thinks the same thing could happen here. He's a man like the rest of us, and he tries to make wise decisions, but it's hard to believe that if he came here that he would want us all gathered up in the lower valley when conditions are better here—where access to water is much better. And we're getting along just fine with the Pah Utes."

Bishop Morrison listened attentively, and something in his nodding, or maybe shrugging, seemed to say, *I know what you mean.* But that wasn't what he said. "I'm sure the President prayed about this. He wouldn't just—"

"I'm not so sure of that," Brother Carpenter said, his voice strident again. "I think he heard that we was thinkin' for oursel's and he don't like that. He got that telegram and he said, 'I'll straighten out them folks I sent down to the Muddy. If they won't bow down to me, I'll shame 'em by tellin' 'em to turn tail and come on home."

"Is that the kind of man you think the President is?"

Brother Carpenter hesitated for a second or two, and then he said in a slightly more respectful voice, "I'm afraid I do. I knew Joseph Smith. He loved his people. He never talked to us the way Brigham does."

A stillness set in, as though all the people had taken a collective breath and were holding it, waiting. Morgan knew that George had gone too far. His judgment of Brigham Young was too harsh. And yet, he knew that George was getting at something that many members had felt—including Morgan himself.

"I heard Joseph reprimand his people when he thought it was necessary," Bishop Morrison said. "People forget that. But I'm not goin' to listen to any more of that kind of talk about President Young. We've needed a strong leader in these perilous years of crossin' the plains and settlin' in the West. We should be—"

"I don't mind a strong leader," Daniel Pulsipher said, and now he sounded as angry as George Carpenter. "But Brigham's a man like the rest of us. Half the things he's tried out here in the West have fallen flat. I don't fault him for looking for answers and using his own good sense, but I also don't happen to believe that every decision he makes is straight from God."

This scared Morgan. He was afraid the entire group would take the same attitude. He didn't want to leave the hard work he had done these last few weeks and start over again, and he didn't want to live in the lower valley, but he also didn't want to break his commitment to serve this mission, and George and Daniel were both sounding ready to turn their backs on all that.

"That's enough," the bishop was saying. "I won't argue with you. I'm tellin' you what President Young has asked of us. You'll have to make your own decisions—each one of you. If some leave, that doesn't mean you all have to go." He stroked his beard with the palm of his hand again, let his eyes move across the crowd. And then he spoke in a softer voice. "But I beseech you, please stay with us. And consider movin' to the bench and helpin' us build New St. Joseph. I know that most of you didn't like that site, but I would hope that you would settle there all the same. We've lost too many people this last year—folks who came in answer to the Lord's call but decided they couldn't stick it out. We've been countin' on yer help. We need the new life you can bring to us. Still, if the only way you can find it in your heart to stay is to move to St. Thomas, we will also welcome you there."

"Could I just pose a couple of questions?" Lyman Hunt asked. "I don't want to argue. I just need to understand."

"Of course you can ask questions."

"Your own counselor, Warren Foote, was the one who convinced us that the New St. Joseph settlement is sure to fail—because of the long canal you're digging. That's one of the reasons we chose to come to this upper valley. How can we feel good about moving onto the sand bench if we suspect we'll soon have to start all over once more, somewhere else?"

"Brother Foote has his opinion," the bishop said, "and there's not a better man in these valleys. That's why I chose him as a counselor. But I do believe things will work out better than he expects. I know it will take work to keep the canal flowin', but I have high hopes that that site, on higher ground, will be a beautiful settin' for a fine city. You'll be plantin' trees, puttin' in orchards and vineyards. Remember, the Salt Lake Valley didn't look like much when the pioneers first arrived, and look what we've done with it."

"One more question," Lyman said.

"Yes. Surely."

"As I understand it, when President Young first advised you to move closer together, those in St. Joseph only moved two or three miles down the river. I believe you're still nine miles apart. West Point isn't much farther from New St. Joseph than St. Thomas is. Why are we in more danger than the folks in New St. Joseph?"

"That's a good question," the bishop said, and Morgan could tell that he saw the difficulty in the logic that they had to move for their own safety. "But here's the thing. Having two settlements, both built in the form of forts, and within a half day's ride of each other, does seem safer to me than three settlements, sparsely inhabited, and spread out over more than twenty miles."

"Is that what Brigham was thinking, or does he even know that the two settlements on the lower river are still so far apart?"

"I'm not entirely sure. But I have to assume that Apostle Snow has made that clear to him."

Lyman didn't sound angry, but maybe a little frustrated, when he said, "But it was Apostle Snow who gave permission to Alma Gibson and his people to settle the upper valley. Is Brigham telling them to leave, too?"

"Well . . . no. I don't think so. Nothing's been said about that. Maybe President Young felt that this new group should bolster the other settlements—and West Point can be built up later."

"But that goes against the whole idea that it's dangerous to live up here," Lyman said. "Can you see why we wonder about all this? I have to think that if President Young came here, he would have quite a different opinion. We've all grubbed brush until our backs are breaking, and we've put our wives to work making adobes. Most of us have houses at least half built. I just wish President Young could have a look at what we've been trying to do. I don't like being told I'm a rebel when I know I'm not."

"Brother Hunt, I understand what you're sayin'. Entirely. I had to rebuild right after I got my first house finished. We started St. Thomas and then realized we had to move it farther up the river. All I can promise you is that the Lord will bless you if you move closer and work with us to accomplish what we were sent here to do."

Alice Hunt, standing next to Lyman, spoke up—to Morgan's surprise—and said in a stronger voice than Morgan would have expected, "We aren't troublemakers, Bishop Morrison. We've accepted a calling, and we've given all we have to get this far. Most of us have planned to start our families here. To be told to fall in line or go home sounds like something said in anger, not in love. Can you understand how that makes us feel?"

"I do understand that. And I know Brother Brigham has a stern way of speakin' sometimes, and he takes a hard line on many things. But I've never known anyone more committed to doing God's work. I promise you, he is thinkin' about what's best for you—and for all the members of the Church. I don't think you'll be sorry if you follow his advice and start over. For now, most of you could move into houses that have been left open in the Mill Point area—or just camp for a month or so. Then everyone will move up to the bench, and you can start the new settlement together. You've learned a lot these last few weeks. You'll find the goin' a little easier next time."

The meeting had come around to a gentler tone, and Morgan

wanted to calm himself and accept this new reality. But then Daniel Pulsipher spoke again. "I'll tell you what I'm going to do. I'm going to pack up and get out of this desert." Brother Pulsipher was not a big man, but he had a barrel of a chest and a voice that sounded as though it had rumbled around inside before bursting out. He stood silent for a moment, with his hands on his hips, and then he added, "Brigham has given us two choices, and I'm going to accept his second option. My only regret is that I made this senseless trip down here in the first place. And I'll tell you what else. The day will come when you'll all leave, because there's no hope of turning all this sand into a beautiful garden spot. Brigham would know that if he came down and took a quick look around."

"That's fine, Brother Pulsipher," Bishop Morrison said. "Plan to leave as soon as you like, but I would do it before spring comes and the Virgin is runnin' high. You have more experience than many of these young men, so I suggest you be the leader for all of those who want to go with you. But be a little careful about where, exactly, you might be leadin' 'em. And those who follow Daniel, just make sure yer not takin' a trip straight down to hell."

And with that, the meeting ended.

• • •

By the time Morgan and Angeline walked away, Angeline could sense that Morgan was trying to stay calm. But she knew how conflicted he was—and she understood. As a little girl, shortly after her family had arrived in the Salt Lake Valley, she had lived in primitive conditions, although she remembered little of that. But her father had built a good home, with a good fireplace, nice beds, a kitchen with a coal stove, and, gradually, nice furniture. Now all she had was this little rectangular, one-room house, built from river mud and salt grass, and yet it had seemed acceptable for the present, partly because she had worked so hard to make the bricks and help set the walls. The floor was nothing but tamped-down clay, but she and Morgan had talked of better things: more rooms added on; a trip north to Sheep Mountain to bring back lumber to make a puncheon floor; plaster to cover the adobe surfaces; furniture brought in from St. George or even Salt Lake City; glass windows and a real door; maybe even a cook-stove.

What Angeline really wanted was to escape this place, return to where they had come from, and build a real house on good land. She knew that was what Morgan wanted, too. But to leave now would be to admit failure, to say to Brigham Young, "We're some of the weaklings who couldn't hold up in the desert." Even worse, they would have to admit that they had done more than fail; they had revolted.

She didn't say a word to Morgan as they walked back, and, inside the house, she still left him to his own thoughts. She knew he was mulling everything over, and he would tell her what he thought when he was ready. She had learned that about him: that if she forced him to talk, he would resent the incursion into his head while he was still trying to make sense of things.

Inside the house were a bed and two chairs. There was also a little table, not big enough for a family, but big enough for the two of them to sit across from one another and eat a meal. But Morgan was clearly not ready to sit across from her at this point. He sat on the bed. So Angeline pulled a chair away from the table and sat near the opening she called her front window. It was lighter there. The day was sunny and was becoming warm. She welcomed the touch of the sun on the side of her face. She didn't look directly at Morgan; she only waited.

When Morgan finally spoke, his words didn't surprise her. "I don't want to go back," was all he said.

"I don't either."

"We're on a mission. We don't just quit because we don't like what we're called to do." Another full minute must have passed before he added, "But I'm fighting not to be angry. Brigham *likes* to tell people what to do. And when people don't fall into line, he passes hard judgments on them."

Angeline's feelings were not all that different from Morgan's, but she didn't want him to sound like George Carpenter or Daniel Pulsipher. "He asks more of us, that's all," she said. "He thinks we should be better than we are. You said the same thing yourself just a few days ago."

"That's fine. We ought to be better. But he should be easier on people. We built this house, Angie. Now we have to give it up and build another one on that sand bench where we don't want to live." Morgan suddenly stood up. "Angie, if I'm not allowed to trust my own judgment, I don't want to be part of this Church. God can tell me what's right, the same as He can tell Brigham. I don't mind starting over; I mind being told that I *must* start over. Do you understand what I'm saying?"

"But sometimes we have to humble ourselves and—"

"That's all I've ever done! I love my father, but the man only understands one thing: Do what the Brethren tell you to do. The trouble is, that's not me. When something makes sense to me, I need to trust my own judgment. Our leaders are ordained to lead us, but they aren't ordained to take away my agency. I can't stand to live that way."

Angeline had never thought Morgan would speak of leaving

the Church. And yet, what scared her even more was that she felt almost the same. And there was something more, something she had always held back. Now she said it: "You think your agency is stolen away; how would you like to be a woman? We're not credited with having so much as a brain in our heads."

Morgan looked surprised. "You don't get that from me," he said. "I know how smart you are."

"Maybe. But you sometimes talk to me as though you're the wise one and I'm just a woman."

"That's not what I think. I don't—"

"All men think that way, whether they know it or not. Church leaders say things all the time that make it sound like only men should have opinions."

And now the whole discussion had come to some sort of dead end. Angeline was pleased, in a way. She was glad to let Morgan know that he wasn't the only one who could be upset with the way things were in the world. But where were they going with all this talk? Had she said things that would change her relationship with her new husband? She didn't want Morgan to love her any less, and she didn't want him to feel that he had to watch everything he said around her.

"I'm sorry, Angie. I didn't know I made you feel that way. If I can blame Brigham for not respecting my decisions, I can't turn around and force you to go against your own will. I never want to do that."

"I know. It's just the way men and women have been for such a long time. Not many women want it any different. I'm afraid I've always thought more like a man than I should."

"No. It's what I first liked about you. You weren't afraid to stand up for yourself."

"But I never should have brought that up—at least not right

now. The important thing is, what are we going to do about this mission?"

"We stay, don't we?" Morgan asked. "We promised."

"But how angry will we be? Can we complete a mission and resent our leaders at the same time?"

• • •

Morgan sat down on the bed again, set his elbows on his knees, and looked at the dirt beneath his boots. The day had started so well, the air outside warm and the farm starting to take shape, with his crops half planted and the house mostly finished. Now, everything had changed. But he didn't want to be angry. "I know I have to humble myself. So I guess it's better we're here, where some of my pride will get crushed." He stopped, then seemed to realize he was talking only about his own struggle. "But what do you want to do? What do you think about all this?

Angeline smiled. "Thanks," she said. And then, "I don't want to stay, not really, but I will stay. Partly to be with you. You're not like my father, and he's the one who made me so suspicious—and resentful—of men. What I want to do is accept God's will, so I need to accept direction. I'll be a better person, in the long run, if I give up some of the resentment I've been holding onto."

"You're an amazing woman, Angie. I sensed it way back when we were in school, but I only understand who you are now."

"It's good we have each other, Morgan. But can we be happy here? Can we give our whole lives to this mission?"

"I can give my life to it, and I think you can too, but that's because we're stubborn and we don't want to be known for giving up. I don't know whether we can be as happy as we would like to be. I do believe that Brigham Young is a prophet, but I'm not sure

I'll ever accept that he knows whether I ought to plant cotton or barley—and which boot I ought to lace on first. He has to leave me some room to be who I am. Right now, I feel like we're sacrificing some part of who we are. Maybe that's a good thing in some ways. Maybe we're passing the test God is giving us. But it's not what I would choose. It feels like a heavy price to pay."

He looked at Angie, almost hoping she would tell him he was wrong. But she only nodded.

CHAPTER 8

Early in the afternoon, Jens Larsen called his company back together. He asked for a thoughtful, respectful discussion about what people wanted to do. But the meeting turned into an angry, accusing free-for-all, with George Carpenter and Daniel Pulsipher advocating that they all pick up and leave, and what seemed to Morgan a majority of the company agreeing. Lyman Hunt, in spite of the questions he had posed earlier, tried to calm the discussion and to propose another solution: that they stay, give New St. Joseph a try, and see whether Bishop Morrison's vision of the future might not come true.

Morgan decided that it was finally time to weigh in. "I just want to say that Angeline and I have already talked things over, and we're staying. We don't like the way some of this has been handled, but we were called to serve here, and we're going to carry out our mission."

"That's all well and good, Brother Davis," George said. "But Brigham changed the rules. I don't think we're held to our original commitment at this point."

"I understand what you're saying," Morgan said. "And I wish you the best, George. I'm just saying that I'd like to stay and see whether we can make some good things happen here."

"And what do you mean by 'here'? Are you talking about New St. Joseph? Are you going to settle on the bench and farm in that sand?"

"Yes. I suppose." Morgan hadn't committed himself to that until that moment, but it was what he thought he ought to do—because Bishop Morrison had asked it. And yet, he hardly knew how that fit with all the complaining he'd done about leaders taking away his agency. Maybe he was his father's son no matter how much he longed to break free.

Some agreed that Morgan was right, but no vote was taken. Jens Larsen asked each family to talk it over and make a decision. Daniel Pulsipher couldn't resist saying, as the meeting was ending, "As for me and my family, we're starting north on the day after tomorrow, and we'll push off early. All who are going with us, let me know. Bishop Morrison was right about one thing: we need to make it back through the Virgin River Valley before the river rises."

Morgan watched several men gather around Brother Pulsipher as soon as the meeting ended. Morgan thought that the majority would join with that group before another day went by. He had seen too many angry faces in the company to think that most would accept Brigham's advice.

What Morgan did was seek out his closest friends: the Hunts and Wilcoxes and Brookses, along with Eb and Mary Ann. He told each of them, "Talk things over, the way Brother Larsen said, but why don't we meet at our house tonight and find out what we're each planning to do."

• • •

When the couples showed up that evening, they all brought chairs. It was something they had learned to do, since no one had

146

enough seats for visitors. Angeline still felt rather sick at heart about leaving the house they had almost completed. She had gone to her garden before the guests had arrived, and she had checked the little plants that had started to grow, but it was too soon to harvest anything. The problem was, she had used up most of the seeds she and Morgan had brought with them. She had no idea how she could start another garden. Men liked to debate about settling here or settling there, digging canals, and the like. But she knew that the decision to come to West Point, and then to leave so soon, had cost more than energy. The sudden reversal had wasted the food they had brought with them, and it had wasted these plants that would soon be dying from lack of water.

She didn't want to be angry, though. If she had learned one thing in life, it was that a farmer could never really count on anything.

When everyone had assembled and arranged their chairs into a circle, Morgan said, "Well, first, let me ask, have you all made a decision? It sounds as though the Hunts are planning to stay, and you know that Angeline and I are doing the same."

"We're staying too," Art Brooks said. "When I first heard that Brigham was giving us permission to leave, I felt like grabbing the chance and getting out of here. But Susan told me that she didn't feel good about quitting. We don't like this country, but we're not ready to run from it just yet."

Angeline couldn't help but smile. It was just like the men to do the talking, but it sounded as though Susan had been the stronger voice in the decision.

"We're feeling about the same," James Wilcox said. "If you're all staying, we are too."

But he and Lydia both seemed changed from the couple Angeline remembered from that first day they had met. James

seemed aged by years, his eyes full of resolution more than enthusiasm, and pretty little Lydia looked like everyone else now, her
simple dress already faded and limp, her hair tied up, not curled.

"We're thinking we may have to leave," Eb said. "We just don't
know whether Mary Ann can survive this place. But right now, we
hardly dare set out for several weeks in a wagon. I'm not sure she
could make it."

But Mary Ann, in her tiny voice, didn't let the statement stand
by itself. "Still, next fall, as soon as I feel better, I've told Eb already,
I want to go home."

Angeline actually found herself wondering whether Mary Ann
would be alive that long. There hardly seemed anything left of her
now. Her arms were like sticks, and her dark eyes had sunk behind
her cheekbones. The smile that Angeline had pulled from her once
in a while lately was entirely gone. More than anything, it must
have been the disappointment in hearing, today, that she might be
able to go home, only to realize that she wasn't up to it.

"Here's the thing I've been thinking about," Morgan said. He
slid forward in his chair, as though he had something important
to say. "We've helped each other get here, and we've talked about
building Zion. I think we need to put all of today's wrangling behind us and just concentrate on keeping each other strong—along
with any others who want to stay."

"Everything broke apart today," Lyman said. "From what I'm
hearing, more people are leaving than staying. I'm not even sure
they have enough provisions to make the trip, but they say they'll
pool what they have and make it to St. George. Even if they have
to stop and work for a while, they figure they can fit themselves
out for the long road ahead after that. I guess that's the version of
'Zion' they've chosen."

"But we have the same problem," Angeline said. "I don't know about you, but I used up most of our seeds in our garden. And I don't think we'll have enough food to get through until crops come in—not by the time we start plowing and planting all over again."

"I've been thinking about that all afternoon," Art said. "If the bishop wants us to stay, he needs to do what he can to provide some supplies. I'm thinking he can go to the members and ask them to help us out until we can get by on our own. I don't know any other way we can make it."

"Maybe Brigham can send a telegram to the folks down here," James Wilcox said. "He can tell 'em they have to feed us."

The sudden sarcasm silenced everyone. Angeline knew that they were all smarting at the command they had received. But she didn't want that spirit to stay with them. "I think President Young does expect the previous settlers to help us," she said. "That's exactly what he believes in. And I think, if he were here, he'd share with us right down to his last sack of flour. I know he's harsh sometimes, but he's also generous."

Everyone was nodding by then.

"Well, that's right," James said. "And maybe it's just as well that some people clear out—the ones that might have struggled to live God's laws. The rest of us will have to work all the harder to look out for one another."

"Where?" Lyman asked. "In New St. Joseph or in St. Thomas? Morgan, did you mean it that you want to settle on the sand bench?"

"I didn't say I wanted to. I said I would. Because the bishop asked us to."

Angeline smiled. She wondered when she would ever come to understand her husband. To those who didn't know him, he must have seemed the most stalwart man they would ever meet, but his obedience was an act of will. She knew that the last place in the world he wanted to live was on that bench.

"Well, let's try it there," Lyman said. He smiled through his red beard, as though he were enjoying some irony he hadn't yet revealed to the others. "And if Warren Foote knows what he's talking about, the place will fail before long. Then we can decide what comes next."

But James couldn't muster a smile. "I don't want to start over another time," he said. "Let's make sure the place does survive."

"I agree," Morgan said. "I think that's how we should look at it."

And then Susan Brooks, who hadn't said a word so far, asked the others, "Could we have a prayer together? I'm really worried, if you want to know the truth. We've got so much we have to do, and we're all having babies. I don't know if I have the strength."

Angeline didn't say anything, but she was thinking that she had the strength—but not the baby.

They did pray, and, to Angeline's surprise, Morgan asked Susan to say the prayer. Maybe he had paid some attention to the things she had told him about the way men treated women.

• • •

Two days later Morgan got up early to see off the company that was pulling out. But the travelers didn't get away as soon as they had planned. Morgan had time to walk along the lined-up wagons and wish everyone a good trip. He wasn't surprised to see most of the young newlyweds—with the exception of his close friends— among those who were turning back. And he wasn't surprised that Charlton Donaldson had given in to his wife's wishes and lined up with the others. What did surprise him was that the angry Wilfred Shupe, his young wife, and his boys were not among the company, nor was Brother Garrick Callahan, the Irishman who had always seemed the least suited to survive the Muddy Valley. Brother and Sister Baker had apparently also decided to stay. Morgan thought that showed some pluck on their part, and he was pleased.

Jens Larsen and his family planned to stay, and so did a few of the others, but the original company would be cut by about two-thirds.

When Morgan came to Ben Gerard in one of the last wagons, he asked him, "Say, Brother Gerard, how can we hold any dances without your fiddle?"

Morgan laughed, but Brother Gerard didn't. "I wish I could stay, Brother Davis. I really do. But I don't think I understood what I was getting into. Rose, my first wife, is up in Brigham City—with our six children. I was planning to bring them all down as soon as we were well established here, but I don't think Rose could live in these conditions. Her health isn't good enough."

"We each have our own situations, Ben. There's a lot for all of us to consider. I just wish you well all along the way, and I pray you'll prosper."

"I don't want to pull my family apart for years and years. You understand that, don't you?"

"I just told you, I do understand."

Millicent, Ben's young wife, said, "It's mostly my fault. Rose and me worked good together. She tried to teach me to cook and to make butter and do all the things a woman has to do. I'm not good at any of those things. I need to be with Rose so she can teach me. Ben knows that."

Millicent was a pretty girl, with lips that puckered when she stopped to think. Ben patted her on the knee. "You'll learn all those things in time," he said. And then he looked back at Morgan. "Rose and Millicent lived in the same house. Not all plural wives can manage that. But those two got along well, right from the start. I'm afeard that Millicent and me, in a half-built mud shack, missed the life we had up north. If Brigham had said to stay, I would've, but he gave us a choice. I jist hope he doesn't think I went against him."

Morgan wasn't sure what President Young would think of those who pulled out. But Ben had his family to consider, and maybe Brother Brigham, if he knew the whole story, wouldn't judge him too severely. "Well, good luck," Morgan said. "In the end, it's the Lord we have to answer to." Morgan shook hands with Ben and walked away.

Then Ben called out, "Brother Rintlesbacher plays the fiddle better than I do, and he's stayin'. You can still have some fine dances."

Morgan thought that might be true. But he wondered how long before a church or meeting place would be built on the sand bench. He found himself thinking, again, that he would rather try his luck in St. Thomas, where a settlement had been established for a couple of years, but he pushed the idea aside. He was going to do what the bishop had asked of him.

Morgan counted twenty-six wagons in the line, and when the stream of them passed by his place, he saw that two more had joined in. He waved to each family, called out his farewell again, but it hurt him to think that the Saints who had come here to build Zion had broken apart in such a short time. He was not sorry to see Daniel Pulsipher and a few others leave, but he had come to like most of these people, and he knew he would miss them.

Finally the draft animals began to plod by. Dry boards in the wagons strained and complained, and wheels squeaked. Angeline came outside and joined Morgan, and they both waved to the people—most of them walking, not riding in the wagons—as they passed by. They waved back, but few of them looked at Morgan and Angeline directly. Morgan knew they were ashamed. The truth was, he was rather ashamed of them himself, but he had to admit that he also envied them.

"I feel like our family is ripping apart," Angeline said, and Morgan realized that was what he was feeling too.

• • •

Those heading south to New St. Joseph took one more day to pack their wagons before they also left West Point. Angeline walked next to Morgan as he led the oxen and urged them along. She looked back, just once, when the little wagon train crested the bluff above the river valley. The new houses were like skeletons, some barely started, some mostly built, but only one had a full roof, and that was the one Morgan and Angeline had built. It wasn't much of a house to miss, but she felt more regret than when she had left her home in Farmington. This one was built with her own hands, hers and Morgan's. They had talked so much about the house it would be someday—when it was all built out and improved—that it was that house, the future one, she felt she was losing.

The families that had settled in West Point earlier, before the Larsen group had arrived, were staying for now. Bishop Morrison had encouraged them to move downriver too, but Brother Gibson still trusted in the permission he had received from Apostle Snow. He wasn't belligerent, but he was firm, and Bishop Morrison, in the end, had not pushed too hard.

For those leaving for the sand bench, things went better when they arrived than Angeline had dared to hope. They camped, at first, at the fort by the river. They would have to wait a time before the move onto the bench could begin, but several houses in the fort had been abandoned, and that meant that the new arrivals most in need—like Eb and Mary Ann—got inside immediately. But the weather was becoming more pleasant all the time, so sleeping in wagon boxes was not a problem for those who had to do that, including Morgan and Angeline.

Angeline also saw the relief in Morgan's face when he learned that the work on the canal had gone well, and the water had almost reached the area where the new town would be. Even though lots and farms had not yet been platted and allotted, Morgan got some men organized, almost all of them from the new settlers, and they began to take their oxen onto the bench each day to clear brush. Angeline was also able to start making bricks immediately; when the time was right, Morgan planned to use his wagon to carry the bricks to their building site.

The actual survey and platting took longer than the new settlers hoped it would, but as soon as lands were assigned by lot, Angeline and Morgan began to build. They constructed a somewhat larger house this time, and Angeline had to admit to herself that it was already nicer than the one at West Point. The view of the valley from the bench was more pleasant than Angeline ever would have expected. The changing angles of the sun from hour to hour altered the look of the place. The pinks flamed to peach and even orange early and late, and the stretch of willows along the river was a green ribbon through the valley. Looking to the north, she could see the pastel-colored bluffs of the Mormon Mesa, and beyond that a distant line of dark-blue mountains, capped with snow.

Angeline began planting her garden with seeds others shared with her, and she imagined a day when roses would bloom outside her front door and her children would run and play with the other children who would live in their little village. She was getting used to the idea that the beauty of the place was in the vistas and subtle colors, not in the sand beneath her feet. Still, she had discovered the bright pink blooms on prickly pears, and she decided those could be her roses for now. She and Morgan had begun to talk again about a nice house and, in time, a fine little city.

The seeds in Angeline's garden germinated quickly in the warm weather. She would have some food of her own cultivation before long, and supplies would hold out until then, as long as they were careful. A first crop of grains and a money crop of cotton would come equally fast, she hoped, and Morgan was talking more optimistically about the long growing season and the number of cuttings of hay they could make each year. He talked of the animals they could own and feed, the surprising productivity of this sandy soil, even if it didn't look dark and rich.

Angeline's only worry was that the older settlers seemed to be dragging their feet. They participated in the drawing for assigned land, but they weren't moving onto the bench. Most had lived in the fort for a season or two, and they didn't like the idea of rebuilding. They also didn't offer their food, didn't make much effort to get acquainted, and actually didn't show much liveliness. They worked hard, but they seemed drained. They didn't admit to discouragement very often, but they looked solemn, and they seemed to conserve their energy, as though they knew they would need all the strength they could muster when the heat came on. When they spoke of summer, it was with awe, as though the very powers of hell were waiting ahead, and only the strongest would survive. Angeline wondered at their reticence, their lack of welcoming spirit, until at church one Sunday—still held at the fort since no building had been started on the bench—a sister rather offhandedly admitted her suspicion. When Angeline talked of the coming year, Sister Connor said, "We'll see if you stay that long."

It was becoming clear: many had been sent to the Muddy, but a majority had given up, usually after one summer. And the people at the fort near Mill Point had already rebuilt their houses after moving from old St. Joseph. No wonder they were in no hurry to build again. Angeline thought maybe she understood their feelings, but she also understood Brigham Young a little better now. He had called people to come here and stay. It was what had to happen if the area would ever prosper, but he wasn't used to pioneers who gave up. He must have seen this generation of members as weaklings compared to the men and women he had led across the plains.

•   •   •

April was wonderful. Days were often quite hot, but livable; nights were cool and, with a couple of quilts on the bed, pleasant. Morgan appreciated how hard Angeline continued to work every day and still liked to go to bed with him at night. He knew she longed to be pregnant, but her closeness was more than practical; it was never merely submissive. He understood her better now, knew that she would accept nothing less than respect, but that was not a problem. He did respect her, and it had never been his nature to command anyone. He liked that she thought for herself, and he loved that she didn't play little games he had seen other women employ: coyly seeking compliments or manipulating their husbands to get what they wanted. Angeline thought about life, felt things deeply, and she made decisions carefully.

Morgan was pleased with his work, too. He got his land plowed and planted, and his cotton starts popped up quickly in the warmth. His wheat and barley broke through the earth faster than he ever expected.

When the canal was completed, a committee of men worked every day to dig ditches to each farm property. Morgan wasn't on the committee, but with all the time he could set aside, he joined the men and helped with the digging. The canal was eight feet wide, two and a half feet deep, and over three miles long. It was a monumental achievement to dig it. The men had used oxen and scrapers as much as possible, but in many places, picks and shovels had been necessary to get through bedrock. The ditches were smaller, but they took more shovel work, and Morgan began to take pride in such a massive community project. The Muddy was spring-fed, so it flowed year round, and once the canal reached the bench, there was adequate water to nourish the new fields. Morgan began to think that Warren Foote had been much too pessimistic about farming on the bench.

But summer was nearing, and Morgan heard every day, from the older settlers, what to expect. By May, he thought he was starting to understand, but as the summer heat came on with full force—each day seeming a little worse than the day before—work could be done only in the early morning or in the evening, and even then, it was almost unbearable. Sensible or not, Morgan felt he had too much to do to stop and rest. He made more adobe bricks, down by the river, and set them out to dry. He wanted a little barn to get his oxen out of the sun in the midday. He also needed to build a chicken coop, and there was no lumber for such things. So he withstood the furnace of heat as much as he could, and for as long as he could stand it each day, he set the walls for the outbuildings he wanted. And Angeline, more often than not, worked alongside him no matter how many times he told her to stay out of the sun. They no longer slept under quilts. They had set the wagon box behind their house, raised off the ground with large stones, and they slept out in the air, where occasionally a hint of a breeze would pass over them.

But the heat was everything Morgan had heard it would be—and maybe more. He had known hot days in Farmington, with temperatures around one hundred degrees, but this was different. The air itself was like the draft off a fire. There was no stepping away from it, and hiding inside the house only took the bite of direct sun off his clothes and skin. Inside, nothing moved; he found it hard to breathe at times. He would lie down for a while, but the bed stored heat and used it to bake his back. His shirt and trousers soaked up his sweat, and so did his stockings, inside his boots. There were times when his vision blurred, his head seemed to spin, and he thought he couldn't survive another minute if he didn't get some relief. But there was no relief. A couple of times he had sat down in the canal and dunked himself, but the water wasn't cool, and when he climbed out, he felt little change.

"How long will it be this way?" Angeline asked him one day. It was what Morgan had been wondering. But he had heard the answer the old settlers gave: it would keep getting hotter through August, and temperatures wouldn't cool much until November, maybe late November.

But Morgan didn't slack off. His answer to stress and worry had always been the same: work hard, keep taking forward steps. And then, just when he was satisfied with his crops, a dry thunderstorm blew through and set off a savage wind. Sand blew across the desert in waves, like sheets of rain in a thunderstorm. The tawny-gray sand covered everything. It blew through the uncovered "windows" of the house and piled up in corners and against walls, inches deep. Worse than that, the sand filled up the irrigation canal so completely it almost disappeared. It had to be dug out quickly or the crops would burn.

The men from St. Joseph dug sand all the next day, sweated through all their clothing, drank the distasteful Muddy River water by gallons, and still felt depleted and thirsty. In a couple of days they had deepened the canal and ditches enough to get some water onto the crops, but the wheat and barley and corn looked devastated and the cotton plants looked like sagging vines. Morgan wondered whether he had hope of harvesting anything at all that year.

After a few days of watering, some of the plants began to recover, but every farmer had been hurt the same way, and the men talked of having to combine whatever had survived just to have enough to eat that winter. "We'll be all right," Brother Handley, one of the old settlers, told Morgan. "Some things grow here year round. We can put in late crops and get enough harvest to get us by."

Brother Aaron Handley was a big, wide-shouldered man who had marched with the Mormon Battalion, had helped to settle the Salt Lake Valley, and had lost his wife in childbirth in those early days. But he had married again, and he and his new wife were raising Brother Handley's children from his first marriage plus three more of their own—eight in all. To Morgan, he seemed an old man, but in truth he was not more than fifty. Still, there seemed nothing too strenuous, too demanding, for him to survive. After all, in his Mormon Battalion days, he had marched through deserts, half-naked and starving at times, all the way across the West. He told Morgan, "After that, nothing has seemed all that trying to me."

But not everyone was so confident. A week after the first sandstorm blew through, another one struck. As the men dug out the canal again, Morgan watched Eb and could see how listless he appeared. And Morgan understood. Some of the clearing could be done by oxen-pulled scrapers, but much of the work had to be done one shovelful at a time, which was impossibly slow. And what everyone knew was that another windstorm would follow, sooner or later. Everything Warren Foote had predicted looked as if it may yet turn out to be true.

Eb took a rest, leaning on his shovel and breathing deeply for a time. "I don't know if I can hold up," he told Morgan. He took another long breath. "I'm losing weight, and there's not a whole lot left of me. But what worries me more is Mary Ann. Have you seen the way she looks lately?"

Morgan had seen her at church, which was now held in a new little adobe building that the men had raised during the last month, but she hadn't lasted the entire meeting. The room was like a cookstove inside, and Bishop Morrison, visiting that day, had preached much too long—laying out doctrines of eternity that seemed a little too abstract and disconnected from the realities they all faced each day. Mary Ann had risen, then dropped back onto the bench she had been sitting on. Eb had had to help her up, and then he had walked out with her, almost carrying her. She was thinner than ever, and yet, under her dress, Morgan could see the ample bulge that meant her baby would be coming before the summer ended. She had been pale as alkaline dust, and her eyes were empty, as though she were only half alive.

"Yes, I've seen her," Morgan said. "It's obvious how much she's suffering." Sweat was running in Morgan's eyes. He took off his hat and wiped his face with the bandanna he wore around his neck. But the cloth was so wet that it didn't help.

"She's just so little, and the baby seems big. I don't know whether she can give birth, Morgan. I'm scared to death about that."

"How long until the baby comes?"

"Three months, I think. But I hope it comes sooner. Angeline comes over every day and wipes her all over with water. I think Mary Ann would be dead by now if it weren't for that."

"We pray for her every—"

"That's all well and good, Morgan. But Brigham sent us down here where no human being should ever try to live. I just don't know how we can pray our way out of such foolishness."

Morgan didn't try to argue with him, and Eb seemed to realize, immediately, that he had spoken too strongly. He shoveled some more sand for a time, casting it behind him, but then he stopped again and said, "I'm wrong to say such things. You know I am. God should smite me right now for speaking that way. But I think Brigham picked the wrong man when he called on me, and I should have known Mary Ann well enough to recognize that she couldn't do this."

Isaac Humboldt, another of the old settlers, had been digging alongside Eb, but he stopped now. "Boys," he said, "I don't know how to tell you this, but you ain't seen nothin' yet. People don't like to tell the new folks, but we've been digging out this canal since before it was even finished. The wind's going to fill it up many times each year. And I'll tell yuh what else. We're losing too much water to the sand. I've heard that the folks down in St. Thomas are worried. Not enough water is getting down to them since we finished this canal."

Actually, Morgan had heard some talk of that kind before. "Isaac," he asked now, "isn't there some way to stop the problem—maybe by planting bushes to block the wind along the canal?"

"I don't know. Some say that. But I'm not the one who decides about such things. Ever'one seems to think they've got more brains than me."

Morgan was taken aback. He had always assumed that the

older settlers got along well with each other. He heard in Isaac's tone a resentment he never would have expected.

But Isaac was quick to say, "Don't pay me no mind. I'm just tired out. I come down here with jist my one wife and two of my childern. But after the first year, I went back and got the rest. I got three wives here now and fourteen childern. It's all I can do to keep 'em fed, and to cover 'em up with some sort of clothing. I jist don't see that we're gittin' anywhere. We take a step forward and then we fall back, over'n over."

"But you finished your planting early," Eb said. "Your farm is starting to produce, isn't it?" He set down his shovel, picked up a water jug, and took a long drink. Then he handed the jug to Isaac.

Isaac took a drink and wiped his mouth. He took off his hat and wiped the inside brim with his dirty hand. "It's doin' all right. But we come down here to grow cotton. Thass what they tol' us, anyway. Each year I hafta plant more grain, jist to get enough to keep us eatin' in the winter. And I ain't makin' much on the cotton I grow. The price has fallen off ever since the War Between the States ended. So I ask myself, what's the use of bein' here if we can't make a living from cotton? I can farm wheat and corn better up in Provo, where I was. I don't know why we're here—'less it's to bake our brains out. Maybe thass why folks think I'm empty in the head. Maybe my brains is all burned up."

"When you start a new place, it always takes time," Morgan said. "We'll make this a beautiful town in time."

Isaac looked out from the ditch, across the expansive desert. "It's what we say. But I think the devil built this country. It ain't even healthy, the way they tol' us it was. Sally, my second wife, an' about half my childern too, is down with shakes and fevers agin right now—an' it keeps comin' back on 'em."

Morgan had no idea what to say. He had been quite hopeful for a time in the spring, but these were all the worries he had been stewing about lately no matter how hard he tried not to give way to discouragement.

"But I'll tell you what," Isaac said. "I ain't leavin' this place 'til Brigham sends word for us to pull out. We're called to a mission. If it don't work out, fine. But I'd rather fry on this hot ground than ever quit. I ain't goin' nowhere until I get a honorable release."

"I think that's right," Morgan said, and then he looked at Eb. "Let's just keep going for now. One day at a time. Muscles get stronger when you use them. We'll all be stronger by the time we get this town built up."

But Morgan didn't tell Eb about his biggest worry. For months Angeline had wondered what was wrong with her that she couldn't become pregnant. And yet, to their joy, it had finally happened. The only trouble was, she was finding out about baby sickness herself now, and she was having trouble keeping food down. She was such a powerful woman, it was disheartening to her to feel any kind of weakness. She hadn't told Mary Ann. She had simply continued to visit her, bathe her, console her, and try to lift her spirits. But by the time she would walk home in the heat, she was ready to collapse, and she had never experienced anything of that sort before. She didn't admit that she was discouraged; he knew she didn't like to complain. But she had lost some of her humor, some of her desire, and he could sense it in everything she did.

•   •   •

After a couple of days, the canal was running quite well again. Bishop Morrison made the trip from St. Thomas on the third day, appearing on the sand bench in his buggy. He told the men who were digging, "You're pushin' yerselves too hard. Let's get by with the canal as it is for now. This fall you can work to deepen it again."

That was fine with everyone, but what did autumn mean in a place like this? Morgan wondered. Golden leaves, ripe crops, crisp air? Those were things he would never see again, at least not if he spent his life here.

As the men began to walk away, shovels over their shoulders, Bishop Morrison stopped Morgan. "I've been thinking about you, Morgan," he said. "You and Angeline have your place in better order than most of the new families—and you don't have any children yet. There's something I was thinking you could do for us."

"What's that, Bishop?"

"Once this heat lets up this fall, and we can see what we have left for crops, a few men need to take wagons to St. George and do some trading and purchasing. The older farms will have some cotton ready by then, and we can use that to buy some of the provisions we'll need for winter."

"We need more plows, too, and tools," Morgan said. "We could even use—"

"We need lots of things, but mostly we hafta be sure we can feed ourselves all right. We can replant a fall crop—that's one good thing about this place—but we need to get some variety in what we eat. If we don't, we'll all get sick. We also need some livestock to replace the cattle the Pah Utes stole from us last year. Anyway, do you suppose you could make a haul like that—up to St. George and back?"

"I guess I could, Bishop. But I don't think Angeline could go with me. She's actually in a family way now."

Bishop Morrison smiled and slapped Morgan on the shoulder. "That's good news," he said. "I know she's been worryin' about that. My wife told me so."

"Yes, it's a good thing for us. She's been sick, but I think by fall she might be doing better—so I could maybe get away. But crossing that Virgin River so many times, with a heavy load, that might not be a good idea with only one team of oxen."

"I know. That's true. We'll send you with another team, and maybe have you take the older Cotter boy. He's a strong young fellow; he can work alongside grown men all day long. We'll decide later how many wagons need to go, but we'll make sure we have double teams for every wagon."

"All right. As long as Angie is doing better, I wouldn't mind making the trip."

"Well, let's see how she's feeling in a few months. And listen, you can take a fee from each of the men who ship cotton with you. That way, you come out ahead a little, and you do a service for everyone in the valley."

"All right. That sounds good to me. I would like a way to bring in a little more income. I could maybe buy some furniture and tie it on top of the wagon when we come back."

"Sure. That's what you ought to do."

CHAPTER 9

Bishop Nephi Barkley was the leader of the New St. Joseph settlement, which was split apart at this point, some people having moved to the bench and others still at the fort near Mill Point. Since the new settlers had arrived, not much had happened to unite them with the previous settlers. Maybe it was for that reason that Bishop Barkley announced a Saturday night dance in the new school and church building on the bench. It was July now, and Angeline could only imagine that a dance would be miserable, but she had been feeling much better the last week or so, and she and Morgan decided they needed to attend. Most of the other Saints also showed up. Angeline thought maybe people chose to come because it was a change from the usual routine, or maybe they felt the same need she and Morgan did to create a better sense of togetherness.

The dance didn't start until nine o'clock, when at least the sun wasn't beating down on the church. But it was a breezeless evening, and the temperature inside the cramped building was overpowering. Still, Brother Rintlesbacher, along with an older settler named Geoffrey Barnard, began to play the fiddle right on time, and another brother, Henry Stoddard, called out the commands for the reels. The fiddles made as many squeaks and scratches as true notes, and the fiddlers didn't know many songs, but they played with enthusiasm, and the dancers, sweating until they soaked through their clothes, pranced and swung with surprising liveliness. They kicked up lots of dust from the dirt floor, and the room became hazy in the lamplight. Only about half the crowd could be inside at once, so, after each dance, most of the dancers would walk outside, and new ones would enter and take their turns.

Morgan had never been a dancer, but Angeline got him through a couple of reels by pushing him in the direction he was supposed to turn and sometimes telling him out loud what he needed to do. She knew he was relieved at the end of each dance and only too happy to clear out. Most of the men were at least as unskilled as Morgan, which Angeline pointed out to Morgan, but that didn't seem to make him any less self-conscious about his mistakes.

Angeline liked seeing all the members together and looking more sprightly than usual. Even Wilfred Shupe was spinning Polly about, rather adeptly, and the two looked happy together. Angeline was glad to see that he wasn't always in a cranky mood. And the Bakers, it turned out, knew their reels and seemed delighted, grinning as they moved lightly through the maneuvers.

Angeline was gradually getting to know some of the Saints who had migrated to the Muddy in previous years—or at least a few of the women—and she had already found she liked them more than she had at first. They had also begun to accept her, she thought. So far, she hadn't told anyone that she was expecting, but hoping that she would be a mother, as most of the women already were, seemed to connect her to them. She knew she would also need to learn from them.

A woman named Beth Millard, who had lived on the Muddy since the beginning of the mission and so far was still living at the fort by Mill Point, fancied herself a poet and welcomed every chance to read her verse. Between dances, early in the evening, Sister Barkley, the bishop's wife, invited her forward to recite. What she presented, from memory, was a lengthy poem in awkward rhythm and rhymes that rang like off-tune fiddle notes in Angeline's ears. Still, the poem was a valiant attempt to memorialize the efforts of the Muddy River missionaries, and Angeline appreciated her sentiment.

Sister Millard was a sunburned little woman with thick, hard arms showing beneath her rolled-up sleeves. Her graying hair was tied up on her head, and the button of her dress closest to her neck was left undone—all this to fight the heat a little, no doubt. But her eyes seemed almost dreamy as she pronounced her lines without so much as a slip.

The poem was about sand and snakes and digging ditches, but it extolled the spiritual purpose of the settlers' efforts, and Angeline liked the mixture of homely images and transcendent ideals. One couplet especially appealed to Angeline: "We came to the desert as we knew we must, to build something holy out of the dust."

It was good for Angeline to think that way. She knew they weren't building a mere town—even with future rosebushes—but a holy place for the Saints to live together. It was not a new idea to her, but it seemed new, spoken by this prosaic little poet. Sister Millard's face was red from the sun, and her forearms were red from washing clothes in boiling river water, but Angeline could see something deeper in her work. She suspected it was what some of the folks who had quit the mission had never quite understood. She did hate the "dust" of the desert, but it could be made into adobe bricks, and adobe bricks could be made into houses, and houses could become the elements of a true town—a Zion town.

So Angeline went to Sister Millard after she had completed her recitation, and she told her how much her poem had meant to her. "Oh, I'm not a real poet," Sister Millard told her. "I just fiddle with words in my head and see if I can make 'em into somethin'."

Angeline didn't hint that her words actually were quite clumsy. She merely said, "You changed my mind about dust. That's a very good thing."

Angeline was not confident that Sister Millard even understood what she meant, but they gave each other a quick, sweaty hug, and Angeline felt happy about that.

By then, Morgan was saying, "Let's walk outside for a few minutes. I'm about to melt into a puddle and turn this floor into mud."

As the two walked out, Angeline noticed a woman standing by herself just outside the door. She looked as though she had stopped to think about something, her face serious—even clouded, it seemed. Angeline said, "Hello, Sister. I'm sorry, but I don't believe I've met you."

The woman nodded politely and said in a quiet voice, "I'm Ruth Nilsson."

"You must live at the fort," Angeline suggested.

"Yes, I do."

"We came with the new settlers. I'm Angeline Davis, and this is my husband, Morgan."

"Yes. I've seen you at church." But she was looking at Morgan when she spoke, and that seemed a little strange to Angeline.

"Have I met your husband?" Morgan asked.

"I don't have a husband."

"Oh," Morgan said, and an embarrassing silence followed.

Finally Sister Nilsson said, "My husband was killed in an accident."

"Oh, my, how awful," Angeline said. "Are you alone now, or—"

"No. I have a son. He's staying with some friends tonight, but I decided just now that I should go home to him."

"But did you have a chance to dance?" Angeline asked.

"No. Or, I mean . . . I had a chance, but I decided I didn't want to. I came to see everyone. But it's so hot, and . . . well, anyway, it was nice to meet you." And once again, her eyes drifted toward Morgan.

"Yes, it was nice to meet you," he said.

Ruth nodded and then walked away. "What an awful thing," Angeline said as soon as the woman was out of hearing distance. "I can't imagine coming to a place like this and then losing my husband. She must be the only single woman in this valley. I wonder why she stays."

"That's what I was wondering," Morgan said. "She's a sad little creature, don't you think? Her face looked as gray as her dress."

"Of course she's sad—and terribly lonely."

"If she's lonely, she certainly made no effort to get to know us better."

"She doesn't need us. She needs a husband."

"No doubt," Morgan agreed. "But who would want to marry her? She looks like a ghost. She came to the dance and then avoided people. What sense does that make?"

"I think she wanted to be part of things, but when she got here, she felt out of place. Who wouldn't in her situation?"

"That's probably right, but I can't picture her laughing and talking, and that's what she needs to do if she wants to have friends."

Angeline understood what Morgan was saying, but she thought she had seen some prettiness in Ruth's dark eyes, and maybe some feeling behind her reticence. She probably did want to make friends but couldn't bring herself to enter into things.

By then another group had exited the building, and Angeline said to Morgan, "Should we go back in and dance one more reel?"

"Not yet. I know it's not cool out here, but at least there's a little air to breathe."

Sweat was still running off Morgan's face, and his shirt was soaked. Angeline didn't blame him for wanting to stay outside, and the truth was, she had danced enough herself. She tired more easily these days, and she was exhausted now. She would have given almost anything for a cool night, even just enough breeze to blow across her sweaty face.

Art Brooks had just bent to make his way through the door and step outside. Susan followed close behind. "I'm about to pass out," she said, but she was laughing. "I think our next dance should be at Christmastime when it feels good to hop around and get our blood flowing."

"That ceiling is awfully low in there," Art said. "I keep thinking that I'll bump my head."

"And that's where the heat collects—up there close to the ceiling," Morgan said.

"That's for sure," Art said, adding as he looked up, "I like this ceiling, out here."

"I like it too," Angeline said. "It's beautiful." These nights in the desert were actually magnificent. The sky was so full of stars that they seemed a smear of dusty light rather than an array of pinpricks. It was one of the beauties of the valley that Angeline had come to love. When they slept outside, as they always did now, she would try to keep her eyes open as long as she could, just to feel a sense of reward for the long day she had put in.

She thought now that was what she wanted to do: go back to her house and take in some sky before she fell asleep. She was about to suggest that it was time to walk home when Bishop Barkley and his wife, Jane, stepped up to them. "Maybe this was not such a good idea," the bishop said. "I think I'm getting heat stroke."

"Well, it was good to get people together," his wife said, "but I think a watermelon bust might be a better choice next time. The last time we had one, though, these black flies down here almost ate us up." Angeline hated those flies that had come on so strong lately. There was no escaping them, and their sting was as sharp as a poke with a needle. But she had seen the wonderful melons that people grew here. She had planted some of her own, and she did think it would be fun to share them.

"Have you gotten to know all the folks who were here before you came?" the bishop asked. He looked around at both couples.

"Not really," Art said. "I think we've met everyone, but it's hard to get acquainted the way we're divided between the bench and the fort."

"I know," the bishop said. "We're still talking about that. We hope, this fall, everyone at the fort will move together up to the new town, where you are."

Angeline admitted the truth even though she knew she probably shouldn't. "I don't think the older group wants to get to know us. They tell us that we'll probably pull out before long, the way so many people have done before."

"Well, it's happened a lot," Sister Barkley said. "We start to get skeptical about new people when they come and go so often."

Susan was standing across from Jane, but she reached out and touched her arm, just above the wrist. "What keeps *you* here?" she asked. "Why do some stay and others leave?"

The question was serious, but the touch was gentle and respectful, and Sister Barkley seemed to respond. She sounded thoughtful when she said, "Most people would say that they stay because they accepted a mission. But all of us did that. I think some of us are just more stubborn than others. We keep telling ourselves we won't let this place defeat us." And then she laughed. "Or maybe some of us are headed to hell, and we think we can prepare for hellfire down here better than anywhere else."

Everyone laughed, but only quietly. Angeline was still thinking about Jane's stubbornness. She actually thought it explained something about herself.

Then the bishop said, "When I think of leaving, I wonder what trials we'll run into in the next place. I think maybe life is supposed to be hard." Bishop Barkley was a compact man, rather short, with serious eyes. He stopped and thought for a time, as though he still hadn't found the right words. "When we were traveling down here, we came to the Mormon Mesa and wanted to go over the top, the way you people did. But our wagon was too big and heavy. We added another ox team, but the animals still couldn't make it up the hill. So we had to back down and go around by way of St. Thomas. That was farther, but we finally got here. We had two choices, and neither one was very good—but we got where we were going." He smiled. "Do you understand what I'm saying?"

"You're telling us we have to make our way the best we can," Angeline said.

"Yes. But that's only part of it." He smiled, and Angeline glimpsed deep dimples under his curly black beard. "We wouldn't like the easy way if we found it. Hard roads are more interesting—and satisfying—than easy ones. We're trying to get to heaven, not just to the Muddy River. "

About then another couple joined the group. Angeline knew that the woman was named Catherine. Angeline had talked to her at church one day. She was a plain woman, with drooping cheeks and a heavy, rather flat nose. But her eyes were animated, and she liked to talk.

"This is Isaiah Groves and his wife, Catherine," the bishop said. "Or maybe you've all met."

"I've seen you," Isaiah said. "And this man sticks up above everyone else, but I can't say that I know his name." He stuck out his hand toward Art.

"Art Brooks, and my wife, Susan."

"I know this is Brother Davis," Isaiah went on. "People all say that he can get more work done in one day than anyone they've ever seen."

"Except for my wife," Morgan said.

"Isaiah and Catherine moved down here with us," Bishop Barkley said. "We came the first year—1865—but we came with the second group. We helped get the old St. Joseph started."

Brother Groves nodded. He was a man of forty or so, with little hair on his head, but a heavy brown beard. He sounded gentle, unassuming, when he spoke. "We didn't think much of this place when we got here, but we're starting to figure it out. At least I hope so."

"These folks have been asking me and Jane why we stay here when so many turn around and go home. What's your answer, Isaiah?"

Brother Groves laughed. "I don't know. I'm not one to ask those kinds of questions. I just do what I have to do each day and hope for the best."

"What about you, Catherine?" the bishop asked.

"We buried a little son here," she said. "Sixteen months old. I don't want to leave him here in this desert, all alone. I want to be close to him."

Catherine looked down at the ground, almost as though the sand beneath her feet represented "this desert" to her. She was a trim woman, with dark hair and eyes, and she had curled her hair for the dance, in spite of the heat. Those curls were drooping now, but she looked pretty, even in a faded green dress that had seen far too much wear.

But Sister Groves wasn't quite finished. "I know we'll have our son again. It's not that I think his spirit is buried under the sand. But it's the sand and the weather—and the ague—that took his life. So I feel that we've paid a price for this place, and now I don't want to think it wasn't worth it. I'll give my own life to this desert before I let all this work go and just walk away from it."

"Do you have more children?" Angeline asked.

"Yes. We have six, four girls and two boys."

"Do you worry the desert will take their lives, too?" It was something Angeline had thought about lately—bringing a baby into this hostile place.

"I do worry. But bad things happen everywhere. Babies die sometimes. It's just that we haven't given so much of ourselves to any other place."

"Do you plan to live with us, up on the bench?" Susan asked.

"I suppose we do. But we've dragged our feet so far. We've gotten settled here at the fort and it's hard to build again—for the third time. But I guess we'll do it."

"We will too," Sister Barkley said. "In the fall."

The little group had gradually formed itself into a sort of square, with one couple on each side. Angeline felt the breath of the Spirit moving among them even if there was hardly a breath of air. She realized she felt love for each person now that she grasped a little better who they were—and mostly, now that she felt connected to their hopes, which were becoming her own.

The bishop said, "We got our crops in before the water was on the bench. We want to harvest what's left of this year's yield, and then we'll join you."

175

Angeline understood for the first time what the settlers in the fort were dealing with. They didn't want to move again any more than the Larsen group had wanted to leave West Point. But they were all going to do it, in time, and maybe Zion could start to take shape.

• • •

Morgan liked what he felt at church the next morning. He knew more of the people from conversations during the dance, and he saw everyone a little differently. They were surviving as best they could, and if they were beaten down, they hadn't given up. But the day was extraordinarily hot. Church services didn't last long, and afterward, Morgan saw children, most of them without shoes, running over the hot sand as though running on coals. They would scramble twenty or thirty yards and then throw something on the sand—an apron or a bonnet or a straw hat—and stand on it until their feet weren't burning quite so badly, and then they would make another run.

Monday morning came on even hotter. Morgan got up before sunup and turned water from the ditch onto his crops, and he cultivated for a couple of hours. But he finally couldn't take the sensation he had that he was burning up, both inside and out. His vision was actually getting blurry by the time he got back to his house. He had looked forward to getting in out of the sun, but the heat was already rising inside the house, turning it into a fire pit. Angeline was doing something he had rarely seen her do. She was sitting down on their bed, fanning herself. "Are you all right?" Morgan asked her.

"I think so," was all she said, but she didn't sound well.

"Lie down. Rest. You can't work in this heat."

"You can't either."

"There's a little shade on the north side of the house," Morgan said. "Let's go out there. This room is going to cook us."

So they took their chairs outside and sat close to the north wall of the house, not saying much. Morgan wanted to encourage Angeline, lift her spirits, but he couldn't think of anything to say that would help her through a day that was going to get even worse before it got better—and a summer that now seemed likely to last forever.

But they lasted the day, and they slept outside in the wagon box that night. Morgan had seen plenty of rattlesnakes over the last few weeks. He always wondered whether they were capable of slipping up and over the side of the box, even though it was propped up off the ground, but he never admitted his fear to Angie. What he did find was that lizards found their way in and sometimes scrambled over him in the night, startling him. And then, awake at night, he would calculate the number of weeks that might have to go by before the weather broke a little. The fact was, he never slept well on these hot nights, and he worked more hours than he should. The schedule was wearing him down, and he knew it, but his greater fear was over what the heat was doing to Angeline. She was putting up a brave front, and she rarely complained, but he wondered whether she could carry the baby through all this strain.

One day in August the temperature seemed to hit a peak. Morgan couldn't believe that it could get any worse. And then a wind came up that offered no relief; it felt like air from a black-smith's bellows gushing over hot coals. Morgan had worked in the fields from very early that morning, and he was walking back toward the house for a rest when he noticed smoke rising from somewhere down off the bench. He walked closer to where he could see into the valley, and then he realized: a house was burning—actually, three or four houses—down at the fort.

Morgan stopped for a moment, not sure what to do. He couldn't tell from that distance whether anyone was fighting the fire. Suddenly the dry reeds on another roof ignited, and he realized that the wind was carrying sparks from one house to another. He dropped his shovel and hoe and began to run. The fire was at least a mile away, but he couldn't just watch the whole town burn up. He had to get down there and help.

Morgan ran too hard at first, his desire to help stronger than his good sense, but soon his boots, grabbed by the sand with each stride, became heavy, and his legs couldn't keep up the pace. He slowed to a fast walk for a hundred yards or so, and then he ran again, this time without pushing so hard. Halfway down the hill, he spotted a man, walking hard but not running, and realized it was Wilfred Shupe. Morgan caught up quickly and walked with Shupe.

"What kind of fool starts a fire in this heat and wind?" Shupe asked.

Morgan had entertained the same thought, but he wanted to get there and do something, not find someone to blame. "The whole fort could go up in flames," Morgan said between hard breaths, and then, as though that were enough explanation, he began to run again, leaving Brother Shupe behind.

By the time Morgan made it to the fort, he was walking again, even struggling to do that. He felt as though he had spent his strength getting to the fire and wasn't sure what he could do now to stop what was happening. But no one was trying to put out the fire. A group of people, men and women and children, had gathered at the south end of the settlement, with the wind behind their backs, and they were merely watching now.

Morgan saw Isaiah Groves in the crowd and stepped toward him. "Can't we do anything?" he asked.

"There's no way to stop it. We're just hoping that the sparks don't jump across and burn the houses on the west side. Brother Jones has a thermometer, and he said the temperature is 119 degrees today. Everything is so dry, we'll be lucky if the whole place doesn't burn up."

Morgan saw what he meant. The south wind had carried the sparks to most of the houses and sheds and outhouses on the east side, but those to the west were not affected so far.

So Morgan watched with the others. Dry roofs burned up in a great rush of flames, and then the burning reeds would drop inside the house. The adobe walls stood firm, but everything inside burned, the flames rising above the walls and flashing out through the windows. That meant furniture, beds, food—everything—would be lost.

When the last of the east-side roofs was gone, the flames still belched from the houses at the north end. "That's our house at the end," Brother Groves finally said. "I had a decent wheat crop, and I had it ground at the mill just a few days ago. I stacked the sacks of flour in that little shed on the back—the one that's burning now. I got some furniture out, but all our flour will be gone."

"I'm sorry, Isaiah."

"It's just one more thing." Isaiah didn't sound disconsolate or angry or broken, just sad. "We'll figure something out."

"We have fall wheat growing now," Morgan said. "Let's hope for a good crop. We can all share and get through the winter."

"There's always food here," Isaiah said. "Our garden is used up now, but we'll plant again as soon as the heat breaks. We'll have enough." Then he added, "But I don't know how we can replace all the things we lost in the house."

Morgan wanted to offer him some of his own things, but he had next to nothing himself.

By then, Bishop Barkley stepped away from the others and approached Morgan and Isaiah. "I think the houses on the west are going to be all right. At least we didn't lose everything."

Morgan could hardly believe what he was seeing and hearing. These men weren't despairing, nor were the others. He saw a few women wiping their eyes, and some smaller children were whimpering, but no one was falling down, no one screeching or cursing.

"It's been this way since we first settled this place," Bishop Barkley said. "Things just happen—over and over. And then we have to figure out a way to get by again."

Wilfred Shupe had finally arrived. He stepped up next to Morgan. "How did this happen?" he asked. He was out of breath and sounding perturbed.

"A couple of boys tried to roast some potatoes in a little shed that used to be right over there." The bishop pointed to a burned pile of rubble nearby. "I guess the wind blew through the cracks in the boards and sent sparks flying. That set the shed on fire, and once it was burning, sparks went everywhere."

"I hope those boys get a good caning before this day is over," Wilfred said.

"Well, I suppose," Bishop Barkley said. "But they both burned their hands trying to put out the fire, and I'm more worried about that than anything else."

Brother Groves said, "The boys told me they were hungry, and I feel bad about that. Food gets a little scarce at times, but I don't want our children to go hungry, ever."

Wilfred seemed ready to say something more, but he glanced at Morgan, who stared back at him. Morgan wanted to remind Wilfred that he had once let his son go without water—on purpose. Maybe Wilfred guessed that was what Morgan was thinking. He said nothing.

"The thing is," Isaiah said, "we were planning to start building a house on the bench anyway. And we were sleeping outside, so this doesn't change things too much. We'll start building a little sooner, that's all."

"I'll start making adobes for you," Morgan said.

"No. You have enough to do. I can do that."

"But I'll help, and my oxen have had it easy lately. I can start grubbing brush on your farm lot—on all of the ones that still need to be cleared."

"That would help," Bishop Barkley said, "but you can't work twelve hours a day in this heat."

"That may be right, but I can start putting some time into it, even at night, and then, when we get some cooler days, I can put in long days again."

"I can help too," Brother Shupe said.

Morgan turned and looked at Wilfred. He could hardly believe what he was hearing, but Shupe nodded. "Morgan, I know you don't think much of me, but I work hard, and when people need help, I'm willing to give it."

"That's good," the bishop said. "It's what we need. Everyone is moving from the fort onto the bench this fall, so we all need to pull together—to get adobes made, houses built, farmland cleared. I don't think our people gave you new folks as much help as they could have when you got here, but if we all work together now, we can get a good town started on the bench."

All the men were nodding. And then they looked back at the houses. Smoke was still rising and blowing off to the north, but flames were visible only in the last three or four houses. Still, Morgan felt all right. He was impressed by the resilience of these people. No one was saying, "This is the last straw. We're pulling out." The idea of sharing appealed to Morgan more than anything. He had spent his young life imagining the family he would have and the things he would accumulate someday: his farm, his house, his animals. But now he was thinking about a people, a town—Zion. He had never really thought much about the meaning of the word until he had come here, but now it seemed the most important word he knew.

• • •

Angeline had noticed the smoke and had walked to where she could look down on the fort. By the time that happened, however, the fire was mostly burned out. She wondered whether she should walk off the bench and find out what she could do, but she knew she could never make it down and then up again, walking in the sand. She hated her new sense of weakness, but she never stopped worrying about the baby she was carrying, and she knew it would be a mistake to tax herself to that extent.

She walked back to the house and sat on the bed. She was breathing hard from the effort. The wind, hot as it was, felt good when it blew across her clothes, wet with sweat. But inside the house, sand and dirt were blowing in, covering everything again. She knew she would have to clean the place once the wind stopped, but for now, it was pointless to start.

Morgan usually came back to the house by this time of day. She hoped he was all right. She was almost sure he had gone down to the fort to help. So she said a prayer for him, and for the people who lived in the fort, and she waited. The heat seemed to be rising up out of the floor, crushing from the roof, filling everything. The wind was like flames licking around her. It crossed her mind that she might die before this day ended. Everyone said the heat would break in time, but they offered no hope that the break would come in September or even October. She didn't know how she could keep going for that long. So she merely sat, breathed—or actually panted—and couldn't think what else to do. The sun would go down eventually, and the temperature would drop a little, but not much. The desert drank up the sun all day and then released the heat back into the air all night. There was no escaping.

Morgan came back after a time. "Do you know about the fire?" he asked.

Angeline nodded. "I went out and looked. Did you go down there?"

"Yes. But there was nothing I could do."

"You're soaked," she said. And it was true. Every inch of his shirt, his hat, even his trousers, was wet. The climb back to the bench had taken the last of his energy.

"They say it's 120 degrees," he said.

"How can we do this?"

"We're all going to work together," Morgan told her.

"I don't mean that. How can we live through this?"

He looked back at her with almost no expression. He wasn't as broken as she seemed to be, but he had no answer.

CHAPTER 10

Morgan and Angeline did make it through the summer, but each day was a trial. Morgan often thought of his growing-up years in northern Utah when summer would slide easily into fall, the days gradually shortening and the angle of the sun deepening. Above all, he thought of cool and comfortable nights. The end of summer was not so obvious in the Muddy River Valley. All Morgan noticed was the intensity of the heat diminishing a bit by the end of September.

Earlier in the month Mary Ann had given birth to a baby girl, and, in spite of the heat and Mary Ann's weakness, all had gone quite well. Angeline was with her during her confinement, and she told Morgan later of the desperate struggle and screams of pain, but Mary Ann had lived through it, no matter how weak she had been afterwards. In the ensuing days, the baby, a little girl they named Eliza, had proven robust and stubborn. Mary Ann even had enough milk, in spite of all she had been through, and she was gradually getting her strength back. Eb was beginning to look like his old self and was even talking more like himself, some of his optimism returning. That was all very hopeful to Morgan.

What also pleased him was that Angeline was doing better. As temperatures dropped a little more in October, she was encouraged, and she was excited about her baby. She jokingly promised Morgan that she was making a perfect son for him: one who would be as strong as he was and eventually as skilled—and maybe, slightly more handsome, "if such a thing is even possible."

She even wondered if she could ride with Morgan to St. George when the time came for the hauling trip he had promised to take. But Morgan wouldn't hear of that. He told her that she shouldn't be bumping along in a wagon in her condition.

"Oh, I know," Angeline told him. "Anyway, I need to take care of the garden and make sure we harvest as much as possible."

"I don't want you to work too hard, though."

Morgan and Angeline were sitting across from one another at their little table. Angeline had cooked their dinner outside—a soup made from fresh vegetables from their fall garden and fried bread made from newly ground wheat from their own farm. She had set the table with dishes, not just tin plates. "What's the special occasion?" Morgan asked.

"I saw Susan Brooks this afternoon. She heard from someone that the temperature stayed below one hundred today—first time this fall."

"Well, that is worth celebrating. But you still need to be easy on yourself."

"I can work, Morgan." She pushed some light strands of sun-bleached hair away from her forehead, which was damp with sweat. He liked seeing that life was returning to her pretty eyes, looking more blue than gray now.

"I don't want you, ever again, to work as hard as you have this year."

"Fine. But I'll say the same about you," Angeline said.

"That's what I'm for. That's what men do. Your job now is to take care of that baby. Life won't ever be the same again, once that handsome boy is born."

"I know. But women work, too. I'm not a princess or a pampered lady. As long as I have no servants, I'll have chores that keep me going sunup to sundown, and children to manage, too. And unless I'm mistaken, I won't ever have any servants."

"But I want to make things just a little easier for you—the way you do for me. You share more of my load than any of the other women do for their husbands."

"Do you love me for that?"

"Absolutely not," Morgan said firmly.

"What?"

"I appreciate your help. But I love you with my heart. And head. And all the rest of me. No matter what you do or don't do, nothing will ever change that."

She smiled. "Then what about windows?"

"What?"

"If you love me so much, could you buy some glass windows in St. George?"

"Maybe. I've thought about that. I'll see what they'll cost—and how much I'll earn from the trip. Would you rather have more chairs, or—"

"Windows. So the wind can't blow through our house."

"All right. I'll find a way to make that happen."

"Now I'm the one in love." She placed her hand over her heart and smiled coyly.

"You only love me for my windows."

"Well, at least you finally know the truth."

• • •

A week later, Angeline wasn't in quite such a playful mood. She watched Morgan leave with a big wagon that Bishop Morrison had provided for him, leading two yokes of oxen, his own and an extra team. Ben Cotter followed behind, leading another four oxen and another wagon. She continued to stand outside and watch until she could see no more dust rising on the road onto the Mormon Mesa, and she knew Morgan was really gone. She thought of sitting down, maybe even crying, but she was not silly enough to do that. She walked out back, grabbed a hoe, and went to work in her garden. Morgan would be gone about three weeks, maybe a little more. It was nothing to fret about. But Angeline had never been alone in her life, and however independent she liked to think she was, three weeks now seemed a very long time.

Angeline was not one to imagine the worst, but she knew that Navajos, from across the Colorado River, sometimes roamed the area and attacked settlers, especially single wagons or small wagon trains. She also knew how dangerous the Virgin River Valley could be. The river could go on a rampage after a thunderstorm, which could happen at any time. There was also the quicksand, the danger of turning over a wagon—even sickness from coming in contact with measles or smallpox or other diseases that struck in larger places like St. George.

So she hacked away at weeds in the garden and dug some carrots and turnips. And she sang. She mixed up hymns with family songs she had learned as a little girl: "The Spirit of God Like a Fire Is Burning," and then "Row, Row, Row Your Boat." It didn't matter what she sang. She simply wasn't going to let her mind dwell on her fears. She would work, and sing, and pray, and the days would soon be gone.

And actually, the days did pass rather quickly. For one thing, the weather continued to get better, and Angeline went to see

Mary Ann every day. She had also added Lydia, Susan, and Alice to her schedule. Lydia had given birth in late September to a boy she and James had named Albert, and a couple of weeks later Susan also had a boy, whom they named Robert. Alice expected her baby soon, and was eager for its arrival. Angeline tried be helpful, just to clean up a little in her friends' houses or even hold a baby while the new mothers had a chance to take care of things they needed to do.

Angeline was not sure she knew much about taking care of a baby, so by watching and talking to the new mothers she felt she was gaining some preparation. Her own baby was not due until February, but she was starting to feel changed, awkward. Still, the truth was, she rather liked it when the sisters at church noticed that she was pregnant and gave her little winks. It wasn't something people—especially men—talked about openly. Women did all they could to hide their condition, and when the time for birthing came, other women said, "She's taken sick." Everyone knew what that meant. Angeline actually thought all that was nonsense. Men certainly knew when their milk cows were expecting, and they didn't pretend otherwise. She was not sure why a woman's pregnancy could only be mentioned in whispers. Fathers certainly bragged enough about their newborns.

Three weeks passed and Morgan hadn't returned yet, but now Angeline was expecting him at any time, and she often looked off toward the mesa to see whether she could spot any sign of wagons moving her way. She had returned to the house after working in her garden early one morning when she noticed that something didn't feel right. She felt sick again, but not like the morning nausea she had known before. Something was happening inside her. She felt weak, distracted, and she heard a buzz in her head. And then a pain struck her abdomen, a clenching pain—it seemed like the pain she had heard women describe when they labored to have a baby.

This couldn't be happening yet. She lay on the bed, trying to rest and let the hurt pass away, and for a time that seemed to help. But then it came again. She twisted on her side, pulled her legs up, and let herself scream. It was fear as much as pain, because she knew now that something was terribly wrong. And she was alone.

Angeline got up. She needed to walk to Mary Ann's house. She was going to need help.

Then she thought a wall of the house was coming at her, or turning, and she struck the floor before she knew where to reach. She hit her chin, hard, on the hard-packed dirt. She knew she couldn't pass out, just couldn't, and she fought it, but light was spinning through her head, turning into dark, and she felt as though she were falling, reaching out, getting hold of nothing.

• • •

When Angeline awoke, she didn't remember exactly what had happened. She only knew that time had passed and that she was on her bed. There were people around her—women—and the pain was still there. "Angeline, Angeline," someone was saying. It was Sister Ballif. "Can you understand me now?"

"What?"

"Do you know what I'm saying to you?"

"Yes."

"All right. Now listen." Someone was swabbing Angeline's head with a wet rag, and most of her clothes were off. Sister Ballif was far away, at the end of the bed. Angeline's legs were bent at the knee, raised, and two women were holding them that way. One of them was Mary Ann—pale little Mary Ann.

"Mary Ann," Angeline said. "You need to rest. You shouldn't—"

"Angeline, listen to me," Sister Ballif said, this time forcefully, like an upset schoolteacher. "You are losing your baby. But we have to deliver it. I want you to bear down and help push it out."

"I don't want to lose it."

"I know. But that's not a choice now. You were on the floor, passed out, and you have lost a lot of blood. We need to get the baby out, and then we need to help you heal. If you don't help us now, you could die. Do you understand that?"

"I don't want to lose my baby."

"Angeline! Do as I tell you. Push!"

Angeline didn't know whether she pushed or not, but she felt a gush, and soon Sister Ballif was saying, "All right. The worst is over, but don't let yourself slip away. You need to live. You need to fight, no matter how weak you feel."

But Angeline was already drifting again. She didn't want to lose her baby. It was the only thought that was clear to her.

• • •

When Morgan arrived at his farm, he had the new glass windows packed on top of the foodstuffs and various orders that families had asked him to fill. He had even strapped some chairs on top, a gift for Bishop Barkley, who had lost everything in the fire. He was excited to tell Angeline that he had her windows—and had even bargained for a good price.

"Angie!" he called from outside, but the woman who stepped from the door was Sister Ballif. Morgan could only think that Angeline had gotten sick while he was gone. "What's happened?" he asked.

"She's going to live," Sister Ballif answered. "I'm almost sure.

But she was very grave for two days, and she's still too weak to get back on her feet."

"What? Why?"

"She lost the baby, Brother Davis. And she lost way too much blood. It's going to take quite some time for her to get her strength back."

Morgan brushed past Sister Ballif and hurried inside. Angeline was on the bed, looking pallid and frail. Her eyes were shut.

Morgan dropped onto his knees next to her. "Angie, look at me."

Her eyes came open, and she smiled, mildly. "Oh, good. Oh, good," she said. "You're here now."

"Yes. And I'm sorry I ever left. I had no idea something like this would happen."

"It's all right. I'm getting better. I'll get up . . . tomorrow."

"No. Sister Ballif says you're very weak. You need to rest. I'll take care of you."

"There's too much work for you to do now. I couldn't take care of everything."

Sister Ballif said, from across the room, "I'll come every day, Morgan. I'll help you look after her."

"Millie Ballif is an angel, Morgan," Angeline said. "I watched her float around this room, and her feet didn't touch the ground. Sometimes she glowed like a spirit."

"I'm very much tied to the ground, sweet one," Sister Ballif said. "And I'm much too fat and short to be an angel—at least according to the pictures I've seen. But I'll walk over here every day until you can manage by yourself, and when I'm not here, other sisters will come. We won't let you work—not at all—until you're recovered."

Morgan stood up. "Thank you so much." He patted her on the

shoulder. Millie Ballif *was* small, and chubby, and one of the oldest women in the settlement, but she looked beautiful to Morgan at the moment. "Was she here alone—you know, when this happened?"

"Yes, she was. But Mary Ann Crawford just had a *feeling* that something was wrong, and she walked over here and found Angeline on the floor. Your wife would have died if Mary Ann hadn't found her."

• • •

Angeline had rarely been sick in her life, and then only for a few days at a time. What she felt now was something much worse. A month had passed by, and, after staying in bed most of the time, she felt feeble. She had no experience with such a sensation. She made up her mind every morning that she would begin to take up her duties, go about her business, but after an hour or so, she would be exhausted. As winter in the desert gradually came on, the temperatures were nice, and she slept well in the mild nights, but something seemed broken inside her. Sister Ballif said that her blood needed to be rebuilt, and that would only come with time. But she had never been a patient person.

Before this, Angeline had come to love being the one who could give others a hand, do their chores when they couldn't take care of things themselves. She hadn't always been that way, but it was something she had learned since leaving home. Now, however, all that was turned around. Even Mary Ann began to visit her, carrying along little Eliza with her. Angeline appreciated the visits but somehow resented them at the same time. She told Mary Ann every time she came that she shouldn't work, but Mary Ann would say, "Would you mind holding the baby for a few minutes?"

as though the task might be too much for Angeline. Mary Ann couldn't have known how much sadness Angeline felt, holding a little baby when her own had died inside her. Still, she took Eliza all the same, and the truth was, the little beauty—with a sweet rosebud mouth and chubby hands that gripped Angeline's finger— did raise her spirits, bringing out a side of Angeline that she had always wanted to experience.

Mary Ann would then take the chance to pick up a few things that Morgan had left about, or she would sweep the hardpan floor. "It's all right," Angeline would say. "I can do that. I need to do it myself."

"No, you don't *need* to. I'm the one who needs to do something for you. I don't know if I'd be alive without the things you did for me." She walked closer to the bed. "Angeline, it's wrong to think you can only give help to others and can't accept a little assistance when you need it."

It was the strongest thing Mary Ann had ever said to Angeline. In fact, it occurred to Angeline that Mary Ann had grown up a good deal in the last year, that it wasn't dancing and giggling with friends back home that was most important to her anymore.

"You're right," Angeline said. "I tell myself that every day. It's prideful of me not to be grateful for you sisters wanting to help me. But the one thing I could always tell myself was that I was strong, that I could work hard, that I could do my share and maybe a little more. I've lost that."

"Not for long, Angie. You're getting strong again. And you *will* be a mother before long. Next time, things will go better. I'm sure of that."

Mary Ann obviously sensed the truth about Angeline's fears: more than anything, she was worried that she wouldn't be able to have a family.

Still, after Mary Ann left that day, Angeline knew that their friendship had deepened, and she respected this new Mary Ann who was becoming the woman she needed to be. Angeline also tried to be more accepting when other sisters called on her. Lydia Wilcox and Susan Brooks both came by, bringing their tiny baby boys. Alice was not up and around yet, but she had given birth to a girl whom she and Lyman had named Patricia. All Angeline's friends had now given birth to healthy babies, and that was a joy. Angeline truly was happy for them, and she resisted the little pangs of jealousy that poked at her feelings at times.

Sisters whom Angeline had never known until these last few months, most of them much older than herself, also paid her visits, and she liked that people were trying hard to look after one another. The new group had proven that they could stick out a full summer and not speak of leaving, and that seemed to bring acceptance for them. The fact that the men had joined in digging out the canal not just those first two times, but several more times now, also had raised the level of trust.

Angeline did begin to attend her church meetings in the little adobe church, and she liked seeing everyone there. Sermons were never very sophisticated, but they were also not nearly so long as they had been in her home congregation. The building was actually too small to allow everyone in the settlement to attend, but most of the new mothers kept their babies home anyway. What also kept the numbers down was the ague that plagued so many people. Three people—two children and an older brother—had died that fall, but most had survived, only to have the "shakes and bakes" reoccur from time to time. When the men were down with fevers, they weren't able to keep their farms going. Morgan and the other young men in the new company tried to help all they could in those cases, but the labor of doing extra farm work as they tried to establish their own farms—and then stopped to dig out the canal—kept the healthy ones busy constantly. Most of the new people had avoided illness so far, and some said it was because the sand bench was healthier than the river valley. Angeline hoped that would turn out to be true.

Angeline had come to love a sister named Lizzie Bachelor. Lizzie was over sixty—one of the oldest sisters in the valley. She had left her grandchildren in Scipio, Utah, and had taken on the desert with the doggedness of a cedar fence. "No, I don't like it here," she had told Angeline the first time she had met her. "How could anyone like this place? But it's not going to lick me. I've got fruit trees growing, and I milk our old cow that shrivels up under this infernal sun, and I tell her she better give me something for my bucket or I'll make a stew of her. She listens, too—just not very well."

This conversation had occurred as Lizzie and Angeline had walked from the church together one day that fall. The two had stood on the shady side of the building while their husbands discussed farming or some such thing. The nasty biting flies had not died off yet, and Sister Bachelor not only slapped at them with surprising quickness but cursed them under her breath as well.

"You're a strong woman," Angeline had told Sister Bachelor.

"I'm not strong so much as I am tough. I'm like jerky meat, hard to bite into. But there's another side to that. Jerky softens up if you don't try to chew it too fast—and I'm the same way."

Angeline liked that image, and she thought she had felt some of that softer side of the woman. "Well, 'tough' is a good thing, if it means you don't bend with every wind that comes along."

"I guess I've bent some from time to time," Lizzie said. She used her sleeve to wipe the sweat from her forehead. "But I have my limits. I still don't like this way of men taking on extra wives. I didn't think it was right when I first heard about it, and I still don't think it is. If you ask me, men thought it up, not God. My husband knows, sure as anything, if he comes home with some spring chicken and wants me to take her in, he can kiss her and love her all he wants, but he won't step into my house again."

"I think I feel a lot the same," Angeline said. "My father had two wives, and he wasn't fair to my mother. That left me with a low opinion of polygamy."

"Well, don't buy into it." Lizzie slapped at a fly, called it a devil, and then added, "Tell your husband, right now, it's not for you, and he better get used to the idea."

"We've talked about it. He doesn't want more than one wife either."

"They all say that. But some of 'em start lookin' around and thinkin' their first wife ain't so soft and lovey as she used to be. You don't see any of them taking on *older* wives. Have you noticed that?"

Actually, Angeline did know a few cases of men marrying older women, but she didn't say that to Lizzie. Mostly, she was glad to have an ally.

Still, that night, after praying with Morgan and then starting her own prayer, she felt a little guilty about agreeing with Lizzie. She didn't want to practice plural marriage, but she didn't want to think that men had thought up the whole idea without any guidance from the Lord and His prophet. If that was true, how could she trust in any revelation? So she told the Lord she was sorry about not saying that to Lizzie.

Still, she really liked the woman. And Lizzie was one of the ones who stopped by to check on her every few days. Lizzie liked to chat—and complain—more than wash dishes or sweep the floor, but she always made Angeline laugh, and that was something she needed these days.

MUDDY

• • •

Morgan was pleased with his crops. Even though the canal had filled up with sand every two or three weeks and had had to be dug out, his grains and his cotton had survived pretty well. Picking cotton was something new for him. It was tedious, and he soon learned that the bolls could shred his fingers, but he was catching on. Even better, he had been able to hire Pah Utes to help him, and they appreciated the wheat they received as payment. Angeline's melons had also been a great surprise. They grew well in the sandy soil, and they had matured in the heat, big and sweet, the best change from the plain-food diet that they were becoming used to.

Morgan now felt he would have enough food to get through the winter. He wished there were easier ways to buy a cow, or to trade for some of the farm tools he needed, but he told himself that would all come in time. If he could make it through this first season, his second year should be better. He still longed for northern valleys, for green, and for a good long talk with his father, but he wasn't one to dwell on such things. He and Angeline both got mail from their families every once in a while, and the letters reminded them that harsh winters weren't so lovely, and troubles plagued people everywhere. A cousin of Morgan's, a woman not much older than he was, had died in childbirth and left her husband with three little children to raise. Angeline's mother hinted in every letter that having a hostile sister wife was a never-ending trial. Morgan was reminded that he should be thankful for his blessings and not dwell on the life he had imagined for himself. Mostly, he thanked the Lord that Angeline had lived. As he watched her stay up longer and work a little more each day, he felt that she would come back to her true self soon enough.

He often talked with his four friends—Eb, Lyman, James, and Art. Their houses were all close together even if their farms were spread out across the land outside this newest of new St. Josephs. The other men all depended on him for advice, and he felt that he was a genuine help to them. He liked that, and he liked that even among the older settlers, he had gained a reputation for knowing plenty about farming, building houses, fixing wagons, sharpening plow blades, repairing harnesses, and even being positive about staying and making the best of this hard place.

He had also found someone to turn to for his own guidance. Bishop Morrison loved the gospel, could give a good sermon, but he also knew about animals, about canals and ditches, even about cotton. And the man also thought about life. He liked to speculate a little about the second coming of Christ, but he also talked about the purposes of the kingdom of God and the place the Muddy River Mission played in that. It was good for Morgan to be reminded of the bigger picture behind their mission; it helped him accept the daily grind of life in the valley.

Bishop Morrison lived in St. Thomas and served as the bishop there, but as president of the mission, he often made the nine-mile trip north to St. Joseph to consult with Bishop Barkley and other town leaders. More and more, however, he visited Morgan when he came to town, sometimes even driving his buggy out to Morgan's farm. He seemed to like their conversations, which was a surprise to Morgan, since there were plenty of others he might have taken interest in.

"I'll tell you what's goin' to happen," Bishop Morrison told Morgan one day that fall. "This railroad line across the continent is suppose' to be finished next year, and when that happens, there won't be any more wagons and mules haulin' people across the plains. People will get on a train somewhere in the States, and a few days later they'll be sittin' down to dinner in Salt Lake. They won't even be dirty or tired. It's kind of a miracle, if you think about it. Look how long it took you to make that out-and-back trip you made to Nebraska—pritty much all summer. Now we can gather folks into Zion easier than ever afore, and more and more people will come. We'll fill up this whole kingdom out here, sure as anythin'."

"Maybe it's too easy," Morgan told him. "The folks I crossed with had to put out plenty of effort. They never were so happy as when they looked down the canyon and saw the Great Salt Lake."

"I know. I agree. But the Lord is at work, opening up the way, and this church is going to grow more than it seems possible right now." Then Bishop Morrison took a long breath and added, "Or at least that's what will happen if the United States government doesn't get in our way."

"They're still after us, aren't they?" Morgan asked.

"I don't think we've seen anythin' yet. Now that the war has ended in the States, congress has started talkin' about us again. The 'twin pillars of barbarism,' they used to say: slavery and polygamy. Now they've got slavery whipped, they'll be comin' after us. Those same trains that bring converts our way will bring in politicians looking to make a name for themselves by puttin' polygamists in jail."

Morgan smiled. "Well, at least you can rest assured, they won't look for you clear down here." Morgan knew that Priscilla, the bishop's wife in St. Thomas, was not his only wife. Delia, the wife Morgan knew from his growing-up years in Farmington, was still living there.

Bishop Morrison was shaking his head, his big beard brushing back and forth across his chest. He looked more worked up than usual, spit turning white in the corners of his mouth. "That won't matter," he said. "They're already tryin' to pass more laws to make our way of life illegal."

"I know that. My father wrote to me about it—and he sent some newspapers."

"But don't worry, the Lord will not let them win this battle. What comes from God cannot be defeated by Satan and his minions. We won't go back on the truths we've received through revelation." He held up a finger, shaking it as though at Satan himself. "Never!"

For the first time ever, Morgan felt uneasy around the bishop. He didn't have the courage to tell him that he and Angeline had made a decision that plural marriage was fine for others but not for them.

What Morgan had noticed as he lived around several families who had chosen plural marriage was that marriages, whether with one wife or more, all depended on the people who entered into the covenants. Wilfred Shupe would make any kind of marriage look bad. He was a harsh man, and he seemed to know no other way than to rule over his wives and children. But another brother, Joseph Wilde, had brought three wives to St. Joseph, and he had built two houses next door to one another, one for himself and his first wife, and another for the other two. Those two, each with small children, seemed to live just fine together. There were two rooms in the house and two entries. Morgan had noticed that Joseph shared time with his wives, moving about on some schedule he had worked out. He was a cheery man who seemed perfectly happy with the arrangement—and, more important, his wives were just as pleased, as far as Morgan could tell.

The fact was, the majority of the settlers in St. Joseph were monogamous, and some were thriving, doing their best, and others were struggling. Tragedy seemed to strike randomly, hurting the righteous as well as the complainers. One family, as righteous as anyone in the town—a couple named Watson—had lost two little babies, both within days after their births. But Sister Watson was expecting again, and she was going about life as though tragedy were part of the scheme. There was also a little girl in St. Joseph named Olivia who had a terrible scar on her face. It had come from burns she had gotten when she had stood too close to a fireplace and her skirt had caught fire. But her father had borne testimony in a church meeting that he felt blessed that Olivia hadn't died. And Olivia went on with life, seeming to have accepted her father's view of things.

The heat was not the only challenge on the Muddy, Morgan had learned, but then, illness and accidents and deaths happened everywhere. If there was one thing he did understand, it was that God did not intend to make this life easy for the Muddy missionaries—or, maybe, for anyone.

• • •

As the winter progressed, Angeline became stronger, week by week. It was around Christmas when she realized the reason she had felt for a few days that she was relapsing. She was almost certain that she was pregnant again. And that was good. Morgan told her to go back to resting more, not to push her body too hard—and Angeline tried to do just that—but her hope was restored enough to bring back some of her optimism. More than anything, she wanted babies—lots of strong sons and daughters to help Morgan in his work, and to serve missions, and build the kingdom, and turn this desert into a garden place. She prayed with new sincerity, pleading with the Lord to help her carry this baby the full time.

Morgan was rejuvenated by the softer weather. His workload was a little lighter, and his energy seemed restored. He talked to Angeline about all his hopes for the farm. "I know some of the first settlers down here are running out of confidence in this place, but we need to get some windbreaks established and see if that doesn't stop some of the sand from drifting into the canal. And we need trees around our houses to make some shade. I think, as much as anything, we have to learn to be thankful for these warm winters—and not complain so much that it gets hot in the summer."

Angeline didn't say it, but she knew Morgan well enough now to recognize the subtle suggestions in his voice. He was trying to convince himself as much as her. He had learned a certain rhythm in the coming and going of the seasons, and everything here was wrong to him—felt wrong, looked wrong. And yet, she knew he wanted to be happy, not dwell on the difficulties. And he wanted her to be happy.

It was March when everything turned in the wrong direction again. Angeline began to bleed—badly—and she lost this baby, too. The physical loss was easier, not so debilitating this time. But Angeline's emotions were brought back to the depths. She wasn't down as long, wasn't as physically weak, but she was almost sure now that something was wrong with her. She couldn't give her husband what they wanted and needed, and she could hardly tolerate going to church on Sundays and seeing children with their hair combed, their old clothes washed and mended, and their mothers fussing over them. It was so easy for most of the women to carry a baby and go on with life. It had never occurred to Angeline that she wouldn't be able to fulfill this most basic requirement for a woman, to bring forth a royal generation.

"It's not true," Morgan told her. "My mother lost some babies. A lot of women do. It doesn't mean you'll never have a child."

She knew all that. She even liked his patience, his kindly tone. But she was letting him down, and he couldn't really hide that. He loved those little trees he was planting, loved to see winter wheat sprouts break the ground, loved to picture the farm he would create in this desert. But a farm was more than crops; it was a family, too. And he wanted a family. If she could never give him that, he would refuse to admit his disappointment, but she would see it in him every day of her life.

CHAPTER II

It was spring of 1869 and already getting hot again when Bishop Morrison drove his buggy up to Morgan's place on the sand bench and found him in the garden, hoeing. "Morgan," he said, "I hoped I would find you here. I haven't talked to you for a long time."

He got down and walked toward Morgan, but the sun was behind him, and what Morgan actually saw was a stretched-out silhouette of the bishop's small frame and a glow through his white hair. Morgan also saw a hand reaching toward him. He shook hands with the bishop, and then the two stepped into the shade of the house. "Looks like your garden's producin' well this year," the bishop said. "It helps a great deal when we get so much yield from our early plantin'."

"That's true," Morgan said, but then he laughed. "We won't say anything about the late crop that gets burned up so bad."

"I guess that's the other side of it." But the bishop was looking serious. "What are you goin' to do, Morgan? Are you stayin' here on this plot?"

"I don't know, Bishop. Does it make any sense to move one more time and build again, just to fit into some plat they've surveyed?"

During the winter, the old survey had been redrawn, and the leaders had asked the settlers to move a little north on the sand bench, to fit with a plan for the future.

"I know it's hard for those of you who built here," Bishop Morrison said, "but our leaders have decided it's a better site. It should be good for those who are still in the fort and for new people arrivin'. In the long run, I think it'll be better for everyone."

"Look up there, Ewan." Morgan pointed to the north. "It's just more desert, the same as right here. I don't see the advantage."

"If you prefer, you could still farm the same acres here, and—"

"And lead my oxen almost two miles over here every day. You know what we call this place now? We don't call it New St. Joseph. We call it Sandy Town, and those of us who built here don't see the difference between living in one Sandy Town or the other."

"Listen, I understan'. But in twenty years we'll want to be organized into one nice town. It won't take you long to build another house, and—"

"Bishop, I don't want to argue with you, but I'll tell you what's really going to happen. We're all going to leave this bench. There's not enough water and you know it. The canal loses half its water into the sand, and that's why you're not getting enough water down in St. Thomas."

"We've started another canal."

"But how does that make any sense? We're fighting between the two settlements for the same water."

"Yes, but we had little rain this last winter. Not every year will be so bad. Apostle Snow and Joseph Young, who's helpin' him lead this area now, both feel that we can get a good system of ditches worked out, and there will be enough water for all of us."

"And where do those two live?"

"St. George, of course, but Morgan, that doesn't matter. They're our leaders."

"Bishop, I didn't plan to bring all this up with you, but I heard what they told this new group that has started to arrive. Twenty-five families are approved to settle up at West Point. God Himself commanded us to leave there last year, and now I guess the Lord has changed His mind."

"Don't start that kind of talk again, Morgan. Most of the new people will settle here in the lower valley. West Point needed more people too, and over time we'll have to spread out a little more."

"Well, somebody didn't seem to know that just a year ago. You know I wanted to stay there and not try to farm on this bench."

"You told me last summer that things were startin' to work out here."

"That was before the canal filled up with sand a dozen more times, and before our ditches started to dry up."

"Well, as I said afore, we didn't get much moisture this year. But the Lord will bless us if we keep movin' forward, doin' what we're asked."

Morgan didn't want to do this. He liked Ewan Morrison too much, and he didn't want to be a problem for the man. But he decided to make himself clear. "All right. I'll stick with this mission. I'll do what's asked of me. But I'm not moving to this new site—and a lot of other men feel the same way. If I build another house, it will be down with you in St. Thomas, or in the old St. Joseph site, but when I move, I'm leaving this bench."

"I understan'. I would welcome you in St. Thomas. But Morgan, don't encourage rebellion. Let the Lord guide you—and use yer skills to help yer neighbors, the way you've done afore. You're a leader, Son, and I need you to help me lead this people in the right direction." A gray lizard darted between the two of them and the movement caught the bishop's eye. But when he looked down, he didn't seem to focus on the lizard. He obviously had other things on his mind. "I didn't come here to talk about where you'll choose to live. In the end, I'll just have to leave that up to you. But there's somethin' else, more important, that we need to talk about."

The bishop sounded hesitant, careful, and that worried Morgan. "What's on your mind, Bishop? Do you want to step into the house, or—"

"No. This is fine. It's just as well if Angeline doesn't hear what I have to say—not yet."

Morgan thought he knew what was coming. The possibility had occurred to him months ago, but he had hoped he was wrong. Still, he knew the answer he would give. He had even rehearsed it.

"You know Sister Ruth Nilsson fairly well, I guess," the bishop began.

Morgan stiffened, stood straight. "Actually, I don't. She never has much to say to me—or to anyone else."

"Yes, I know. She's had a hard go of it, and it's changed her manner. She was friendly at one time."

Bishop Morrison had told Morgan Sister Nilsson's story before. She had married a Swedish fellow, Bern Nilsson, who had accepted a call to the Muddy Mission back in 1865. Nilsson had gained a reputation for being disagreeable, argumentative, and unwilling to accept direction. Ruth had given birth to a baby boy—Jefferson— the first year in the Muddy Valley, but about a year later Brother Nilsson had met with an accident. He had tipped over a wagon and fallen under it, and it had crashed down on his neck and head, killing him instantly. Morgan and Angeline had tried to be friendly with Ruth after that first night they had met her at the dance. Ruth had always been polite but never exactly receptive. She looked after her spindly, pale son, and she tried to do the best she could with her farm—but couldn't have managed without the help of the men in the settlement. Morgan had helped her as much as anyone, and she always thanked him but said little more.

"Why does she stay here, Bishop? This is no place for a woman on her own."

"She has no place to go. Her family didn't join the Church. She came west on her own. At least she has a house and a garden here. She doesn't know where she can go and get a fresh start for herself, all alone the way she is."

Morgan could see the logic now. But the bishop would have to find someone else. Morgan was *not* going to do this.

"Sister Ruth is a good woman, Morgan, and what she needs more than anythin' is a good husband. I've come here to ask you to take her as yer wife." Morgan had begun to shake his head even before the bishop's sentence was completed. "Don't answer yet, Morgan. You need to think about this. Ruth could help Angeline while she's gettin' better again, and you've caught hold here the best of all the new men. No matter where you choose to farm, you'll do well. And you have a chance to make some extra money with the hauling you do. For now, Ruth could stay where she is, down at the fort, and then later, if you wanted, you could expand yer house a little—wherever you end up—and let her move in with the two of you. If you decide to move to St. Thomas, there's a good house, not far from mine, that's abandoned. With a little work, you could move right in, and there would be no grubbin', with the land already open."

Morgan stared at the bishop. Did he really think it was that simple—just a matter of houses? Morgan didn't want another wife, and if he had wanted one, he certainly had no interest in Sister

Nilsson. She was not an attractive woman. She was probably seven or eight years older than he was, and she was sullen, dreary.

"I was thinkin', we need to have you make a long-haul trip all the way up to Salt Lake City sometime soon. There's items we can obtain there that we cannot get in St. George. You could take Ruth along with you and marry her in the Endowment House."

"Wait a minute," Morgan said. "I'm not doing this. I don't want another wife. Angeline and I talked about polygamy before we got married. We decided—and I promised her—we won't enter into it. I know it's a principle given to us by the Lord, but I don't think it's the right thing for everyone."

"Listen to yerself, Morgan. Is that how you live the commandments—pick and choose the ones you like? Choosin' a location to live is one thing, but celestial marriage is quite another."

"There never has been a better man than my father," Morgan countered, "and he chose to have only one wife. If that's wrong, fine. But I'll follow my father's example."

"Times have moved on since yer father made his choice. The Lord is expectin' more of us. I'm not *suggestin'* you take Ruth as yer wife; I'm callin' you in the name of the Lord—and I have the approval of Apostle Snow and Brigham Young himself. Will you accept God's will or go against it and live with the consequences?"

Morgan could not believe what he was hearing. He had not expected force from such a mild man. For a few seconds his reaction was surprise, maybe even a little shame. But resentment began to rise in him. "There's no way that all men could take on plural wives, Bishop. It's simple arithmetic. There aren't enough women. Some will live the principle and others never will. And I can tell you right now, no matter how hard you talk, I'm not going to be one of those who does."

"You need to go back to yer arithmetic book, Brother Davis. There are not enough stalwart men among us—strong, noble men who can raise up the generation that will lead the Church, build the kingdom. The men who are worthy and who are called to enter into the principle must not let down the good women of the Church. I have prayed about this, and I know that you're the best man to give Sister Nilsson children, to take care of her, and to look after her little son. So that's the arithmetic you have to think about. Are you one who accepts a sacred call when it comes—or do you choose to think about yer own comfort and yer own desires?"

"Wait a minute. You say you have your answer, but I have a right to get my own. If I have no interest in Sister Nilsson, no thoughts of her that way, do I have to push all that aside and marry a woman just because you think I should?"

"I'm goin' to walk away from you right now, Morgan. I'm goin' to let you think about what you've just asked me. And I'm goin' to let you think whether you don't sound selfish and self-servin' even to ask me such a thing. What I want you to do is ask the Lord what He expects of you. And once you've prayed and listened to the Lord's will, then I want you to talk to Angeline. If you both turn me down, that will be the end of the matter. But Morgan . . ." He stopped and took a long look into Morgan's eyes. "Yer decision is not just for now. If you say no to the Lord, think what that might mean in the eternities before you."

Morgan said nothing. He was furious. He knew good men— strong, wise men—who chose not to live the principle. Maybe the convenience was all on the bishop's side. The man had people to worry about, and Sister Nilsson was one of them. What he needed was a way to push his responsibility off onto someone else. *I won't do it,* Morgan told himself. *And I'll leave this place if Bishop Morrison keeps pushing me.*

But Morgan's anger didn't last long, and his worry set in rather quickly. He had never said no to the Lord—not directly—and the idea of doing so frightened him. He couldn't stand to think of a life with two women, of trying to share every aspect of marriage with someone who was a stranger to him. The bishop wanted Morgan to give babies to Sister Nilsson, but Morgan couldn't even imagine being alone with her. It wasn't just that he didn't find her desirable; he didn't even find her someone he wanted to pass the time of day with. Morgan didn't want to turn down the bishop—and especially the Lord—but he also knew he wouldn't do this. He simply couldn't.

• • •

Most of a week went by and Morgan didn't say anything to Angeline, nor did he give Bishop Morrison an answer. Above all, he didn't pray about it. He was in no mood to talk with the Lord about this. Certainly God should understand Morgan's heart well enough to know that this wasn't a matter of choice. Maybe other men could have more than one wife, but Morgan only wanted Angeline. And now, after a year of marriage, he loved her more than he had ever imagined he could love anyone. How could it possibly be fair to love Angeline and marry Sister Nilsson? It wasn't fair to Angeline, but, even more, it wasn't fair to Ruth. She would always know that he felt nothing for her. How could he be so close to her . . . and feel so distant?

So Morgan didn't change his mind, but he also kept delaying. He didn't say it to himself, but he was haunted with the idea that if he turned the bishop down, didn't capitulate, some disaster would befall him—or, worse yet, would strike Angeline.

And then, on Sunday, Bishop Morrison showed up in New

St. Joseph and presided at church services. After the meeting, he pulled Morgan aside. "Have you decided about Sister Nilsson?" he asked.

"I already told you that I can't—"

"Morgan, have you prayed about it?"

Morgan looked at the floor. "I don't need to pray about it."

"Yes, you do. Face the Lord. Once you've done that, come back and face me."

Morgan felt his anger return. But he said nothing, simply left. And it was another full day before he walked up toward the Mormon Mesa, far out of sight of anyone on the bench, and knelt down. "Lord, I don't want to do this," he said. "Can that be so bad? Please don't make me marry her. It will break Angeline's heart. Don't put this burden on my shoulders. I promise, I will serve Thee in every other way."

But it didn't work, and somehow he had known it wouldn't. At church, he had looked at Ruth and felt sorry for her. She did need a husband, and, try as he might, he could not think of anyone else who might be in a better position to marry her.

It was as he was walking back to the house that he realized the Lord was not taking away his call. But he knew something else as well. Brigham had taught that a man should never take multiple wives without the consent of his first wife. He didn't want to put the burden on Angeline, but he thought she would agree that it was wrong, and together, they could support one another in the decision they had made when they first married.

So Morgan walked into the house. He found Angeline sitting at the table, sewing a shirt for Morgan. He had worn out everything he had, and although Angeline had admitted that she wasn't much of a seamstress, she said she would do what she could if he brought her some cotton fabric from St. George. So he had done that, and she had taken apart his one other shirt to make herself a pattern. It touched Morgan that she tried so hard to take care of him.

He pulled up a chair in front of her. "I need to talk to you," he said.

"Yes, I know."

"What do you mean?"

"It's about Sister Nilsson, isn't it?"

Morgan didn't answer. He had tried to think how he would bring up the subject, but he hadn't expected this.

"I know that the bishop has talked to you lately, and I know that your mind has been somewhere else, night and day. I also know that Ruth needs a husband and that you're the most likely choice. I realized that almost as soon as we met her that first time, but I had hoped she would leave—or that some other answer could be found."

Morgan slid forward on his chair and looked into his wife's eyes. "I can't do it, Angie. I have no love for her, no desire to enter into plural marriage. We promised each other. We don't want that kind of life. I'm going to tell the bishop I can't do it."

"I was hoping you would say that," Angeline said. "It relieves my mind."

"Well, then, that's settled."

She was looking down at the shirt in front of her, but she wasn't sewing. After a time she said, "No. I don't think so."

That brought Morgan out of his chair. "What do you mean?"

"You *are* the best choice. And Ruth does need you. I've thought and thought about it. I don't want to share you, but we can't turn our backs on a sister who needs help, and we can't reject a call from the Lord."

"Angeline, don't do this to me. I can't—"

"To *you?* How do you think *I* feel? It's the worst thing I can imagine, and I get sick to my stomach just imagining what it will be like."

"But you would do it?"

"I don't know. But I keep thinking, it's what I have to accept."

Morgan sat down again, and he took hold of Angeline's hand. "But we've said all along, we can think for ourselves. The bishop has no right to take that away from us."

"What about the Lord? If the Lord is speaking to the bishop, can we ignore that?"

"You know how I feel about that. I don't think the Lord talks to people as much as they claim. Maybe the bishop just sees me as the most likely man to accept. If I turn him down, he'll go to someone else and say that God has called that poor fellow—and keep saying it until someone gets so scared he agrees to do it."

"Morgan, you said things like that about moving to this bench—and then you did it. You obeyed, whether you liked the idea or not, and things have turned out all right."

"But they haven't, Angie. The canal isn't working—and that was why I didn't want to come here. It's turned out just the way I feared it would."

"I don't mean that. What I know is that I could have died, and the Lord sent Mary Ann to our house. The Lord is looking out for us, and I think it's because we obeyed."

Morgan had thought about all that. He knew he wanted to keep the Lord on his side. But he just couldn't do this one thing. "Angie, I won't be able to treat her the way I treat you. She'll know I don't feel for her the same way."

"Maybe you can learn to feel more for her as you get to know her better."

"Do you want me to love her?"

"No. Of course not. But I don't want to live in this desert, either. And I don't want to give my life over to the Lord. Something in me fights against it. But the Lord hasn't blessed me with what I want most, and maybe that's because I hold back. Maybe, if I accept Ruth, love her in spite of myself—and let you love her too—finally, I'll be able to give you children."

"Angie, I don't think the Lord is that cruel. He wouldn't—"

"It's not cruel, Morgan. He just wants me to be His obedient child." She looked down for a time. "Ruth's a good woman. She knows lots of things I don't—like sewing." Angeline lifted the shirt, as if for proof. "She can teach me things I need to learn. Maybe most of all, humility. She's had to learn plenty of that."

· · ·

It took Morgan three more days—days of hard praying, hard thinking. And days of trying to humble himself. But he didn't have much success. What he felt more than anything was resentment and anger. Why would God give him a brain and a will and then require that he ignore his own conclusions and simply bow down to another mortal? He felt bullied, diminished. He could not think without revulsion of the future that was being pushed onto him. The idea of helping Sister Nilsson was appealing. He could help her plow and plant and harvest. But sleep with her, love her, share his deepest self with her? That's what he had learned about marriage so far, that it pulled him out of himself, opened him up to an intimacy he had never understood before. How could he duplicate that—especially with a woman who didn't even appeal to him?

More than anything, he tried to think of a justification he could give that the Lord would accept—and one that Angeline could live with. She was so desperate to do the right thing that she was willing to take upon herself a way of life she had hated since she was a child. She wanted the Lord's blessing, and this to her was the way to receive it. Morgan hated that idea, too, but—as he always had—he feared standing up to God.

And so he gave up. He accepted that he had lived out his last happy days and would take on a burden that would surely weigh him down forever. When he told Angeline what he was about to do, she broke down. She hugged him and sobbed for a long time, and then she said, "Yes. Go now. It's what we have to do."

Morgan walked down to Sister Nilsson's house and called through a blanket that was hung up for a door, "Sister Nilsson, are you home?" When she pulled the blanket aside and looked out, he saw an initial hint of surprise, and then acceptance, as if she knew exactly what this was about.

"Could I talk to you for a few minutes, Sister Nilsson?" he asked.

"Yes. Of course. Come inside." But she wouldn't look at him, not directly. The whole situation was painfully awkward, embarrassing to Morgan and, he knew, to her.

Like most of the houses, this one contained only a bed, a table, and wooden chairs for furniture. Sister Nilsson pulled out one of the chairs for Morgan, and then she walked to the other side of the table. She sat down on the opposite side, still not looking at him. Jefferson, her three-year-old son, was playing on the dirt floor, making a little wood-carved horse gallop about. He was also glancing at Morgan warily, as if thrown off balance by having a man in his house.

Morgan sensed the pain in this situation—the emptiness of Sister Nilsson's life. He felt sorry for her, just as he had in church on Sunday. Someone really did need to lift her burden, to look after her.

"Sister Nilsson, I know we're not well acquainted, but I've come to ask you if you would be willing to be my wife. I've talked to Angeline, and we both feel—"

"The bishop asked you to do this, didn't he?" She finally looked up, took him on with her eyes. But there was no anger in her challenge. What he sensed was that she was humiliated to have a man so bluntly ask for her hand when he hadn't bothered to call on her a time or two to get acquainted. Morgan had thought about that; he had even considered bringing Angeline along to make a friendly visit. But that all seemed too obvious, and he was a man who liked directness.

Morgan thought of denying that the bishop had asked him to approach her, but she was clearly too perceptive—and honest—to allow such pretense. So he said, "Yes. The bishop suggested that an arrangement of that kind might be better for you." But that sounded awful. "What I mean is, it might be the best way to . . . I don't know. You wouldn't be alone, and your son would have a father. Angeline feels it might be nice for her to have a companion in the house—and a help to her, I guess you would say. She wouldn't expect you to do all the—"

"I understand, Brother Davis. I understand completely."

Morgan heard the resignation in her voice and saw the sorrow in her eyes. She was a little woman, seemingly meek, opposite of Angeline in almost every way. Her face was not really unattractive, but it was stolid, expressionless. She seemed to be holding the world at bay, excluding all the people who might want to come near her. Her hair was dark, as were her eyes, but there was a colorlessness about her, like the faded dress she always wore.

"Would you like me to call on you a few times, so we can get better acquainted?" Morgan asked.

"No. This is fine. I'll marry you. But if you hadn't been honest with me, I wouldn't. I'm glad you admitted that it was what you've been asked to do."

"Well . . . yes. But maybe I would have thought of it . . . in time."

"No, Brother Davis. You wouldn't have. And I understand that. But I do need a husband, and you are my own first choice of all the men here. I will never expect you to love me. And I will always understand that Angeline will be your true wife. But this will be better for Jefferson. And I will try to make life as good as possible for Angeline. I like her very much. There's no one else I would rather accept as a sister wife."

A hint of life had come into her face, embarrassed as she clearly was by what she had had to say. But she looked a little better, and Morgan was surprised at how much he suddenly liked her. She was as straightforward as he was, and she was also accepting a situation she wouldn't have chosen for herself.

"All right, then," he said. "I'm leaving sometime in the next couple of weeks to carry goods to the Salt Lake Valley, and to bring back some essentials. If you would be willing to travel with me that soon, we could be married up there."

"That would be fine."

"Before too long, I'll add an adobe room to our house, if you would like."

"I could stay here, if you would prefer."

"Angeline and I talked about that. She would rather have you with her."

"I think that I would like that better myself. I've been very lonely here."

"Angeline will look after your son while we travel north. I'll sleep on the ground, on the way there, and you can sleep in the wagon. We can be married in the Endowment House in the new and everlasting covenant. The bishop tells me that you never were sealed to your first husband—only married for time."

"That's right. And I don't want to be sealed to him."

"And you don't mind being sealed to me?"

"Brother Davis, I like you very much. I know I'm older than you, and I know that I'm plain. But you are a good man. I've noticed that in you ever since you came here. So yes, I would like to be sealed to you. But as I said before, I don't expect you to feel the same way toward me."

The words pained Morgan. He couldn't, in good conscience, deny them, but he knew he had to show some sign of understanding. "What I've learned, Sister Nilsson, is that love grows with time. It doesn't just grab you and hold on."

"Thank you for saying that." She smiled just a little. "I'll try not to disrupt your life and bring you unhappiness. I can be almost unnoticeable. That's become my strongest trait."

"No. I don't want that. Be part of our family. Let's find joy in this." And at the moment he believed himself.

But as the next week passed by, he tried not to think of trading off, sleeping with one wife and then the other. The very idea of it was repellent. Still, he called on Sister Nilsson with Angeline several times, and he found that she could talk, that she was not so sullen as he had thought. He couldn't bring himself to call her Ruth just yet, but he did begin to feel a little more relaxed when he was around her.

• • •

Angeline watched as Morgan got his wagon ready and loaded the items that men in the settlement wanted to sell—mostly cotton. Some of his friends had agreed to look after his spring planting and to check on Angeline. But Angeline knew that Morgan was not at all sure that anyone would take care of his farm as well as he could. He kept saying, though, that he could make some money from the trip and maybe bring back some pieces of furniture for Angeline. What he didn't say was that this was a honeymoon trip like the one that had started their marriage. The thought of that made Angeline cry, but she never shed any tears in front of him. She had agreed to this arrangement—even encouraged it—and, as much as she disliked it, she wasn't going to make him feel guilty.

When Morgan and Ruth Nilsson set off for Salt Lake City, the parting was much more difficult than ever before. This would be a long trip. Morgan might be gone two months or more, not the three or four weeks he had been away on his trips to St. George. But even more, there was no doubt in Angeline's mind that life would never be the same. Angeline had been talking to herself every day, committing that she would make the best of this and accept her new reality. Others had made this adjustment, and she would too. God would help her do it.

She had also come to like little Jefferson, and she thought she would like having a child around to take care of. He was less excited about the idea, and he cried hard for a while after his mother left, but Angeline soon involved him in some little activities, and even though he wouldn't nestle in her lap, he seemed to like her telling him stories. And yet, all the while, Angeline wondered what Morgan and Ruth were talking about. She remembered her own trip to the Muddy as a newlywed, and it was painful beyond belief to imagine that the return trip for Morgan and Ruth would repeat that experience. She tried to console herself by assuming that Morgan would never feel the same things for Ruth that he did for her. But what if Ruth gave him babies, and what if Angeline never could?

• • •

Ruth was self-conscious the first few hours of the trip. Morgan was not a talkative man, and she had no idea what to say to him. He commented a few times about the oxen and the road they would travel, and he warned her about the difficult river crossings they would have to make in the Virgin River Valley, but he seemed wary of engaging in personal talk. And she thought she knew why. It seemed a little to her—and certainly must seem more so to him—that they were doing something wrong. He was a married man, and she was spending time alone with him. True, they would be married before much longer, but that was only more awkward, not less.

Morgan had explained to Ruth that they couldn't make it over the Mormon Mesa with no one to help them lower the wagon down the steep slope, so they would have to take the long way around, through St. Thomas and across a stretch of desert. It was an extra three days of travel, but he saw no other choice. So the first day took them to St. Thomas, and most of that day, Morgan walked and led the oxen. But on the second day, as they followed the Santa Fe Trail, he climbed onto the wagon. Ruth, by then, knew that they should talk. She felt that they needed to know each other better before they returned as husband and wife. "There's something I wanted you to know," she told Morgan.

"What's that?" he asked, but he sounded a little nervous,

maybe worried that she was going to break through some barrier he was trying to hold onto.

"I need to tell you a little about Bern—my first husband."

"Sure. If you think you need to."

"I do, Morgan." It was the first time she had called him by his first name. She watched to see whether he accepted that all right, but he showed no reaction. His eyes were focused straight ahead, toward the oxen. "I was only sixteen when I met him, seventeen when we married," she went on. "He was ten years older. He had come from Sweden and then had settled in Beaver, Utah, where I lived. He was a good-looking man, and he was very nice to me. I had only moved to Beaver because I had crossed the plains with some people who settled there. They liked Bern, and they told me he would be a good husband. I thought that might be right, even though I never really loved him. After we married, he changed. He went back to some of his habits. Lots of men break the Word of Wisdom, but he loved his drink too much, and he drank hard liquor when he could get it. He would denounce the Church at times, and then go off with me to meetings on Sunday. He swore, took the name of the Lord in vain, and he cussed his animals in language I could hardly stand to hear. He promised to take me to the Endowment House, but I don't think that mattered to him. That's why we were never sealed. He accepted the call to come to this mission, but once he got here, he was more than disappointed. He kept talking about going on to California, and I kept saying no to that, but I think, if nothing had happened to him, he might have left me and gone there without me."

"Well, you've been through a lot."

"I just wanted you to know that my heart is not broken. I don't think life with him ever would have been happy—especially not for Jefferson. Bern was unpredictable, kind one moment and mean the next. Jefferson was scared to death of him."

"Actually, the bishop told me some of those things."

"That's good. But what I've wondered is whether you really want to be married to me for all eternity, or whether that was just what the bishop asked you to do. I know we have to go to the Endowment House to enter into a plural marriage, but maybe you would rather marry me only for this life. Is that possible?"

"No. It isn't. And it's not what I want. You'll be married to me for all eternity, the same as Angeline."

"All right. But what I told you is still true. I don't expect you to feel about me the way you—"

"Let's not talk that way, Ruth." And that was the first time he had called her by *her* first name. "We'll just have to grow closer— with time."

"All right. I would like that."

"Tell me about yourself—about your growing-up years," he said.

"All right. My father was a farmer, a plain man, not educated, not a preacher, not a leader. But he worked hard, and I always knew he loved me. He called me his little 'gleaner.' I didn't know what that meant until I grew old enough to read the story of Ruth in the Bible. He used the word as though it meant 'queen' or something of that sort. Mother told me that she loved the story of Ruth, who accepted the covenant and was loyal to her mother-in-law. I'm not sure what Father thought about all that. But he knew Ruth gleaned the grain fields, and I suppose he thought that was a good thing."

"Were you the only one in your family who joined the Church?"

"Yes. Missionaries came to our town in Ohio. My family went to a meeting and heard them preach. Father didn't seem to pay much attention; Mother thought they were sent by Satan. But I felt something I'd never known before, so I kept listening, and then I was baptized. Mother was very upset by that, but another family in my town had joined the Church, and they wanted to go west, so I traveled with them to Florence, Nebraska, and then on across the plains."

"What did you like to do when you were a young girl?"

She loved that he wanted to know. Morgan was such a handsome man, with those beautiful blue eyes against his dark skin, and she had watched many times how he treated Angeline. She longed to feel the same attention from him, but she told herself over and over not to expect it. It was good, though, that he wanted to know her better. "I was like most girls, I guess. My friends and I went to the dances in our town, and we talked about the boys. Most of the boys were farmers, too shy to say anything to us, but we still tried to decide which ones were the best looking and which ones we might choose for husbands one day. We were silly. We laughed at everything, and we were thrilled by a new ribbon for our hair or a new school dress each fall when school started."

"Did you like school?"

"I did. I was good at reading, and even at numbers, so I thought I could be a teacher. I had a picture in my head of a well-mannered woman, demanding in my way, but full of love for my students. Who knew I would turn out . . . the way I have?"

"What do you mean?"

"I don't know exactly. I lost myself somewhere along the way."

"Well, we're going right through Beaver on this trip. Let's take a look. Maybe we can find the old you along the road somewhere." He looked over at her and laughed, and then, surprisingly, he patted her hand.

Ruth was charmed. Morgan was nothing like Bern. She thought maybe he did want to look for her and find her. She hoped now that they would talk about lots of other things. She had stayed within herself for such a long time, it felt good to reveal a little of who she was.

CHAPTER 12

Morgan felt awkward around Ruth the next morning. He actually felt good about their conversations so far. He had found her more likable, more understandable, than he had expected, and they had moved a long way toward becoming friends. But as he had lain under the wagon that night, with her breathing softly just above him in the wagon box, he felt guilty. He had told himself, until now, that he would do his duty when the time came. He would marry Ruth, even have babies with her, but he would hold back, never be close to her the way he was with Angeline. He knew that the ideal the Brethren taught was equal love for all wives, and that made sense, in theory. But he had promised Angeline that he would never be unfaithful to her, and becoming close to another woman, even if only mentally—verbally—seemed to break his vows. He didn't like to think of Angeline sharing her thoughts, her feelings, her secrets with anyone but him. And he was quite certain that Angeline was worrying about that very thing: that he was linking himself to someone new and would come home changed, not "hers" in the way he had been before. So he told himself to be careful today. They would certainly talk along the way, but he didn't have to tell her everything.

Ruth busied herself preparing a pot of oatmeal mush and

cutting thick slices of bread, but she didn't say very much. Morgan thought maybe she sensed, too, that she had intruded herself into Morgan's marriage, talking to him like someone who was courting her. It was easier for him just to be quiet, and either Ruth knew that or she was withdrawing in the manner she had taken on in recent years.

Morgan did sense after a time, however, that he needed to say *something*. "Pretty morning, isn't it?"

"Just right," Ruth said.

"I guess, by next week, we'll be into the mountains and wishing we had brought a little of this Muddy Valley warmth with us."

"No doubt," was all she said, and now he suspected that she was spending some time with her own thoughts. This was something new to him—a little strange—and he found himself curious about her. He wondered what she might be thinking. Was she missing Jefferson? It seemed likely that she had liked the little breakthrough they had experienced but hesitated to demand anything more. Morgan liked that. It seemed as though she understood his discomfort, or maybe she felt just as uncomfortable herself. She was the one who probably felt more out of place, more pressured to do just the right things.

The two packed things up after breakfast, and then they set out in the wagon. But when silence set in this time, Morgan asked, in spite of what he had told himself earlier, "What are you thinking about this morning, Ruth?"

Ruth's head twisted quickly toward Morgan, and he heard a little gust of breath from her. Then she laughed. "Morgan, you just keep surprising me. I don't think any man, in my whole life, has ever asked me that question."

"Why would that be?"

"I don't know. I think a man feels like he doesn't want to get a woman started. If he asks what she's thinking, she'll actually tell him—and never stop."

Morgan laughed too. "Well, yes. I understand what you're saying. Sometimes Angie tells me more than I really want to know."

"I like that about her, Morgan. She's straightforward. She doesn't say one thing and mean another."

"Well . . . maybe. Most of the time." But now he really had betrayed Angeline. He had criticized her—or at least hinted in that direction—and he knew he had to be careful about ever doing that again.

"Do you really want to know what I'm thinking?" Ruth asked.

"Maybe. Now I'm not so sure." He laughed again, and so did she.

"Well, I won't tell you everything, then. I'll just tell you one thing, and I'll leave it at that."

"That sounds about right."

But she didn't say anything immediately. The oxen continued to lumber along, their hooves dragging through sand and gravel, their labored breaths like moans, and the wagon wheels made another kind of crushing sound—all of it in a sort of rhythm. The road ahead seemed long and slow at the moment, but Morgan knew the bends in the river were coming. Crossings would not be easy with the wagon heavily weighted and the river a little higher now with the spring runoff beginning.

"The thing is, Morgan, I'm scared," Ruth finally said. "When you asked me to marry you, it sounded like an 'arrangement' we were making. It was the best thing for me and Jefferson, and you were a good man, so you wanted to be generous—especially because you had been asked. I thought I could live with that. I would be your wife, but not really, not the way Angie is, and I wouldn't ask for anything more than that. But yesterday, I found out I like you very much. I'm sorry that I do, but I can't help it, and yet it makes the whole situation more difficult than I thought it would be."

Now Morgan wished he hadn't asked. He had actually known all this, but he didn't know what to say about it. So he only said, "Don't worry about it. It seems difficult now, but maybe, after some time passes, everything will be normal to us."

He knew he had actually said nothing. More than anything, she was probably hoping he would tell her that he liked her. And of course, he did, but the words would seem to mean much more than that. So he addressed the other part of what she had said. "If you want to know the truth, I'm scared too. It seems like I always am. My father is one of those men who can do anything and everything. I've always wanted to be like that, but I'm not sure about things. I make a decision and then I question it."

"I'm surprised you would admit something like that. Bern was scared, but I don't think he knew it—or at least he never said it."

"I suspect most people are like that. In school, one time, I answered a question—I don't even remember what it was—and my teacher, Miss Holmes, told me, 'Morgan, before you answer a question, you should make sure you understand what you've been asked.' Those were her exact words. I'll never forget that. All the kids in the class laughed. After that, I didn't want to take chances. I figured out it was easier to keep my mouth shut than to say something stupid and embarrass myself."

"It's not a bad thing to be quiet," Ruth told him. "Too many people babble on and on and hardly know what they're saying. I used to talk a lot when I was in school, and the teacher liked what I said. But after so many things went wrong in my life, I realized that people didn't want to hear me complain. So I started keeping my feelings to myself."

Morgan nodded. He heard bravery in Ruth's words, and he admired her. He took the chance to glance at her. It was true, she really wasn't very pretty. She had a rather square face, with a mouth that seemed a little too severe, lips that bent downward in the corners. But he had found out now that she could smile, and when she did, her face lightened considerably. Her eyes weren't all that noticeable from a distance, but up close, they were hazel, almost green, and her lashes were naturally dark and long. He liked her voice, too. It was a little lower than most women's voices, yet gentle. He had always detected sadness in that voice, those eyes, but even if life had subdued her, he liked that she wasn't allowing herself to be broken.

As it turned out, while the oxen trudged along, the two talked a great deal that day as well as in the days after. There were many hours to fill, and Morgan was surprised that they kept finding new things to say. They were quiet for long stretches, and during river crossings they turned all their attention to the tough task of getting the oxen and the wagon through the water and the dangerous sand in the bed of the river. Much of their talk was about the weather, the state of the river, preparations as they neared the river and got ready to cross, and the practical matter of making meals. At first, personal matters—leaving the wagon to find a place to relieve oneself, or washing in the river—were embarrassing to Morgan, but Ruth wasn't all that self-conscious about such things, and gradually Morgan gave them little thought.

One afternoon they talked rather extensively about Jefferson and his timid way of approaching life. Jefferson had feared his own father, but it had been worse for him when Bern was suddenly gone and Ruth was set adrift. Morgan thought he understood the little fellow better, and he told himself he had to be a father to the boy, not just the man in the house who was out working most of the time.

"He'll like you, Morgan," Ruth told him. "Don't push him too much at first. Just let him feel that you like him. He'll warm to that."

"All right. I'll take it slowly. Thanks for telling me more about him. I'm a little too much like my own father. If there's something that needs to be fixed, I like to get at it and solve the problem immediately. But sometimes that doesn't work."

"That's where Bern was different from you. He paid no attention to Jefferson. And then he would suddenly shout at him for the smallest things."

"I won't do that. But remind me if I start asking too much of him, too fast. That's kind of how I am."

"It's been interesting to hear you say things like that. I've been saying things—understanding things—about myself I'm not sure I knew before." She hesitated, looked at the road ahead for a time, then finally said, "I wonder if it's not the normal state of all of us to be afraid. We worry what others will think of us, or that we're not quite competent to do the things asked of us in life. I watch other women—women like Angeline—and I think that they can manage anything. I'm always scared they'll look beneath my skin and find out there's not much inside."

"But you seem confident to me," Morgan said. "Quiet, but ready to do what you have to do."

"That's what I've learned. If I don't say too much, people assume that there's more to me than there is. It's words that let people see through my skin."

Morgan chuckled. "Yeah. That's about right. That's how I think too. But I'm not so much that way as I used to be."

"That's because you're finding out—you can do lots of things. And you're a leader. People look to you for guidance."

"Maybe. I'm not sure. But you need to know, you can talk to Angeline about all these things. She likes to work, likes to get things done, but she has her fears too. Right now, she's more frightened than anything that she won't be able to carry a baby. And that's got her feeling weak instead of strong. It's terrible for her."

"I'm glad you told me," Ruth said.

"It's going to be important for all of us to understand each other."

"Yes." And then, after a few moments, she said, "Morgan, we'll manage it—because of you. You're not like any man I've ever known. You think about things. You have feelings. You care about people. The men I've known in my life all seemed ashamed to admit any weakness, or even to question themselves. My father made me feel that there was something wrong with me because I had strong feelings. I think you understand me better already than he ever did."

"Well . . . I hope so."

But this worried Morgan again. Was he saying more to Ruth than he ever had to Angeline? And was he sharing things about Angeline she wouldn't want him to share? He had to wonder what life would be like when he and Ruth came home. Could he continue conversations like this? Could they all three talk together? He had set out on this trip thinking that he would accept Ruth as his second wife and then return to his real love. But now he wondered whether he weren't splitting himself apart.

• • •

When Morgan and Ruth reached St. George, they stopped an extra day while a blacksmith removed and tightened a metal tire on one wagon wheel. Then they pushed on to higher elevations and into the mountains. They passed through Beaver, and Morgan offered to stop, but Ruth had thought about that ahead of time; she didn't want to see her old friends. She had written to them about Bern dying, but there was so much more to the story—more than she wanted to tell—and she really didn't want to introduce Morgan to them until he actually was her husband. So they kept going.

In the mountains, a spring snowstorm struck suddenly. Ruth was glad that Morgan had warned her to bring warm clothing, and she was thankful that he knew how hard he could push his oxen, when and where to stop, and how to keep them safe on the bad road. She had always doubted Bern's judgment about such things, and he, knowing that, would become furious with her. She learned that Morgan could get frustrated too, could even swear—although mildly—at his oxen, but he didn't take out his irritation on her. She actually took some pleasure in hearing him get after his oxen. She liked knowing that he wasn't quite so controlled as she had thought, and she remembered her own father speaking to his draft horses in much the same way. It seemed part of being a man to use a few words he wouldn't say at church. As far as that went, when Ruth was alone, she sometimes said things she wouldn't want her bishop to hear. Maybe the bishop did a little of that too.

The storm didn't last long, and once they got past the precarious descent off Beaver Summit, the weather cleared, and Morgan told her the worst was over. Then, when they passed Provo, he assured her that they had only one more day to travel.

That brought all Ruth's fears together. They had learned to be around one another, to relax and talk, but once the wedding ceremony took place, she wondered how uncomfortable the days that followed would be. She knew that Morgan was wrestling with himself. He had more or less admitted what he feared most: that this new marriage would come between him and Angeline. She loved to hear him express his love for his wife, but at the same time it was hard not to feel jealous about that. Angeline was not exactly a beauty, but she was tall and striking, and she attacked life as though it were just a series of challenges that she was certain she would conquer. Ruth had heard both women and men in the settlement talk about Angeline's strength and her willingness to take on any work. Ruth felt insignificant by comparison.

What also seemed obvious was that a man should always love the woman he had first loved, first proposed marriage to. He shouldn't even try to love more than one woman in the same way. She had always believed that. She had never wanted Bern to marry anyone else, regardless of how difficult he had made her life. And yet, however much she told herself these things, she wanted Morgan. What she realized, after traveling in the wagon day after day, was that she had fallen in love. The fact that she would never "own" her husband made her hurt, even though she told herself she had no right to him.

This jumble of feelings was not just confusing but angering. Just when life seemed to have offered her something better than she had experienced these last few years, she realized her new situation might turn out to be worse. What if he took her for a wife, but only thought of it as a way to help her, and something he would rather have avoided? He had suggested, indirectly, that he wanted her to have babies, but what if that happened without her feeling any love from him?

Ruth knew that lots of women faced the same trial. She wondered if all of them felt these same emotions. Leaders sometimes spoke of the relationship of men to women as though it were only a matter of breeding, producing offspring. What happened in bed was for procreation, and if pleasure entered into the act, that was something to control, to master, not to make the main issue.

"What day will we be married?" Ruth finally asked Morgan. She wanted to have some sense whether they would stay in Salt Lake City a day or two, perhaps sleep somewhere other than the wagon, or whether he would take care of matters of trade and then marry her just before they left.

"I'm not sure. I'll have to make some arrangements for that. And I have an awful lot to do while we're here. I really want to be back on the road just as soon as possible and then see if we can't make better time on the way back." He didn't look at her—didn't seem to want to look at her. "We need to get back to Angeline and Jefferson just as soon as we can. And back to our farms. I'm worried that things have turned hot down there, and Eb can't keep up with his farm and mine, too."

Ruth nodded, but she didn't say anything. This did seem to be a matter of business for Morgan.

• • •

Morgan and Ruth were not in Salt Lake City very long. Morgan wanted to continue on to Farmington and see his family, but he just couldn't justify taking that much time. He knew the river would be rising. So he told himself he would surely come again, and he would visit them then. Of course, he also knew he was self-conscious about showing up at home with another wife.

Morgan sold the cotton he had hauled to the city, and he purchased the items that people had ordered, and then, on the second afternoon, he and Ruth were sealed. He knew that after the ceremony, he should show her some affection. She even walked close to him, touched his hand, but he still felt strange about those things.

He knew he would have to be a husband to her now—soon—but he didn't know how that should happen. "I think we better start out this afternoon," he told Ruth. "I packed Angeline's furniture on top, and I hate to leave all that sitting on a street here in town. They tell me Salt Lake's not so safe as it used to be—with all the foreign gandy dancers here working on the railroad that's coming through."

That was his way of saying, *We'll stay in the wagon, even tonight.* He hoped it was also a way of saying that he didn't want things to change too much for now.

"That's fine," Ruth told him.

But once they were in the wagon, he felt her silence and knew very well that he had hurt her. He decided he had better be open with her and not just send little signals. Still, he waited for a time, tried to think how he could say just the right thing. Finally, he told her, "Ruth, this is a little strange for both of us, I think. We've never thought of each other as husband and wife, and now, all of a sudden, we're pronounced 'one flesh' when we've had no real time to go through courting and all the usual things."

"If you feel that way, I understand."

But that left too many questions. Again, he waited. The sun was angling low out in the westward desert. He knew he would have to stop and get a little camp set up, but it must have seemed strange to her to ride only an hour or so out of town when they might have stayed in a hotel for one night. "So how are you feeling . . . about everything?" he asked her.

"I just want what you want. You didn't propose to me because you couldn't wait to be married to me. I told you from the beginning, I understand that."

Morgan had told Ruth the story about Brigham asking him to serve a mission and to get married before he left. Now he told her,

"I didn't really court Angie, either, but we had known each other all our lives." He didn't connect the statement to any particular conclusion, but he hoped she would understand that he was struggling with this adjustment.

"There was another difference, too," she said. "You didn't have another wife at the end of your trail."

"Well, yes. That's true. But don't you think it's wise to spend some more time together—actual married time—before we. . . ." But he couldn't think what he wanted to call it.

"That's fine, Morgan. I love being with you. That's good enough for me. But will you do one thing for me?"

"Sure. What?"

"Will you sleep next to me in the wagon—at least when we reach the mountains again? I got very cold some nights, coming here."

Morgan had already thought that he ought to do that. But he had never slept next to a woman other than Angeline. It was more "closeness" than he felt ready for. By now, he pictured Angie, at home, wondering about that very thing. Angeline didn't know where he and Ruth were in their travels, but she must have been guessing that they would be married by now. More than anything, what was bothering him was the thought of the feelings he would have if Angeline were traveling—and sleeping—with some other man. The idea of it almost made him angry. So he picked a spot, set up camp, and said very little to Ruth all evening. She was painfully patient with his behavior, but that wasn't reason enough for him to change what he found himself doing. And yet, when it came time to go to bed, he couldn't bring himself to sleep under the wagon—and hurt her that much. So he lay next to her, felt her warm softness under the quilt—and hardly slept at all. Mostly, he tried to think of Angeline.

• • •

Angeline was ready for bed, but she stayed up a little longer. She had not slept well while Morgan had been gone. That had been a problem for her when he had traveled before, but this time it was worse. All day she did pretty well at keeping her mind on the things she had to do. With Morgan gone, she was spending a good deal of time doing farm work. Eb was doing his best to get their fields and his own planted, but Angeline soon realized he would never manage it if she didn't help with the sowing, and sometimes even the plowing. She asked Mary Ann to look after Jefferson on those days, and she was good to do that, but the boy struggled at being passed along again. He would cry when Angeline left him. So she hurried and did all she could on the farm, and then she tried to spend lots of time playing, singing, and telling stories to little "Jeffy," as she had begun to call him. He was a mild boy, obedient, and not hard to look after, but he needed attention, and Angeline wasn't used to such a demand on her time.

Still, she pushed hard, as always, and she felt that Morgan would be pleased when he got back and saw that she and Eb had managed all right.

She managed her feelings pretty well—until night came. She would get Jefferson bedded down on some quilts on the floor, and then she would let her candle gutter out, and still, she would sit in the dark. The days were already getting hot, but the nights cooled dramatically. She knew she would sleep better if she let herself get tired and a little cold before she pulled a blanket over herself. But there in the dark, sitting in her chair or on her bed, she could not stop asking herself what was happening between Morgan and Ruth. She had learned, before they left, what a nice woman Ruth was. She wasn't as opinionated and certainly never as forceful as

Angeline. She probably made Morgan feel good about himself. And maybe Ruth knew more about married life, about pleasing a man. Maybe he was already finding out that Angeline didn't understand a man's needs as well as Ruth did. She was afraid, when she thought of that, that she would have to compete for Morgan's attentions when he returned.

• • •

One of Morgan's great worries was the difficulty of the Virgin River crossings that lay ahead. The days were getting warmer, and that meant the river would be running higher than when they had come through before. As it turned out, however, the early crossings were not too bad. Ruth had not worked with animals much, so he asked her to stay in the wagon and hold on tight while he led the four oxen across the river each time. Water had been deep enough to splash over the sideboard and get Ruth's feet wet, but Morgan felt, if things got no worse, they would make it through the river valley just fine. But he kept pushing, putting in long days. It was toward the end of the valley, with only two or three crossings left, that the river suddenly took a substantial rise. The runoff from the mountains was picking up now, and Morgan was well aware how dangerous the river would be from this point on.

When they reached a turn in the road that led to another crossing, Morgan halted the oxen and got out to survey the situation. He walked out into the freezing water to the middle of the stream, bracing himself against the current. As he walked back, still thinking, he said, "Ruth, I could unpack a lot of things and haul them across one at a time, but that would take a long time, and each crossing would be dangerous. So I think I might as well try to get the wagon across, full, but I don't want you to be in it.

I'm going to put you on Ben and lead him across. Once you're safe on the other side, I'll hitch Ben back on with the others and see how they can do."

"Maybe Ben could carry some of the other weight across too, so the wagon wouldn't be quite so heavy," Ruth suggested.

"You're probably right. But it could take us the rest of the afternoon to unpack the right things, and I was hoping to get out of this valley by the end of the day. I think I'll start the wagon in and see how everything holds up."

So Morgan had Ben carry Ruth across first. The water washed over the ox's back sometimes, and Ruth was soaked and very cold by the time she got to the other side. But she was safe, and Morgan felt good about that. So he crossed back, hitched up all his oxen again, and led them into the river. The wagon sat a little deeper in the water than usual; still, all seemed to go fine. But the water became more forceful as the wagon reached the middle of the stream, and the oxen began to labor hard to pull on through. And then the current tipped the wagon just enough for the load to shift. For a moment, Morgan thought the wagon was turning over on its side, but everything held just before the tipping point. The problem now was that the oxen had no chance of pulling the off-balance load on through, and Morgan had no hope of righting the wagon and its load.

For a few seconds Morgan waited to see whether the load would shift any farther, but everything held. He knew he couldn't panic. He had to think what to do. He shouted, "Ruth, I've got to untie some of the load off the top, and carry all I can up to the bank." He was thinking that once the load was lightened, he could use a rope to pull the wagon upright again. But he didn't take time to explain that. He only worked his way to the upside of the wagon and began to pull off anything that was loose or could be untied.

Angeline's furniture—some chairs and a bigger table and chest of drawers—were strapped on top and hardest to reach, but they were also the reason the load had been top heavy. So he climbed onto the upside of the wagon, unlashed a chair, and then dropped back into the water, still holding the chair above his head. The water pushed him against the wagon and banged his ribs, but worse, the wagon shuddered, and he thought it was going over.

But it held again. Morgan fought his way toward the north side of the river, where he found that Ruth had waded into the water, up to her waist. She was reaching for the chair. "Hand it to me," she yelled, her voice barely audible over the sound of the rushing water.

"Be careful. Step back a little."

But she didn't do that. She grabbed the chair, held it high, the way he had done, and fought her way out of the water. Morgan could hardly believe she was that strong, but he didn't wait. He waded back to the deeper water and brought down another chair. When he turned, Ruth was ready for him again, and she took the second chair. But the heaviest weight was in the table and the chest of drawers. Morgan couldn't see yet how he could manage those two, but he knew that was his only chance to right the wagon, so he climbed back onto the side of the wagon, untied the table, and slid down to the water, letting the table slide with him. Once he was in the water, he pushed the table out and away, upside down, held up by the water, the legs sticking in the air. He was against the wagon box, the water pushing him hard, and yet the wagon still held, and Morgan pushed the table ahead of him.

This time Ruth had come deeper into the river, and she held one end of the table as the two resisted the force of the water. Morgan was amazed that Ruth could lift and fight the current at the same time, but she did it, and the two pushed the table out on the bank.

Morgan turned back and looked at the load. The chest of drawers was more than he or Ruth, or the two together, could manage. He told himself he would have to push it off the top on the downriver side and sacrifice it to the current.

"Take out one drawer at a time," Ruth shouted.

Morgan had considered doing that, but getting high enough on the wagon to pull the drawers out looked impossible, and way too dangerous. If he were up on the wagon and it rolled, he might be cast downstream with the load, and his oxen might be pulled into the mess. He knew better than to try it. But the chest was for Angeline, and he had already imagined her joy in getting it. He couldn't get himself to cast it off without at least trying to save it.

• • •

An hour later, Morgan and Ruth were sitting on a little patch of grass. They had saved the chest and had also carried out some of the sacks of seed and some of the tools. With two plows still in the back of the wagon box, they had used a rope, and both had pulled fiercely until they had righted the wagon. By then, Morgan had realized that the wagon was caught in quicksand, and that was what had held it from tipping over. He feared, however, that his oxen were mired. But the oxen were beyond the soft sand. They found footing enough to pull, and the two wheels that had been out of the sand held the wagon up enough that the oxen were able to pull on through.

After resting for a few minutes, Morgan had found his matches dry in the front of the wagon. He gathered some firewood and started a fire. It would take a while for him and Ruth to dry off, but Morgan was astounded that they had saved everything and made it across.

"Ruth, I hope you know, we just watched a miracle happen. That load should have gone over, and even though it didn't, the oxen never should have been able to get the wagon out of that river."

"I guess you're right, but the whole time, I was thinking, *Morgan will know what to do. He'll get us out of this trouble.*"

"Me? What about you? You were practically up to your neck in water, hoisting furniture over your head. I never imagined you could do such a thing."

"I don't think I can, usually. I just did."

"Were you praying the whole time? *I* was."

"Yes. Of course. But not for the wagon or the furniture. *Don't take Morgan from me,* I kept saying. *Keep him safe.*"

Morgan took a closer look at Ruth. Her hair was still matted, and her white collar was soaked in mud. But he saw the look in her eyes, saw how deep her feelings were. He brushed a little drying mud off her cheek. She looked back at him with such a hopeful, loving intensity. "Thank you," he said. And then he kissed that same cheek. He hadn't even kissed her at the end of the marriage ceremony, or along the way, but this little kiss seemed to change everything.

• • •

The warm air and the fire helped the two to dry out. And then Ruth gathered together what food she could salvage, and the two ate, hardly talking. Ruth thought she knew what would happen now, even though she didn't want to get her hopes up too high. But she noticed a couple of times that evening that he touched her shoulder or her arm, and he kept telling her how impressed he was by her strength of will.

They made a bed on the ground that night, the wagon still much in need of drying and repacking. They laid quilts on the grass and pulled two more quilts over them. At first, everything seemed as it had been each night, but Ruth couldn't resist letting him know that it was time. She touched his chest and then stroked his side. "How badly did you hurt yourself?" she asked. But she didn't stop stroking.

He didn't answer. He only rolled more toward her, and he kissed her again, but this time it was a real kiss. And then she knew that the time really had arrived.

CHAPTER 13

Morgan and Ruth had not been back long before Morgan sensed the change in Angeline. He had come into the house, embraced her, and asked her about everything that had happened at home. She had told him some things about the crops, about Eb helping her, but she glanced time and again toward Ruth, who was holding Jefferson on her lap, talking to him, asking him questions about his time without her. Morgan wanted to tell Angeline how much he loved her and how much he had missed her, but it was uncomfortable to say that sort of thing in front of Ruth. He didn't want Ruth to think he was happier to be home with Angeline than he had been with her. He knew Ruth had told him, time and again, that she understood that Morgan would never love her as much as he did Angeline, but he certainly couldn't express that feeling when both were in the room.

He had known before he got back that this would be a difficult adjustment, but he hadn't realized how reticent and self-conscious Angeline would be to express herself when Ruth was with them. Angeline seemed happy when Morgan told her about the furniture he had bought, but when she walked out with him to help take it down from the wagon, Ruth walked out too, and she carried one of the chairs inside. Angeline glanced at Morgan, looking confused, as though she wondered whose furniture it really was.

When Ruth came back outside, she told Angeline, "You wouldn't believe what we went through to save your furniture. We almost tipped the wagon over in the river, and we fought that river for over an hour, unstrapping the furniture—especially those big pieces—and then hauling them onto the bank. Morgan kept climbing up on the wagon, and I was scared every second that the wagon would roll over and wash him downstream with everything else. You'll never know how relieved and happy we were when we finally got the wagon out of the river. We were both soaked to the skin and exhausted, but we knew the Lord had been with us. It was a great feeling."

Morgan watched Angeline, who listened intently at first, but then he saw her eyes leave Ruth's when she talked about them being wet and tired and relieved. Surely, she sensed that this had been a moment of closeness for the two. And surely she had noticed how many times Ruth had said "we." This was all new. Ruth had never put so many sentences together, never spoken so enthusiastically, in all the time Morgan had known her. She even looked prettier than she ever had before. Morgan knew that Angie was noticing all of that.

And then, when Morgan took hold of the table, it was Ruth who stepped forward and took one side. Morgan watched Angeline shrink backward, taking a step away as though her place in the family had been stolen from her. Angeline walked back into the house and spoke to Jefferson, patting his head. She didn't help with any of the other furniture or supplies that Morgan and Ruth carried in.

Morgan brought in a mirror in a dark chestnut frame. "Angie," he said, "I know you told me you didn't want one of these, but I thought you ought to have one." He turned it around and let her look into it. But the timing was wrong.

"Oh, don't. Turn it away," she said. "I look so awful."

Morgan had no idea what to say. He set the frame down, leaning it against the wall with the mirror side hidden. He wished he had waited to give it to her—and had said something about seeing herself as he saw her. But that wouldn't work at all right now.

Morgan wasn't sure what to do next. He needed to get back in the wagon and drive Ruth and her things—and Jefferson—to their own house, but he hated to make that separation too soon. He found himself splitting the distance between his two wives so neither would think he was linking himself more with one than the other. What he wanted to do was hold Angeline in his arms again and tell her that he loved her, but that would have to come later, and he wondered whether she would even want him to hold her by then.

Angeline was saying, "You must be very tired, Ruth. It's such a long ride. Sit down and spend some time with Jeffy. I'll fix something for dinner. You won't want to cook when you get home."

But all this was just a little too "gracious." Morgan knew Angeline was trying to do the right thing, but the word "home," applied to Ruth's house, must have reminded Ruth that this house was not yet her home. Maybe, without acknowledging it to herself, that was exactly what Angeline wanted to say to her.

"It is a long ride," Ruth said, "but it hasn't been too bad. We found lots to talk about. The river was difficult, but we stopped a few miles from here last night, so this day was an easy one."

Morgan had no idea what was intentional and what wasn't, but he wished she hadn't mentioned how much they had talked, and he knew what Angie must be thinking about the "stop" they had made the night before. She certainly had to know that he and Ruth would sleep together in the wagon on the way back, but Ruth had referred to their last night together with such ease, as though this were part of life now. He wasn't sure that Angie was ready for that reality. And now that he was back, he wasn't sure that he could speak at all of nights with Ruth.

What also came to Morgan's mind was the trip he and Angie had made—their honeymoon. He looked at her, trying to reassure her somehow that this new trip together had not replaced those wonderful moments they had shared. But Angie didn't look at him at all.

"Well, that's good," Angeline said to Ruth. "But you need to eat. I'll see what I can put together quickly."

"All right, but let me help."

"No. That's fine. Play with Jeffy a little. He's missed you so much. He asked about you every day . . . especially at first."

"Oh. . . ." Ruth didn't ask the question that was in her eyes. "But let me peel some carrots or—"

"No. Please. Just relax." And Morgan half expected her to say, *"I am, after all, in charge around here."*

So Angeline fixed dinner and Morgan got out of the house. He walked to his farm and looked over the crops. He wasn't entirely pleased with what he saw. The growth in the fields was in patches, with whole sections looking as though they had been flooded or blighted somehow. He would also have Ruth's land now, and he hoped it was in better shape, but it would not be easy to farm both fields, especially since they were more than a mile apart. Somehow, all this hadn't hit him until now: how much work he would have to do to keep two wives supplied, and probably more children. Work was something he could face, at least. It was the delicate, unstated tension he had felt in his home that scared him. He wondered whether he should build a room for Ruth immediately. It might be better to have her stay in her own home. But going back and forth, the way some polygamists did, seemed disruptive and competitive. It was what Angeline had always said she hated about her own father's divided life.

Morgan stood for a time, looking beyond his land to the bluffs beyond, and he thought how differently everything had turned out from what he had expected. This was still ugly land, no matter how hard he tried to accept it, and even though he felt more for Ruth than he had thought he would, she was now a never-ending reality in his life: a division that he would not be able to escape. He knew he had to take one day at a time and not dwell on his fears, but he felt a strange sorrow—even regret—that he had never known in his life. Angie, more than anyone, had convinced him that he should marry Ruth, but surely, neither one of them had known what they would feel now that their new way of living had begun.

Morgan said a prayer: just a few words. He asked for help, for a better attitude. Then he walked back home. He ate dinner with two wives for the first time, and a child, now his, whom he hardly knew. Not much was said, or at least not much of importance, but he heard little stings in some of the words the two women chose.

"Thanks so much for taking care of Jefferson," Ruth said at one point. "I can tell how much he likes you. You'll be a wonderful mother one day."

It sounded innocent enough. Maybe it was. But Angeline didn't need reminders that she had failed to carry her babies so far. And Morgan knew Angie well enough to know that she was probably already worried that Ruth would have another child before she did.

After dinner, Ruth did insist on helping with the dishes, which was probably a good thing, if nothing else to let Angeline know that she had a will of her own. When everything was cleaned up, Morgan showed a little of his own will by taking Ruth and Jefferson back to their own house. He knew that, more than anything, he had to spend some time with Angie—both for himself and to let her understand that they were not as disconnected as she might be thinking.

When he got back, though, Angeline seemed to be going through the motions, trying to talk normally but seeming a little too careful, just slightly formal. After a few minutes of that, Morgan finally took her in his arms and held her. "I've missed you so much," he said. "I thought of you every minute of every day."

But Morgan felt resistance. Angie didn't let their bodies form to each other, and she didn't respond to his words. Finally, she pulled back and, without looking him straight in the eye, said, "Ruth said you had lots to talk about."

Morgan took hold of Angeline's shoulders and waited for her to look at him. "Angie, we were in the wagon all day. You know me. I wasn't talking all the time. I like to look around and just think about things. But sure, we talked. We hardly knew each other. We needed to get acquainted."

"I know. I understand all that." She stepped back and gently pulled away from his grip. "She's your wife now. I've known that you would have to . . . treat her right." She raised her voice a little more. "Morgan, you have to love her. That's what you've been called to do. And you couldn't love her until you knew her better. I've thought about all those things. I've lain awake at night and thought about the two of you. And I knew that you would do the right thing. You've been called, and I'm the one who told you this was what we should do. I can live with our decision now."

"But it's hard, isn't it?"

Angeline nodded. "Of course." There was a resoluteness in

her voice but something more: a tone that hinted at resentment. Morgan knew she was fighting with herself.

"This is hard for me, too, Angie. Harder even than I thought it would be. I feel caught in the middle, and I'm not sure how I'm supposed to behave."

"If you don't mind, Morgan, I'm going to withhold just a little pity for you. All in all, I would say you have the better part of this arrangement."

"No. I don't think so." But he did know. Two women loved him, and he felt far more for Ruth than he had ever imagined that he could. It divided him, complicated his life, but he knew that in some sort of arithmetic of polygamy, his situation was an addition and Angie's was a subtraction. And there was nothing he could think of to change that.

The following days were full of such moments. Morgan kept trying to act as though nothing had changed, and he showed Angeline more affection than usual. But she seemed suspicious of that, and he could guess what she was imagining. In bed, Angeline seemed more hesitant than ever before. Morgan told her over and over how much he loved her, but the very words seemed to limit her response to him, and he decided he had to be careful about that. The truth was, he had actually never felt so much love for Angie. He needed her to love him the way she had before. And yet, he couldn't shake the feeling that he had betrayed her back there by the Virgin River. He had done more than his "duty," and he knew it. She seemed to know it too.

Each day, Morgan stopped by Ruth's house. He made sure that she had food and water, and he played with Jefferson for a few minutes. He purposely didn't stay very long. He didn't want Angeline to wonder what he had been doing there. But he did kiss Ruth as he left each time, and he felt her clinging just a little, as though she wanted him to know that what had happened between them was good—and something she was more than happy to continue.

When Morgan came back from visiting her one day, Angeline asked him, "How are Ruth and Jeffy doing?" She had set the table for dinner, and she motioned for Morgan to sit down.

"Oh, they're fine," he replied. "I think she's still a little tired from the trip, but who wouldn't be?"

"Wasn't she able to sleep very well in the wagon?"

Morgan knew, of course, what Angeline was asking. He had told her that he would sleep under the wagon and let Ruth sleep inside—on the way to Salt Lake City. They had never spoken about the arrangement for the home trip. "I think she slept all right. But I wanted to get back as fast as I could, so we put in long days. I pushed the oxen about as hard as I could."

"She said you stopped early that last night, though."

"Not early. It was just getting too late to push on in the dark and make it all the way home. And the oxen were worn out."

"She didn't seem tired when you got here. What I noticed was that she's happier now than I've ever seen her before."

"Yes, I think she is. Her life was quite empty after Bern was killed."

"I'm glad it's better now."

"Are you?"

And now the moment had come. They had needed to talk about their new lives, and they just hadn't done it. They hadn't yet started to eat, but now Angeline looked down at her empty plate, and tears were suddenly on her cheeks. "I didn't know I would feel this way!" she said. "I thought I could do what my mother did, but it's so much harder than I thought."

Morgan came around the table and knelt by Angeline's chair.

"Angie, I think you're wondering if I slept with her on the way back. I didn't at first. It took me a while to feel like I could. But I did. We're married now. I don't know what else to say. You are my first love, and you always will be."

"But not your only love. I thought you would look after her and her son, and try to make her life better. I didn't think you would fall in love with her. I saw it in both of you when you got back. You were fresh off your honeymoon, and you were closer to her than you are to me."

"No. I'll never be as close to her as I am to you."

But he had to be careful. Ruth wouldn't want to hear him say that. He had to walk a middle path, feel connected to both, treat them the same. He couldn't pit one against the other, saying things that weren't true just to placate them. He did love Angeline as much as ever, but he had begun to feel love toward Ruth, and he could never tell Angeline that he didn't.

Angeline ran her hands over Morgan's hair, and then she put her fingers under his chin and raised it so he could look at her. "You should be close to her, Morgan. You're married, just like you said. And I told you I would be all right with that." Tears filled her eyes and then flowed onto her cheeks. "But I feel as though I've been robbed, that you'll never be mine again, not the way you were. It's breaking my heart, Morgan. I don't want to feel that way, but I do."

Morgan stood and pulled her up from her chair, held her in his arms, said he was sorry, even said he wished he had never agreed to marry Ruth, but even that seemed more than he should have said. Life stretched before him like a long, hard, uphill climb from now on—maybe leading to heaven, but feeling quite the opposite.

· · ·

Ruth continually relived her trip with Morgan, letting it all pass through her mind: the conversations, the sense of freedom, the quiet evenings together, the budding intimacy. Now it seemed gone. She knew she would never have Morgan entirely to herself again. He had promised to be with her next week, but his mind would be on his work, and it would be on Angeline. Ruth had sensed the change in Morgan as soon as he was back with his wife—that is, his first wife. He seemed tense, maybe embarrassed, or guilty. She wondered: if she went to live in the same house, would it always be like that?

She had initially hoped for kindness from Morgan and perhaps friendship from Angeline. She had never expected that she and Morgan could share so many thoughts, never imagined that he would be so interested in what she had to say. Above all, she had never expected him to show her such physical warmth. She had never expected to be as happy as she had been that night on the bank of the river, out under the stars. She hadn't slept that night. She had kept one hand on him, just to keep that much touch between them. Maybe that was what he had been ashamed of when he had faced Angeline, and she knew already that nothing quite like that night would ever happen again. So she savored those memories now, remembered every detail, and she lay in bed at night longing to have him with her again.

Jefferson was clinging to her since she had returned. She never called him "Jeffy," the way Angeline had begun to do. It didn't seem exactly right to Ruth, even though she appreciated Angeline's love for her son. But the first night alone with Jefferson, he had asked Ruth to tell him a story, and when she tried to invent something, Jefferson had said, "No. Like Aunt Angeline. Tell me stories like that."

Ruth couldn't think what to tell him. She had loved to read

all her life, but she didn't know fairy tales—or whatever Angeline had told him. So she thought of Bible stories, and she told some of those. Jefferson sat still for that, but afterward, he said, "Aunt Angeline talked funny. She made me laugh."

That was all right. Ruth couldn't hold such a thing against Angeline, but Jefferson was *her* son. Angeline would have to understand that. She knew that it was hard for her not to have children of her own, but Ruth couldn't help that.

And then, of course, Ruth recognized her own pettiness in thinking such things. How could she expect so much from Morgan and Angeline if she wasn't willing to think the best of them?

• • •

The heat was coming on now, and Morgan had hills of work to catch up on. His crops seemed puny compared to the year before, and he wasn't sure why. There had not been much rain, but Eb had done his best to keep the field watered.

On Morgan's second day home he had sought out Eb on his farm. Eb had been turning water, running it down the furrows of his own field. "Morgan!" he shouted. "You're home. I can't tell you how glad I am to see you." He pushed his shovel blade into the sand, left the shovel standing, and walked toward Morgan.

"I'm sorry I left you so much work," Morgan said. "Thanks for taking care of things." They shook hands, and then Morgan grabbed Eb by the shoulders and gripped hard. "I mean it. Only a true friend would make such an effort."

"I did make an effort, but I don't know, neither field looks as good as last year. You knew what to do better than I do."

"You did the same as last year, didn't you?" Morgan asked.

"I tried. But here's what the men are telling me. The water

from the Muddy has too many minerals in it. The ground builds up a layer of that stuff, and it hampers the growth. They say you have to rotate crops here more than in other places."

"How do we do that? Half my acreage is so alkaline, it only grows lucerne for hay. I don't have anything left to leave fallow."

"I know," Eb said. "It's the same for me. Some of the farms, especially down in St. Thomas, are doing quite well. The soil itself isn't so bad, I guess. We seem to have the worst of the problems here on the bench. And Morgan, I don't think we'll have enough water to get through the full summer. The canal is down to a trickle some days."

Eb walked back to his shovel and grasped the handle. He leaned forward and let it take some of his weight. Morgan noticed how used up he looked—his face thin and burnt, his hands almost skeletal. "We can try fertilizer, I guess. From our oxen. But I didn't know how much to apply, and Brother Westfield told me to go easy on that. It can burn up young plants when the heat gets bad."

Morgan knew something about spreading manure, but not here, not in this situation. He hoped someone knew.

"The canal filled up with sand twice while you were gone, and we dug it out again. People are getting tired of that. Six more families pulled out—all from here or down at the fort. Brother and Sister Baker, after all they've been through, went with them. He told me that this country wasn't meant to be farmed. But he's like me. He didn't really know what he was doing. He'll be better off someplace where he can build and repair—the things he's trained to do."

"But he knows the scriptures backwards and forwards," Morgan said. "We need people like that, too, and someday we'll need skilled tradesmen. I wish, after everyone helped him so much, he would have stuck it out." Morgan tucked his hands into his trouser pockets, looked down at the ground. "I don't blame people for wanting to leave. I think about it all the time. But promises ought to mean more than they do to some people. I'm not leaving until Brigham tells us to go. I was tempted, up in West Point, to take his offer to head home, but I knew darned well he wasn't giving us permission; he was telling us to leave if we weren't up to the calling—and I've known ever since then, I will *not* give up."

"I guess I won't either, Morgan. Mary Ann and I talked a lot about it after Eliza was born, but we decided that most of the people we love are here. Besides, we don't want to be accused of being quitters either. Or at least that's what we said all winter. But Mary Ann is with child again, and sick again. I wonder what this place will do to her. If it kills her, I'm not sure I can forgive myself for staying."

"Has she started talking about leaving again?"

"No. But she doesn't say much of anything right now. It's all she can do to stand up without running for a pail. And the heat, even though it's not so bad yet, is wearing her down again."

"Eb, don't stay just because your friends are staying. You can't sacrifice your wife just to show you're not a quitter."

"Listen, I've thought about all of that. But when I ask God, He doesn't offer me a release. He just keeps making me feel that I have to stand up to this valley—and sometimes I see Mary Ann in a few years, ten times stronger than she was, because she didn't give up."

Morgan wasn't sure. But he respected Eb, who himself seemed much stronger than he had ever been while he was growing up, no matter how thin and wasted he looked.

"What about James and Lyman and Art?" Morgan asked. "What are they saying now?"

Eb removed his hat and wiped his face with a bandanna tied around his neck. "I've got to get out of the sun. I feel like I'm going to turn into butter and melt. I'm going to block up the water now and call it a day."

Morgan took the shovel from him and did the back filling, and then the two walked back toward the settlement. "Boy, what I wouldn't give for a tree to hide under once in a while," Eb said.

"We've planted plenty of them. They'll shade us all we want in a few years."

"I guess so." And then, as they walked, Eb said, "You asked about our friends. Lyman stuck a pitchfork into his foot, right through his boot, and he's had a bad infection. There for a few days, I thought we might lose him. Alice usually takes things well, but she was beside herself. He got through it, though, and he's up and around a little. He just can't work in his fields yet."

"So who's looking after his field?"

"All of us. We take turns."

"So you've had that on top of planting my crops?" Morgan asked.

"Art helped some with that. His field produces more than most—without too much work. So he's always looking to help anyone he can. Susan is expecting again too. Art told me that just a couple of days ago. So far, she's not sick—trouble is, their little Robert doesn't handle the heat very well. He has a fever, or maybe the ague. Susan is worried about that, and I think she was hoping another baby wouldn't come along quite so soon."

"I've got to call on everyone. I hadn't heard about these things. I don't think Angeline knew."

"She knows. I've talked to her about everything. Maybe she just didn't want to drop everything on you all at once. She knows that you'll be running around, trying to help everyone."

"You mean, like you?"

"No. You're a real help."

What Morgan didn't say was that he wasn't sure Angeline had wanted to talk to him about much of anything. "What about James and Lydia?" he asked.

"They're doing all right, but Lydia got word that her sister died having a baby, up in Salt Lake. She would give anything in the world to go home for a while, just to see her folks and offer what help she could to the family. But you know how long it takes to get up there and back, and no one wants to make a trip like that in the summer."

"Do you ever get the feeling this world is too full of troubles?"

The two had arrived at Eb's house, but Eb didn't go in. He stopped Morgan and walked him around to the shady side of the house. "Speaking of troubles, I'm just wondering, how are things working out for you and Angeline—and Ruth?"

Morgan didn't know where to start, or whether to start.

When he hesitated, Eb said, "I had the feeling, while you were gone, Angeline was having second thoughts about the whole situation. She hasn't seemed happy, Morgan, and sometimes she would say little things that didn't sound quite right. 'I hope Morgan and Ruth are doing all right,' she would say, but the way she said it, I kept thinking she was scared that you *were* happy."

"Yeah. I think that might be what she was thinking—and then hating herself for feeling that way. It's one thing to accept a calling; making it work is another."

"I know you didn't really want to marry Ruth, and I've always noticed how glum she is. I've got to say, I don't envy you. I can't believe you were good enough to enter into a marriage like that."

"Ruth isn't at all what you think," Morgan said. "She's a good woman. She was sad before because she was alone and never had been treated right. But she's doing better now. She talks more than you would ever think. And she's smart. It was a long ride, and uncomfortable at first, but we got to be friends. I'm glad I can help her."

"Don't you have to be a lot more than friends, though?" Eb asked.

Morgan had said what he said on purpose. He didn't want to add anything more. What Eb heard would surely go to Mary Ann, and from there it would leap like sheet lightning, straight back to Angeline.

"She's my wife, Eb. So yes, she's more than a friend. I just hope I can be a good husband to her."

"Can Angeline accept that? I think maybe she expected that you were only doing a favor to a widow—a woman you had no interest in."

"It can't work that way, Eb. You can't treat one wife a certain way and the other one, completely opposite. That just wouldn't be fair."

Eb nodded a couple of times, as though he were trying to get used to a new way of looking at things. "Well, I'm glad it's you, not me," he said. "I don't think I could manage a life like that—no matter how much Apostle Snow preaches that I've got to accept the principle."

"Maybe I can't either. I guess I'll find out."

Morgan had intended to step inside and wish Mary Ann well, but he wasn't feeling like it now. It hadn't occurred to him that everyone would be watching him, curious about things he didn't really want to talk about. What did occur to him for the first time was that not only did he have to watch what he said to his wives, he had to watch what he said to his friends.

• • •

Angeline had spent a long day at home. She knew that she had more time and energy now, and that she ought to visit some of the sisters who were not doing so well. But she couldn't bring herself to do it. She didn't feel happy enough to cheer up anyone. She also knew that all her friends—really, most of the women in the settlement—had babies. She liked to hold the little ones sometimes, but then she only had to return to an empty house. Morgan was working hard again, putting in long hours, and now she didn't have Jeffy to entertain. What she also knew, even though he hadn't said it yet, was that Morgan would take a turn living with Ruth before long, or he would finish the extra room and move Ruth and Jeffy into the house. She didn't like to think of either possibility.

The heat was also becoming difficult again. Early in the morning the house was quite cool, but as the day stretched on, hot air filled it, and outside was only worse. Angeline had taken pride the previous summer in telling herself she could manage somehow, but her pregnancy, however miserable, had given her something to look forward to. She dreaded the summer now, and she wondered how she could live with all the summers ahead for the rest of her life.

The rest of her life.

What if she never had a baby, if she had to watch Ruth have one after another?

But Angeline knew she couldn't think this way. She had to pray more, believe more, trust, read her scriptures, keep her garden, smile. She had to. All the same, tears were on her face, and she couldn't stop them from flowing. When Morgan suddenly walked into the house, she turned away quickly, using her apron to pretend she was wiping away sweat, not tears.

"Are you all right, Angie?" Morgan asked.

She turned back toward him, smiling. "Of course." But she knew that her eyes must be red.

"I'm sorry, Angie—about what's happened to us." He walked to her, took hold of her arms, and looked into her eyes. "Let's take care of each other, all right? Our marriage is always first."

Angeline had no idea what that meant, but she appreciated Morgan's efforts. "We'll be fine," she told him. "Some things just take some getting used to. Lots of people are worse off than we are."

Morgan sat down on one of the new chairs. "Eb told me about Lyman sticking a pitchfork in his foot and about Mary Ann being sick again."

"I didn't want to tell you all that the minute you walked through the door. I guess he told you about more people leaving."

"Yes. Six families, he said."

"And Polly Shupe."

"What about Wilfred?"

"He's still here. I don't know everything about the situation, but I guess she told Wilfred she wasn't going to put up with the ugly way he treated her. People say that she talked to Bishop Morrison, and he told her that Brigham has announced that sisters don't have to stay in plural marriage if they don't like it. He'll grant them a divorce, if they're sure that's what they want."

"What about the men? Can they back out?"

Morgan was smiling, but Angeline saw nothing funny in his question. "Which one of us would you divorce?" she asked. She turned and looked across the room. A lizard was climbing up a wall, but she was used to that now. She gave it no thought.

"Angie, you know better than that. I'm not backing out on anyone. I'm just feeling that my life has changed, and I wish it hadn't. I told you before, I'll always love you. And I do mean *always*. For eternity."

Angeline believed that. But her eternities seemed to start every morning, and they lasted far into the night. She needed something in her life, some sense of fulfillment that she couldn't grasp right now.

CHAPTER 14

Morgan had made up his mind that he was not going to mope around the rest of his life. He had to accept his new situation and make the best of it. His farm needed attention, Ruth's room needed to be completed, and Lyman and Eb needed his help. So he threw himself into his work. Without exactly intending to do it, he felt himself creating distance between himself and both his wives. Their needs were important, he knew, but he didn't know how to relieve the tension and make everything right for them. He was taking turns, spending a week with one and then the other, but he found it easier not to be home very much.

The fact was, Morgan had another worry that was insisting on his attention. There had been little rain, and summer was coming on, when storms would be rare for many months. All the farmers were depending on the canal now, and there simply wasn't enough water. Dry winds had come often lately, and the canal had filled with sand several more times. Water turns had been shortened, and that was creating some hard feelings between brothers. It was hard to watch young sprouts burn up in the sun and yet to hold back on taking enough water to reach an entire field.

As summer came on, the desert—the heat, the sand, the blowing dust—seemed like an enemy that had been lurking during the winter, just waiting to inflict its violence again. This was not some goodly earth that brought forth its fruits; it was a lone and dreary world.

Morgan got up very early one morning, planning to let Angeline sleep a little longer. He slipped outside to feed his oxen, chickens, and a young sow he had purchased recently from a neighbor. As he was standing outside the door and pulling his boots on, he saw a man riding toward him on a big mule. "Morgan," the man called out, and Morgan recognized that it was Bishop Barkley. "The canal is filled up again. Grab your shovel." Bishop Barkley had built a house on the bench now, but a number of the people were staying at the fort. The bishop looked after the members on the bench as well as the ones by the river.

Morgan had heard the wind in the night. He wasn't surprised that the ditch had filled up again. He had had enough of this. The canal was the source of most of their problems—so much of their water leaching into the sand—and it was hopeless to dig it out time and again.

But what he said was, "Where do you need me, Bishop?"

"North, maybe half a mile, is the worst."

"If you don't mind," Morgan said, "I'll feed my animals before I head up that way."

"That's fine. We can't start until the sun rises anyway—but that won't be long."

By then Angeline had come to the door. "Is it the canal again?" she asked.

"Yes," Morgan said. "Another day wasted—and another day without water. I see no point in going on with this."

Angeline would normally have had something to say about that, but in these weeks since Morgan had returned from Salt Lake

City she had lost some of her feistiness. "Don't work too long in the sun," was all she said.

Something in the flatness in her voice seemed to extract the life out of his own spirit. He didn't answer. He merely went about feeding his animals, and then he walked north in the dim light. He hadn't gone far before he saw someone ahead of him—someone limping just a little. He knew it had to be Lyman Hunt.

"Lyman, is that you?" he called out. Lyman stopped and turned back. "Should you be walking this far on your bad foot?" Morgan asked.

"It's getting better," Lyman said, but his voice sounded as wilted as Angeline's. "The question is, should any of us be digging out this useless canal one more time?"

"I've been thinking that for months now," Morgan said. When he caught up, Lyman turned, and the two walked on together, each with a shovel over his shoulder. "We have to do what we can to save this year's crops, but I don't see any reason to stay on the bench another year."

"You're not the only one who feels that way, Morgan. I think we need to call a meeting and figure out what we're going to do."

"That's exactly right," Morgan said. "I talked to Bishop Barkley about this a few days ago. When Joseph Young came down this spring, he said Brigham wants some folks to move to that area where the Virgin River and the Colorado come together. He thinks a southern train line is going to be built through there. The trouble with that is, people keep pulling out of this mission, and if it keeps going that way, who's going to be left here to keep this canal, or any canal, running?"

"That's not the worst of it. Erastus Snow says we ought to give up this town and move farther north—but stay on the bench."

"I know. Bishop Morrison told me that, but I told him then,

and I'll say it again, I'm not obeying this time. We've been told what to do so many times our heads are spinning, but I'm going to do what *I* think is best this time around."

"Most of the men are saying the same thing," Lyman said. "Some want to move down off the bench closer to Mill Point. They're calling the place Overton. Others are saying they'd rather go back to the old St. Joseph."

"Well, I've got a different idea. I'm going to go with what I wanted to do when we left West Point. I want to move to St. Thomas. It's the only town that's starting to get somewhere. There are empty houses down there that we could move into and fields that have been grubbed and planted before."

"That sounds like the best idea I've heard," Lyman said. "What about the new people who came in during the winter? What are they going to do?"

"The ones I've talked to say they'll probably help get this Overton site established."

During the winter a small group of new settlers had been called to the Muddy. Most of them were from Nephi, and they were experienced pioneers and strong families. Morgan had been especially impressed with Alexander Hart, George Clairmont, and Tobias Carrington. These men had realized from the beginning that the sand bench was no place to farm, but they and their wives were committed to fulfilling the callings they had received. They added new life to the mission; Morgan was sure they would become leaders. Bishop Morrison had hinted too often lately that Morgan should lead, and that idea still didn't appeal to him.

Morgan could see, even in the dim light, that Lyman had trimmed his beard and cut his hair higher in back so that it was off his neck. It was what most of Morgan's friends were doing now as they got ready for their second summer. Morgan had always kept his hair quite short, and he troubled himself to shave quite often. He sometimes told people it was what Angeline preferred, but the truth was, he looked at himself in a looking glass now and then, and he thought he looked better—younger—without a beard. What he didn't do was ask himself why he cared.

Lyman and Morgan walked on and found other men just beginning to dig. They spent all day clearing sand. But all the talk was that, when fall came, with permission or without, they were leaving the bench.

• • •

The early crops had produced meager yields. Cotton survived the drought better than other plants, so the hope was that the Muddy River farmers would still produce enough cotton to sell in St. George, where provisions could be obtained to replace the lost crops. But most of the men had planted more grain this year, knowing that it was what they needed to feed their families, and the price of cotton had fallen off even further. Morgan knew that the only way they could survive was to help each other. He felt that no one would go hungry if everyone shared.

By July the heat had turned vicious again. Morgan had finished the walls on Ruth's room before the worst of the heat had come on, and he had gathered marsh reeds and mesquite limbs to build a roof, but he hadn't found time to do it. The truth was, he wasn't motivated to do so. He had become accustomed to the pattern of staying in one house at a time, and he thought maybe that was easier than trying to bring Ruth and Angeline together. But Angeline visited Ruth one day, and afterwards she told Morgan, "We need to move Ruth and Jeffy over here. Their house is hotter than ours. I don't think her first husband made his adobes thick enough."

"I don't know how a house could be hotter than this one," Morgan said. They were sitting at their new table, but neither was eating much supper, and both were soaking with sweat.

"I've had a wicked thought lately," Angeline said. "Sometimes I want to take my temple garments off. It would be such a relief not to wear them until the end of summer."

"We all have that thought, no doubt. But—"

"I know. I would never really do it." Still, she had unbuttoned some of the buttons at the top of her dress, and now, instead of eating, she used her old fan to create a little air on her neck.

"Do you actually want Ruth to be here?" Morgan asked.

"Morgan, don't ask me that. What I want is to do the right thing. Jeffy looks as though he can't take much more, and Ruth is beside herself with worry. You should know that."

"I guess it's gotten worse this week." He hesitated, let her look at him directly, before he asked, "Why did you go over there?"

"I just wanted to see how they were doing."

"You like to tell me what a good man I am, but, Angie, you're better than I'll ever be. Thanks for looking after them." He was already thinking about the difficulty of crowding them into the house. The extra bedroom would help, and if they all ate dinner together, or spent evenings in the main room, there were four chairs and a bed, but hardly enough room for Jefferson to play. Morgan had always wanted to plaster the walls, but he hadn't found the time, and he hated the way the packed mud looked inside—as though they lived underground, not in a true house. He had always liked to imagine having a family, and he supposed having Ruth and Jefferson in the house would be the start of that, but he didn't like to picture his family in this place, which to him was still a sort of hovel, like the mud houses the Pah Utes lived in.

"Don't call me good," Angeline said. "I know what I've been feeling about Ruth."

"I'll call you good if I want to. It's what you are."

Angeline rolled her eyes and turned away from him, but then she asked, "Can you finish the roof on her bedroom one of these days?"

So later that evening he worked on the roof, and a couple of days later he had it finished—in spite of the heat and in spite of everything else he had to do. Then, early the next morning, he drove his wagon to Ruth's house, loaded her bed and furniture, and brought her and Jefferson to the house.

Life together began.

Jefferson still suffered with the heat. He couldn't play outside except early in the morning, and by afternoon the temperature inside was debilitating. Everyone slept outside on a little platform that Morgan had built to replace the wagon box. It kept them off the ground, where snakes and tarantulas and scorpions could move among them. This meant that Morgan shared no bed with either woman, and, for the present, that seemed the least of anyone's concerns.

• • •

It was just after sunup on a September morning, and Angeline was harvesting a few dried-up squashes from the garden. Morgan was getting ready to head to the farm lot outside town. Ruth had fried him some eggs on the outdoor fire and then served them to him in the house. After eating, Morgan had walked out to the garden. Ruth was still inside, and Angeline was glad to have the chance to talk to Morgan alone.

But it was Morgan who had something on his mind. "I've been wanting to ask you something," he said.

Angeline was kneeling in the dirt, but she looked up at him now. She heard something she liked in his voice: a little more lightness than she had heard for a time. "So ask me," she said, smiling at him.

"Bishop Morrison asked me to make another trip to St. George. I'm thinking I can maybe get away in a week or two. I was wondering, would you like to go with me this time?"

"What about the garden?" she asked, even though she knew how much she wanted to go, wanted to be alone with Morgan in the wagon again.

"Most of the garden is burned up already," Morgan said. "Ruth can harvest what's left."

"I guess. But I hate to leave her alone. It's such a lonely life when you're gone." She stood up and stretched her back.

Morgan stepped closer to her. He smiled. "So don't you want to go? You always told me before, you wished you could go with me."

"I know. And I do want to go. But—"

"No 'buts.' I'll talk to Ruth. She'll be fine with it." He touched her cheek. "We need this, Angie. We both do."

"All right," she said, and she felt an old swelling inside her that she thought she had forgotten. She loved Morgan. She could hardly believe how much that little touch of her cheek meant to her. Morgan was a practical man who would rather work than sleep, but there was tenderness in him, too. Sometimes she didn't see it for weeks at a time—and she knew that was because he was hiding now, not knowing how to live with two women. But it was still there, and it wasn't something she detected in most of the men she had known in her life, or that she saw around her now, here in this settlement. Men seemed to take on a manner of living that was handed down to them from fathers, or from other men around them, that made them feel "less than a man" by showing a bit of emotion, admitting to fear, expressing softer feelings to women. But Morgan, as distant as he could be at times, seemed to understand that a touch or a whisper could change everything. She didn't want half of Morgan; she wanted all of him. But she was still thankful she at least had her part.

Angeline's spirits rose considerably as she prepared for the trip to St. George. The actual experience, however, was not as joyous as she had hoped it would be. The heat didn't go away, even if it lightened a little, and the river still had to be crossed. Morgan had borrowed a second yoke of oxen for this trip, but that only meant that he could push the animals longer and put in more hours trudging ahead. Still, there was time to talk, and Morgan—whenever he wasn't preoccupied by the river or the needs of the oxen—did talk more openly with her than he had even on that first newlywed trip. That hadn't been very long ago, really, but so much had changed that it seemed another time, another life. Angeline liked the reminiscing they found themselves doing. It linked them back to the time when there had been no Ruth.

One evening, after stopping rather late, Morgan said, "Let's not bother with a fire. We don't need any more heat tonight." Angeline was fine with that. The heat took her appetite away. In the shadow of the canyon walls, with a little breeze blowing through the river valley, she did feel refreshed. What she missed was the light of the fire, but Morgan got out a coal-oil lamp and lit that. They sat with the lamp in front of them, and then they stretched out on the grass next to one another.

"Morgan," Angeline asked, "do you think we'll spend the rest of our lives on the Muddy?"

"I never ask myself that question," Morgan said. "I can take one day at a time—or one summer at a time—but when I think of the long term, I feel as though we've been sent to purgatory and surely our punishment has to end someday." He chuckled.

"If you ask me," Angeline said, "it's the other place. And we've been sentenced to burn forever."

"I know. It seems that way." His voice sounded wistful. "But we'll be all right if we stay, don't you think?"

"I don't know, Morgan." She could see a strip of stars straight above, and she thought of her nights in Farmington. Sometimes she and her brothers and sisters had slept outside in the summer, and they would look at the stars and try to remember the names of the constellations. But nights had always cooled there, and by morning she would be pulling a quilt tight around her. She wished she could have just that much—gentler air at night. It was the relentlessness of the heat she found so exhausting. "You told me once before that it's our stubbornness that will keep us going. I'd rather be somewhere else, but I still like to think that we're doing something hard and we're not quitting, even though so many others have backed out."

"I agree. But there are things that don't add up for me. All our leaders told us that if we left West Point and moved to the bench, we'd be blessed for our obedience. But it didn't happen. I believed it was a bad decision, and now I know it was. And everyone agrees with me now. Almost every man living on the bench has agreed to leave this fall—some of them say they're leaving the mission entirely. I won't do that. I'll keep my promise, if you will, but I won't keep digging out that canal."

This was nothing new for Morgan to say. He and Angeline had talked the matter over many times, and they had decided, at least tentatively, to move to St. Thomas in the fall. Bishop Morrison had promised them a house and farm—and he was no longer telling them that he wanted them to stay where they were.

"If either Apostle Snow or Joseph Young asks me why we're moving," Morgan said, "I'll tell them that we were called to the Muddy Mission, and we're keeping that commitment, but they have to let us choose where we live. I'll say the same thing on Judgment Day, standing before the Lord."

"That's how I feel too. But I can only think like that when I picture the whole of eternity and remember what life is for. What I feel most of the time is that an August day on the Muddy is like a month in northern Utah, and it's those miserable days that make eternity seem too long."

Morgan laughed. "Well, I guess we're assured of having long lives."

Angeline rolled her head to the side and smiled at Morgan. She liked to have time to talk to him, but life did look long and difficult at the moment. She looked back at the stars. She tried to think about eternity, how space and time stretched on and on forever. It was impossible to understand. But now, if she understood what the Brethren called "celestial marriage," she would also be with Ruth forever. That seemed more of a test than August heat or dust storms. Day by day she was dealing with her new reality, but seeing the big picture only reminded her that she would never have Morgan again, not in the same way. Even as she lay here next to him, Ruth was there, always part of her life. "I guess polygamy is the same way," she whispered. "It's our test. And the Lord will praise us for it."

"I hope so."

Angeline was thinking that the reward for staying on their mission was to live in a better place, but polygamy didn't work that way. It simply continued. She wondered whether Morgan was thinking that too, but he didn't say so. What he did was roll on his side. And he touched her neck, softly. For now, she wanted to think about that, and not measure her life by the many days that made up eternity.

● ● ●

Life felt a little better to Morgan after he and Angeline returned from their hauling trip to St. George. He felt they had reconnected during the time alone with each other. And as fall began, he became more confident that he would have enough food to sustain his family through another season. But now he was busy again. The home he and Angeline had been promised in St. Thomas had been vacant for a time, and it was full of drifted sand, lizards, and spiders. The roof had mostly blown away and needed repair, and Morgan also needed to add a room for Ruth, as he had done in their house on the bench. His five-acre farmland would need to be plowed again for planting winter wheat, and he had been allotted a two-and-a-half-acre plot for planting an orchard or a vineyard or both. He spent his days harvesting his grain and picking cotton on his sand-bench farm, but he tried to set aside one or two days a week to work on his St. Thomas property. It was a ten-mile trip to St. Thomas from the bench, so he usually walked down in the evening, slept there, worked the next day, and returned the following evening. Or, if he needed his oxen, he drove the wagon there.

He did feel, now, that when everything was finished, he would have a better house and a better farm—a place where he would have a chance to prosper. The big worry for the present was that St. Thomas was getting inadequate water from the canal and the drought was continuing. Erastus Snow had introduced a plan for a new set of canals that would share the water more fairly and avoid some of the difficulties of the long canal on the bench. Of course, that meant more digging, but at least there seemed a chance that better days might be ahead. So far, except for the small profits he made from his hauling excursions, Morgan felt that he was making no progress. He was getting by, and that was all. He had hoped to make a trip to Sheep Mountain to bring back timber, but he had not found time for that. What he wanted to do was to build a house that looked and felt more like the house he had grown up in. He had removed the window frames and doors from the house on the bench and reinstalled them in the St. Thomas house, and he thought he had learned enough about roofing with willows and reeds that he could stop leaks when rain finally came. But it was still an adobe house that felt primitive, and, for now, there was nothing he could do about that.

As the weather cooled a little, he noticed that Angie seemed more at ease. She and Ruth also spent more time together. Their conversations were less awkward lately, and they had parceled out household chores.

One evening, when Morgan returned from St. Thomas, Angeline and Ruth were sitting outside on chairs they had taken from the house. "What are you two up to?" Morgan asked as he approached them.

"Stargazing," Angeline said. "It's such a nice night."

But Ruth got up. "Good night," she said. "I need to check on Jefferson, and then I think I'll go to bed."

Morgan knew that was her way of giving him and Angeline some time together. It was Angeline's week, and Ruth and Angie had gradually learned to be generous in granting one another privacy with Morgan.

Ruth said good night, and as soon as she had walked around the corner of the house, Angeline stood and embraced Morgan.

He knew immediately, from the quickness of her motion and the tightness of her arms around him, that she was happier than she had been all summer.

"I have something I want to tell you," she said.

"If you give me three guesses, I think I could tell you what it is."

"Only one guess. But don't say it. I want to say it myself." She tightened her hold around him again, and she whispered in his ear, "I'm expecting."

"That's good, Angie." But Morgan knew he had to be careful. He didn't want her to think that he was only satisfied with their marriage when she was able to have babies.

Angeline stepped back. "Do you think God will bless us this time?" she asked.

"It's hard to say. Just don't worry so much about—"

"I think He will. We're trying to do all the right things. I know we're moving off the bench, but we're sticking with the mission. It's also the best time of year to be with child. I can have the baby before the summer heat comes back—in May, I think. I haven't been terribly sick, either. I feel really good this time."

Morgan hoped she was right. But he had already learned one thing: trouble sometimes came to people who tried to do the right things. Morgan had talked to a man named William Preston in St. Thomas that week. He and his wife had come to the Muddy with four children, and they had had a fifth since then. But this summer, when the ague came on, all of their children had fallen sick, and two had died. They had lost their youngest little girl, not yet a year old, and a six-year-old son. Brother Preston had tried to talk about it without emotion, but he had suddenly broken down at the mere words "William Junior." Morgan had patted Brother Preston on the shoulder, not quite knowing what to say. Since then, he had been telling himself that life was full of heartaches, and he had no reason to think he and Angeline would be spared such pain. Still, Morgan had not said anything to Angeline about the Prestons. She believed she would carry this baby, and he promised himself to trust in her faith.

• • •

In late November, the house in St. Thomas was ready, and the Davises moved off the bench. The house was slightly larger but no nicer than the one they had been living in. Still, that had been Ruth's way of life for many years now, and she no longer thought much about it. At least the town was bigger, and the members there were mostly tried and true at this point. Morgan and Angeline's friends had become her friends, and Ruth was glad that all of them had chosen to move to St. Thomas with the Davises. Their families were spread out across the settlement in homes they had been able to take over, but Ruth had begun to reach out to them, to offer help where she could or merely visit on her own, without Angeline always going along.

Ruth was learning some things about herself. The time alone, when Morgan and Angeline had been gone on their trip to St. George, had been good for her. She had managed alone before, and she found she could do it again. She even worried that she had let herself become too dependent on Morgan. She felt that she needed to build up her own self-confidence now. Morgan would always be pulled away from her at least half the time, and she couldn't feel sorry for herself every time he spent his week with Angeline.

The church building—along with the congregation—was larger in St. Thomas. During meetings, Ruth found herself singing hymns with more enthusiasm. She had always been a good singer, but for years now, she had sung softly or hadn't sung at all. It had been part of her desire not to be noticed, to live among her neighbors without intruding her sadness upon them. Now she was accepted in a new way. Everyone liked Morgan and Angeline, and Ruth had become part of them. Or maybe, Ruth wondered, it was the opposite. Maybe she felt different now that she was Morgan Davis's wife, and perhaps she related to people in new ways.

What she hadn't expected was to be asked to sing with a choir that was preparing for a Christmas concert, and then to be chosen to sing a solo. After rehearsals, almost everyone had told her at one time or another that she had a beautiful voice. And Sister Humboldt, a lovely older woman, had said to her, "Ruth, I never noticed how pretty you are—not until lately. When you sing, your countenance brightens, and those beautiful eyes of yours start to shine."

Ruth denied it all, told Sister Humboldt that she was not pretty, that she never had been. And yet, she believed it a little. She wasn't pretty; she was sure of that. But how many women were? She looked good enough, she supposed, and Morgan made her feel pretty when they were alone.

Jefferson was doing better too, as the heat diminished. And she had stopped worrying about the boy liking Angeline's stories. Ruth liked them too, and when Angeline became animated and involved in her tales, she seemed happier than at any other time. The truth was, it was nice to have someone help to entertain Jefferson. Ruth never had been good at thinking up stories, let alone telling them.

One night in December, after Jefferson was in bed, Ruth stayed in the main room of the house. "Thanks so much for playing with Jefferson," she said to Angeline. "I think you love him just as much as I do, and that means he gets double love. It's just what he needs."

"Oh, Ruth," Angeline said, "it's what I need more than Jeffy ever does." This was a new tone of voice for Angeline.

Ruth looked across the room at Morgan, who was using a whetstone to sharpen a butcher knife. "And Morgan," Ruth said, "you're very kind to Jefferson too. He can hardly wait for you to come into the house at night."

"That's good," Morgan said. And then he laughed. "Well, now, aren't we a happy family?"

Ruth laughed too, and she saw Angeline smiling. She supposed they were all thinking the same thing: it was an odd arrangement, but it was starting to feel fairly comfortable.

• • •

A couple of weeks later, Morgan was in bed with Ruth when she whispered to him, "Morgan, I haven't said anything, but I've known for a time, I'm in a family way."

Morgan had sensed that, and he had been waiting for Ruth to say something, but now he told her, "Don't tell Angeline just yet."

"I think she knows. Women can see it in each other."

"All right. But let's give it as much time as we can. You understand, don't you?"

"Not really. She told me yesterday that she's with child—and she's very happy about it. Mine won't be so hard for her this way. I didn't say anything about my own condition. I wanted to tell you first."

"What I know is that she's still fearful, whether she says so or not. It would be very difficult if she had the same trouble as last time and you carried your baby."

"All right. I understand that. But I don't want us to know things she doesn't. I would rather be honest with her."

Morgan tried to think about that. He finally said, "But it has to be that way at times, Ruth. I can't tell you everything that Angie and I talk about. I don't know how to do that. And we don't have to say *everything* to Angeline."

Ruth was quiet for a time, her soft breath the only sound. "It's strange," she finally said. "We're not all married to each other. Angeline and I are each married to you."

That, of course, was the case, but Morgan had never grasped until now what inherent imbalance was caused by that state of things. He had entered into a life he hadn't understood, but he was realizing that it was too much to ask of him to keep things exactly even and balanced.

"Morgan?"

"Yes."

"You didn't say how you feel about the baby."

"I'm sorry, Ruth. It's wonderful. I'm very happy about it."

And that was true. He wanted children, wanted to be a father. The truth was, though, right now it still seemed that Angeline's babies would be *his* children and that Ruth's would be, somehow, a little different—maybe like Jefferson. He knew that was a terrible way to think, and something else he could never admit to Ruth. So he told her again how happy he was, and he held her in his arms, even though he still worried what it would do to Angeline if Ruth carried her baby and Angeline didn't.

CHAPTER 15

Another mild winter passed away, and the good weather helped everyone in St. Thomas feel better. Angeline had felt a sudden stab, sharp but quick, when she had first learned for certain that Ruth was pregnant, but her growing confidence in her own pregnancy was now softening the emotion. As days went by, the two found joy in their similar circumstance. When Morgan wasn't in the house, they often talked about their satisfaction and their discomforts, and Angeline found herself feeling closer to Ruth than she ever had expected to be. It was also good that they could share their chores and ease each other's burdens.

Angeline's fear, of course, never really left her. If something should go wrong again this time, and Ruth delivered her baby next summer, she knew how difficult that would be. But she didn't want to think that way, didn't want to blame anything on Ruth. Mostly, she hoped that all would be well for both of them. Her silent prayers became loud in her own head and so continual that she felt as though her every moment was filled with beseeching.

Ruth was also reaching out more all the time, visiting the sisters in the settlement, singing in church, and taking on an openness to others that no one had known from her before. As strenuous work for Angeline became increasingly difficult, Ruth carried more of the load. Angeline had never been one to shirk her duties, but Ruth gradually spoke with more command. She told Angeline to lie down and rest for a time each day. Ruth's kindness touched Angeline, and, even though she resisted being guided, she liked the good will behind the advice, and she began to accept guidance more than she ever had in her life.

Ruth could be interesting, too. She had experienced hard challenges and had gradually become willing to share her thoughts and feelings with Angeline. The more the two talked, the more they understood one another. They didn't exactly talk behind Morgan's back, but sometimes they laughed at his little quirks. Angeline told Ruth one day, "He claims every morning that he has more to do than he can keep up with, but then I hear from people that he's been over to their farm helping out. The truth is, he loves to be busy—and he hates more than anything to admit that he's actually a good man."

"He also likes to get away from us, I think," Ruth said, and they both laughed.

"We chatter too much. I heard him say that to Eb one time, but he would never say that to us."

"He's too polite for that. He apologizes every time he burps. He's taught Jefferson to do that too—and I never could."

"He gets all that from his father," Angeline said. "Brother Davis was hardworking, the same as Morgan, but he was always quick to open a door for a woman, or to say 'please' and 'thank you.'"

"It's nice. I'd swear that some of our men were born in a barn. They snort like hogs when they blow their noses, and they scratch themselves in places that I'd rather not look at."

Angeline had also noticed the crudeness in some of the men. Bishop Morrison was a polite man, and so were a few others, but most Mormon men, she thought, had been away from fancy parlors and dining rooms for a long time now, and some of them had grown up in log cabins in the middle of forests, where the society was made up of hoot owls and raccoons.

"What makes me laugh," Ruth said, "is the way Morgan pretends not to know how handsome he is, and yet he shaves two or three times a week, and he combs his hair nice and neat before he plops his hat on top."

"It's not just that. At church the women all like to look him over. I told him that one time, and he said he'd never noticed. And then he grinned and said, 'Well, some of the unmarried girls talk and giggle a little when I come around. I never have figured that one out.'"

"Maybe he'll like that more and more as he gets older," Ruth suggested.

That stopped the laughter. What Angeline knew was that some young women liked a mature man better than the boys their own age—the ones who still had to get started in life. She worried about that. Ruth was turning out to be a sister she could live with, but Angeline hated to think about some pretty young girl competing for Morgan's attention.

But Ruth told Angeline, "I don't think Morgan will look around for another wife. I'm quite sure he feels he's got his hands full, just dealing with the two of us. My guess is, he'll never want any further complications in his life."

"I think you're right."

Angeline knew exactly what Ruth was saying. Clearly, Ruth loved Morgan, and she didn't want another competitor any more than Angeline did. Angeline still didn't like to think that another woman loved her husband, but at least Morgan hadn't gone looking for that second wife—he had accepted a call. Back in Farmington, Angeline had known a woman, Sister Reed, who had watched her husband take on a second and third wife at the same time, both under twenty. After that, he'd made a fool of himself parading them around, one on each arm, grinning with pride and tolerating their silliness without ever correcting them. Angeline had heard her mother tell a friend, "Ol' Franklin Reed goes from one of those young girls to the other, and never spends a night at home. It's disgraceful."

Angeline had thought so too, even as a little girl, before she had understood everything about sleeping at one house or another. One thing she could tell herself was that Morgan would never be like that.

•   •   •

In March of 1870, after having spent the winter in St. George, Brigham Young finally made a trip to the Muddy Valley before he returned to Salt Lake City. He brought George A. Smith, his First Counselor, and Smith's wife, Bathsheba, and also Joseph Young, his nephew.

The weather was getting warm, but it didn't seem bad yet to the settlers who had spent some summers there. Still, Brigham was obviously surprised by how far the season had already progressed. Morgan heard him say that it was much hotter at the Muddy than it was in St. George.

Joseph Young, along with Bishop Morrison and some of the other leaders, had worked hard to prepare for Brigham's visit. They had built a boat, at his request, that they could use to take him across the Colorado River. He had written ahead that he wanted to look for possible settlement sites there. But the word that spread through the settlements as Brother Brigham traveled along the Muddy was that he was disappointed by the country he was seeing.

By the time he reached the Colorado River, he had decided not to bother with crossing over to see more of the same kind of land.

The stunning news Morgan heard was that Brigham had actually told the group traveling with him that he was not sure he saw any commercial or agricultural future in the Muddy Valley. Morgan—and everyone else—could hardly believe that he would say such things. Was Brigham changing his mind about the mission itself? As word of Brigham's disillusionment spread, the Saints were perplexed, even a little insulted. They had worked so hard to make the best of their plight, and they were actually starting to take hold, it seemed. They had been called to serve by Brigham, assured by him and other leaders that their call was inspired, and now they wondered whether Brigham was regretting his decision.

Morgan saw Lyman Hunt one evening as they were both walking back from their farms. Lyman looked around, pretending to check for anyone listening, and then he whispered, "So has Brigham decided to change God's mind—or is it the other way around?"

Morgan couldn't laugh. He had wrestled hard over his own decision to keep his commitments to this mission; it was painful to think that Brigham would make a quick visit and start hinting that he had made a mistake.

Meetings were held the following day in St. Thomas, and, in spite of the rumors, it was a grand moment for the settlers to see the President of the Church among them. Brigham rode into town in a carriage drawn by four horses, with his other Salt Lake City visitors with him. Brigham was a stout man, but he looked small when he stepped down from the carriage and stood next to President Smith, a man of greater proportions. Sister Smith looked not only small but considerably younger than her husband, although President Smith, cousin of Joseph Smith, was not, as far as Morgan could reckon, too many years beyond fifty. Sister Smith was nicely dressed, which would not have been noticeable in Salt Lake, but here in St. Thomas she looked like a grand lady. She wore a dark taffeta dress that glimmered in the sunlight and a lacy shawl over her shoulders—in spite of the heat.

Morgan had almost forgotten how much he liked Brigham Young. The man began greeting everybody, one by one. When he came to Morgan, he shook his hand with a hard pumping motion and said, "Brother Davis, I've heard great reports about you. Thank you for staying with this mission. Most of the folks I sent down with you turned tail on me, but you stayed."

Morgan nodded. "I wasn't the only one," he said. "Quite a few of us stayed."

There was a great deal he could have added, but he didn't say any of it. What he felt was the satisfaction of hearing the President speak well of him.

"I remember when I asked you to find a wife and you told me you didn't think you could. But look at you, standing here with two wives," Brigham said. He smiled at Angeline and then Ruth, shook both of their hands. "I remember approving your application to marry this fine sister." He put a hand on Ruth's shoulder. "I love and respect you young people who embrace the fulness of the new and everlasting covenant. The Lord will bless you and prosper you—all three of you." Then he laughed suddenly and deeply. "You'll prosper greatly, Brother Davis, and prove to be such a fine leader, wherever you are. You'll be sending in more applications in time. And that will be a blessing for all of you, over and over."

Morgan couldn't bring himself to tell Brother Brigham that he had no such intentions. He only laughed, and then he did say, "We've had a tough go of it in this valley, but we're all trying our best to make a good town here."

"Yes, yes. I know what you're saying. I've had much to think about since I laid eyes on this desert and this dirty little river. I don't think I ever understood why so many gave it up, but I guess I can see it now."

That was a good thing to say, in some ways, just to know that the President understood the challenge, but he did sound as though he had changed his mind about the mission—and that raised all sorts of questions for Morgan.

Brigham kept shaking hands, remembering people, greeting them warmly, and then he invited everyone to come into the little church building. Once inside, Joseph Young conducted the meeting, but after the opening hymn and prayer, he turned the entire time over to Brother Brigham.

Brigham laughed when he stood up, and he said, "I'll have to admit, you folks look a little worse for wear down here. I've seen two men wearing bedding sheets for trousers, and both told me the same thing: 'Better than nothing, President.' And I must say, I agree with them entirely. I've been down to nothing a few times in my life, and that made any sort of breeches look mighty good."

Then he told the Saints how much he appreciated their noble efforts, their hard work, and their sacrifices. He told them they were the best of the best, people who made covenants and kept them, people who were willing to battle the elements, no matter how challenging. He made comparisons to the Saints who had sacrificed everything they possessed in Jackson County, Missouri, and then again in Nauvoo, Illinois. "It's harder to find that kind of true pioneers anymore," he said. "We've had things too easy in recent years. Some of you lived through those harder times, and they made you strong, but you younger folks are made of the same stuff your parents were. It's on the shoulders of people like you that the kingdom will continue to take shape here in these mountains and valleys of the West."

Morgan liked all that, and he could see Angeline and Ruth nodding their agreement. Angeline's eyes even filled with tears, and Morgan knew why. She worried that she and Morgan had complained too much, doubted the Lord, and it was good for her to hear that they were some of the strong ones.

But Morgan could hear something in Brigham's voice, in his carefully chosen words. He seemed to be building toward some sort of announcement.

And finally it came: "As you know, I've been traveling about this valley, assessing the work you've done here and trying to determine what the future might hold for the Church in this region. I must admit, this area was somewhat misrepresented to me. I thought it would be suitable for commerce, with river travel on the Colorado connecting here from the Pacific Coast, and I thought we could extend the cotton mission here and do very well. But I have my doubts after looking at this dry desert and this puny river. You have worked against the heat and the lack of water, and you've done your best, but I'm not certain that we have a good future here."

The room was still. All Morgan could hear was the flies buzzing in the room. The people seemed to be holding their breaths, as though they didn't quite believe what they had heard. Some might have been waiting to hear that they were released from the mission, and they might have been happy about that. But Morgan was still thinking about the word *misrepresented*. What did that mean? Where had Brigham sought his information?

But Brother Brigham didn't announce that he was closing the mission. He mentioned that a question had come up about whether the Muddy settlements were actually in Nevada, not in

Utah or Arizona territories. That brought up questions about taxes. He said that he had to get a ruling about state and territory boundaries before he made any recommendations about what the people should do. He admonished them to work on, continue to make the desert blossom, and he would advise them further before much longer.

People left the meeting in an obvious state of wonder. They glanced at one another as though they hoped someone would interpret the things they had heard. Should they be resigned to stay, hopeful to leave, or frustrated by not knowing what they would do? Everything was suddenly as murky as the Muddy River, which was bad enough, but what had they all heard for so long? The prophet had called them, and he was guided by the Lord.

Morgan walked with Angeline and Ruth, but they too seemed to be waiting. Morgan knew he had to be careful what he said. Once in the house, he sat down at the table. For a time he merely stared ahead. He didn't want to say something rash or bitter, but he was remembering everything that had been said by leaders, and everything he had said to convince himself he had to stay here. His confusion, with each step, had been turning into anger as he had walked away from the meeting. He didn't want to be angry with Brigham Young. Brigham was called of God. He was a good man. Morgan liked him. But how could he contradict so many things that Morgan and the others had been told when they had been called to come here?

It was finally Angeline who asked the crucial question. "What did he mean when he said this valley had been misrepresented to him? Who misled him?"

Morgan chose his words carefully. He took a long breath before he said, "I guess some of the Brethren had been down here. I think he sent people to look the place over. They must have told him it looked like a good region to grow cotton. That's the only thing I can think of."

But then Morgan stood, abruptly. He caught himself again, didn't say what he was thinking. He merely stood in the middle of the little room and tried to calm himself. So much had been said to convince him to come here, and then to convince him to stay. What was he supposed to feel about that? Angie was sitting on the bed, and Ruth in one of the chairs. They both looked up at him. He couldn't stop himself from asking, "Didn't Bishop Morrison tell us to leave West Point because Brigham told us to, and he was guided by the Lord?"

Angeline seemed to know that she had put a match to dry kindling. She and Ruth were both nodding, accepting Morgan's words but at the same time seeming to say, *"But don't get too upset. Don't be angry at President Young—or God."*

Morgan still couldn't stop, though. "All I wanted to do was stay off that sand bench where I knew we couldn't get enough water, and what did they tell me? 'Brigham and Erastus know best. We need to gather up so the Indians won't attack us.' Well, look at what the Indians have been doing. They may steal a horse once in a while when they're hungry, but they haven't bothered the families that are living in West Point—or here. It sounds to me like Brigham was misled about Indians the same as he was about living in 120-degree heat in a place where there's not a tree for a hundred miles in any direction."

Morgan was still looking at his wives. Angeline, seven months pregnant, was swelling in front more than Ruth, but they mirrored each other, each with hands clasped together, each clearly frightened by the intensity of his voice and, surely, the only slightly controlled fury behind his words. And over in the corner, Jefferson had begun to cry.

So Morgan walked out. He didn't want to upset them any further. But he wasn't ready to calm down, either. Grabbing a hoe that was leaning against the house, he raised it in the air and was about to slam it into the ground, but he suddenly thought better of it. There was no way to buy or even make a new handle in this desert. He dropped the hoe and bent forward, with his hands on his knees. He tried to understand what he was feeling. He had told himself since he had first received his call to the Muddy that he had to be humble, had to listen even when he held different opinions from his leaders. And he had obeyed. But now Brigham wasn't bringing God into his decision at all. He was saying that someone had told him this was a good place, and he had believed it. How could Brigham send hundreds of people down here, commit them to make the desert blossom, then arrive, take a look around, and say he might have made a mistake—that the Muddy Valley had been *misrepresented*? The word itself was stunning, infuriating.

"I'll do what I want to do from now on," Morgan said out loud. "And the first thing is to get out of this desert. I'm going home." He waited a few moments, testing the idea against his emotions, but he was already wondering whether he could do it. He could defy Brigham, perhaps, but everyone said the Lord was standing close behind the prophet, looking over his shoulder. Morgan wasn't sure he was ready to take them both on.

• • •

Angeline heard Morgan's rumbling voice outside. She didn't know what to expect, how he would deal with this new reality once he had calmed. Or maybe he wouldn't calm.

"Ruth," Angeline said, "I don't know how to tell you what this has cost Morgan. He never wanted to leave home in the first place, and he made up his mind, as soon as he saw these valleys, that West Point was better for farming than the sand bench was. He went against everything that made sense to him because all our leaders said he needed to be obedient."

"I know, Angie. We talked about this when we were in the wagon, heading up to Salt Lake. He needs so much to be himself, and sometimes he's not sure who that is."

"It's more than that, Ruth. He carries his father on his shoulders. Brother Davis taught him day and night to be humble and follow his leaders. And now he's carrying the two of us, too. I don't know a man who tries harder to be a good husband. Everything inside him tells him to rebel, and yet the Spirit whispers to him that that way is destruction. He's struggled with this for a long time—maybe always—but I don't know what will happen this time. He might finally kick everyone aside, even God, and strike out on his own path."

Jefferson had come to Ruth, and she was holding him and rubbing her hand over his back. She kept whispering to him that everything was all right. "But what about you, Angeline? You went through all that building and rebuilding too. How do you feel?"

"I don't know, Ruth. But the next time someone tells me I should do something because it's what God wants, I'm going to do more asking and see whether God has anything to say to *me*."

• • •

Ruth had lived in the Muddy Valley for almost five years now, but she had never seen people quite so confused or upset. President Young had praised the Saints who had stayed, and his words had moved many to tears. Ruth herself had felt that she had exercised faith, even when she had lost her husband—and her faith had been rewarded. But Brigham's final statements left everything up in the air. He wanted them to stay for now, continue to consider themselves missionaries, but he had raised serious questions about whether that call would be rescinded. The President hadn't thoroughly explained the situation in the meeting, but he had told some of the leaders that the United States government was claiming that the Muddy settlements were in Nevada. Boundaries had been redrawn twice in the last few years, but local leaders had taken the position that they lived in either Utah or Arizona. Surveyors would be arriving before long to settle the question, but if the Saints were living in Nevada, that could mean trouble. Officials might be forceful in collecting back taxes.

The unsettled state of things left people wondering about whether they wanted to face another summer in the desert if they were only going to pull up and leave before long. Even some of the most ardently committed pioneers were now discussing whether it wasn't time to give up the effort. What had been proven was that some good crops could be raised, that orchards could be established, and cotton crops could be productive. But if cotton raising was their main purpose for staying, low cotton prices made the venture less promising than it had once seemed, and grain and fruit crops could surely be raised more productively in many other places. Why hadn't Brigham just told them to pick up and leave instead of suggesting that as a possibility and then getting back in his carriage and heading north?

Ruth didn't care much about all the details of the discussions she heard. What she cared about was the insecurity she felt—and she heard the same thing from all the sisters she talked to. "It's men who get their hard heads together and make all these decisions," Sister Bridehead had told her. "They don't even stop long enough to think what they're doing to their wives and children."

Ruth was sitting in one of the larger adobe houses in St. Thomas. But it was large only because Brother Bridehead had three wives, and all three had separate bedrooms. There was nothing fancy about the house, with the same unplastered adobe walls that everyone else had. Sometimes Ruth longed for a comfortable couch or chair to sit on. No one had much more than straight-backed chairs. Sister Bridehead had covered her chairs with old quilts to soften them, and she was sitting by a window where she could get a little sunlight as she mended a dress for her four-year-old daughter.

"I've fixed this dress so many times, I'm patching over patches," she told Ruth. "And now, with my new little boy, all the baby clothes I used to have are wore right out. It's lucky he doesn't need to wear much of anything right now, with the heat getting so bad." But then she laughed. "Don't I sound pitiful? You didn't come here to hear me complain. When's your baby due to come?"

"About three months, I think. But Angeline should be ready in three or four weeks."

"I know you two are feeling the heat more than any of us—except for about a dozen other sisters in the same condition. We may not get a good crop of cotton or wheat every year, but we surely do get all the babies we need."

Ruth laughed. Mary Bridehead was only in her early forties, but she had a grandmotherly quality about herself and an older woman's way of saying what she thought without worrying whether others approved.

"So, tell me this, Ruth," Mary said. "How do you like that young, good-looking husband of yours? I've never seen you so happy."

"Morgan's a good man. I feel blessed that he asked me to marry him."

"But he doesn't bother you now, does he, when you're in a family way?"

Mary had always been forward, but she had never asked anything quite so personal before. What Church leaders taught—at priesthood meetings, not during regular services—was that the purpose of being with a woman was for procreation. Once a wife was expecting, it was not good for her health, or the health of the baby, to indulge in physical pleasure for its own sake. Bern had not listened to such ideas, and she had never dared to deny him, but Morgan had been careful to adhere to the advice—and right now he had two wives he wasn't "bothering." Still, Ruth was not about to say anything to Mary about that part of her life. "Morgan is very kind to me—and careful of my well-being," was all she said.

"Well, that's fine. But men can fly from one flower to the next and make all the honey they want. They don't worry much about what the flowers want from them."

Ruth was not entirely sure what Mary meant by that, nor did she ask. She tried to change the subject. "What I hope more than anything right now is that my baby comes soon, and that everything will be all right with him—or her. Angeline and I both hope that one of us can give Morgan a son of his own. He hasn't said so, but I know he would be pleased by that."

"Yes, men always want sons. I guess that's to keep their name spreading, and they figure a boy can work alongside them. What they forget is that most of the work on a farm happens in the house and garden and corrals and barns and chicken coops. Men throw some seed in the ground and then talk about how hard they work. It's dirt and water and God that grow the crops. But it's women who milk the cows, more often than not, and then they have to make it into butter. Men ought to be praying for daughters if they're looking to get the work done."

Ruth laughed about all this, and actually, Mary seemed to know that she was entertaining Ruth with all her irreverent talk. "Well, there's plenty of work for all of us," Ruth said. "And Morgan never stops. When he isn't working on his own place, he's helping his friends."

"I know that about him. I've seen him do it. And how are things between you and Angeline? Do you get along all right?"

"Yes. Very well. It was uncomfortable for both of us at first, I think, but we've worked things out."

"What happens is, you come to a standoff. You learn to put up with each other. It's hard enough for me to live with two women I didn't choose. We each have our own way of doing things. But what makes it worse is that we all want our husband to pay us a little attention, and after all is said and done, we're just plain jealous of each other."

"I guess I've felt some of that." Ruth didn't want to admit how deeply she had felt it at times.

"Polygamy is not for weaklings. It's a cross to bear, if you ask me. Especially for the older wife, who started out thinking she had found herself a man and didn't have to hand over two-thirds of him to younger women."

"What about me? I'm the older woman but the new wife."

"Well, each situation is different. All I can say is that if I ever make it to heaven, I'm going to have a good chat with the Lord. They say He thought this whole thing up, but I'd like to know whether He just had a whim one day and decided to give it a try, or if He knew how complicated it would be."

Ruth smiled. "He knows everything, doesn't He?"

"That's what they tell me. It must be true."

Ruth stood. "Well, Sister Mary, I'm glad I stopped by. I was wondering how you might be doing after having another baby, but I think you're full of as much spit and vinegar as ever."

"Oh, yes. And I'm getting ready to be old. After fifty you can say pretty much what you want. No one pays any attention anyway."

"Well, you've started early. It's what I love about you, Mary. You speak your mind."

"Well, then, listen to one more pearl of wisdom."

"I would be happy to."

"Don't drive poor Brother Davis away. What women do is join forces after a while. They make a peace treaty, and they gradually worry more about their children than they do about their husband. As years go by, that young, handsome man becomes an old farmer, and when he comes home, he walks into a bees' nest of noise and confusion. Wives and children are all saying, 'Here, look at me.' So he just pulls away. It's too much for him, and he realizes he didn't have any idea what he was getting himself into, picking out extra wives. He'll want you once in a while, just to be with a friend, just to share some ideas or some feelings, and you'll say to yourself, 'Oh, oh. If he comes around too much, we'll make another baby, and I've got enough for now. If you're not careful, the day will come that you don't know each other, don't even need each other. And you'll both wonder why you aren't as happy as you're supposed to be."

"I think I've noticed just a little of that starting to happen already."

"Well, take care," Mary warned. "The best thing in life is having a close companion. I've lost that, and the worst part is, it's my fault as much as his."

It was something Ruth knew she had to think about. Amid all the talk and fuss about leaving the Muddy or not leaving, Ruth hadn't thought enough about being happy wherever she ended up. But she had started to miss Morgan lately. They didn't talk as much or as openly as they had on that long wagon ride to Salt Lake City and back. She wondered whether it would ever be possible to feel that close to him again.

CHAPTER 16

Morgan had thrown himself into his work once more. For the first few days after Brigham Young had met with the St. Thomas settlers, Morgan had been agitated night and day. During that time, he hadn't been able to bring himself to pray. But prayer had always kept him going. He didn't like to hear people who claimed that they had gotten "impressions," or "received answers," and then came out with some silly idea that God never in this world would have thought up—or at least that was how it seemed to him. But he had been turning to God all his life, and he couldn't bring himself to stop. He prayed with his wives before the family went to bed at night, then said his own prayers, and he prayed out on his farm or almost any time he was alone. Sometimes he just said, "Lord, help me understand this," but other times he explained everything he had been thinking—about being humble, about taking direction, and about trusting in his own power to reason—and he asked the Lord to help him sort everything out and find some sense in what he had experienced. Still, Morgan remained confused. He only knew that he felt better when he was praying than when he wasn't praying.

On Sunday, after church, Bishop Morrison called Morgan aside. They stood on the shady side of the church building, but the heat was everywhere; shade didn't help. The temperature had suddenly spiked to over one hundred degrees—and it was only May. The worst was still ahead, and the sudden change—a sign of what was to come—was numbing to Morgan's mind.

The bishop had put his hat on after coming out of church, but he took it back off now and held it in one hand while he used a handkerchief to wipe his face. Morgan could see sweat glowing in his hair and beard. He also felt dampness soaking through his own shirt under his arms and down his sides.

"Morgan," the bishop said, "I know you don't want to stand out here long—"

"It's just as hot in my house, Bishop. There's nowhere to hide this time of year."

"That's true. But I won't take long. I just wanted to ask you about something. I've been hearin' things."

"All right."

"Are you pullin' out?"

Morgan looked away from the bishop, out across the desert. The sun was turning the air into shimmering heat waves, and the mountains, even the nearby bluffs, all appeared a hazy gray. "I don't know what I'm going to do," Morgan said. "But what's Brother Brigham saying now? Are we all going to leave?"

"He hasn't said anythin'. This issue with the state border is what he's waiting to hear about. If we're declared citizens of Nevada, I'm thinkin' we probably will leave."

"All of us—all at once? Or what?"

"Yes. I think we should all stay or all go," Bishop Morrison said. "I hate to see people movin' off in a slow trickle. If that keeps happenin', we'll have no hope of keepin' things goin' here. And if you leave, a lot of folks will follow you."

"So you want me to stay to convince my friends to stay. Is that it?"

"I do."

"Even though we're all likely to leave before long anyway?" Morgan asked.

"Yes."

"Explain to me how that makes any sense."

"Don't do this, Morgan. This isn't like you."

"Because I'm a good boy and I do what I'm told. Is that it?"

"You are a good man, Morgan. And a leader. People look to you for guidance."

Morgan leaned against the building. It was hard to think with the heat filling up his head. He didn't want to be obstinate, not with this man he loved, but he really felt he needed to get away from this place. "Bishop, I'm having a hard time right now. You told me God wanted us to settle on the sand bench, so I did that. And how long was it before we found out there was no hope to get adequate water up there? It was what I had said all along. I followed your advice—even though my own good sense told me it was the wrong thing to do." He finally looked the bishop straight in the eye. "So now you tell me I ought to stay here, and I'm thinking that maybe it's time I listen to myself and stop taking orders."

The bishop straightened a little, lifted his chin. Morgan knew his words had gotten under Bishop Morrison's skin this time, but the bishop didn't sound angry when he said, "I'm not orderin' you, Morgan, and I never will. I never tol' you that I knew what God wanted. What I tol' you was that it was Brigham's advice, and I thought it was better to follow the prophet."

"And why is it better to follow the prophet? Isn't it because he has all the right answers? He prays, and then God sends him a telegram with the information he needs. Well, this time the telegraph lines must have been down."

"That's not how the Lord guides us. You know that, Morgan. Our plan is to inhabit all this land we've been provided here in the West. What Brigham sees is the eternal view of things, and he makes decisions that guide us toward buildin' the kingdom of God, bein' a Zion people—to work together and to prosper."

Morgan had thought plenty about that, and he wanted to be fair in his judgment, but it just seemed that too many things had gone wrong. "Brigham makes decisions that affect a lot of people—to start a sugar business or an iron business. He even told some of the Utah Saints to grow grapes and make them into rum. None of that worked out."

"And that's what I'm sayin'. God tells us to build a kingdom, but He doesn't give us all the instructions how to do it. He lets us work it out, and we learn from each try we make."

"But, Bishop, settling on the bench was a bad idea, plain and simple. And it's looking more and more like settling this valley was a bad idea in the first place. So why didn't Brigham know that?"

"Think about that for just a minute. How do gentile settlers conduct themselves? They grab for land, each on his own, and then every man works for himself. If we'd come down here and then scattered out, each man choosin' his own place to farm, how would that have worked out? We build our towns with our people gathered together, circlin' our meetinghouse, and we farm outside the settlement. We work together. We share what we have. We don't just build a city; we build people. And someone has to lead out, make decisions about where we'll settle. Others, even if they disagree about the site, have to be willin' to accept that leadership."

Morgan breathed in that answer for a time. He saw plenty of truth in it, but he didn't feel at peace. He took off his hat and wiped his forehead with his sleeve. "But how far should that go?" he asked. "Brigham sent us down here without knowing enough about this valley. He admitted that when he was here."

"That's not exac'ly right. He had good reports. Those first missionaries who settled down by Las Vegas Springs tol' him the Muddy would make for a good settlement, and then Anson Call, when he got here, praised the place highly and advised that we could build up two or three towns. He tol' Brigham that cotton—and everything else—would grow well here. And remember, that was when the price of cotton was high. The fact is, the men Brigham listened to were not wrong. I know we don't like the heat in the summer, but the growing season lasts year round. President Young can't go everywhere and see everythin'. He has to put trust in the good men he sends out to study a situation. What else can he do?"

"So where does the guidance of the Lord come in? Didn't he ask the Lord about this valley before he made his decision?"

"I'm sure he did, Morgan. But the Lord doesn't send telegrams. He lets us work, and He lets us figger things out for oursel'es. Sometimes we fail, but we learn from mistakes. Do you really believe in a God who sends us a map and then forces us to stick to the road He chooses for us?"

"No. Of course not. But you didn't say anything to us about figuring things out when you asked us to farm the sand bench. You told us it was what God wanted us to do."

"No. I did not say that. I said that our leaders had chosen this place, and I asked you to support that decision. And I told you God would bless you if you did that."

"He blessed us with an empty canal, and then He sent us a drought."

"I know." It was the bishop who looked down at the ground

this time. But after a time he said, "Sometimes, there are reasons to do things that we never understan'. This desert has been a test for us—a refiner's fire—and it's culled out the strong from the weak. Maybe, now, He has somethin' else to do with us, and maybe we've been prepared for it."

"But that's like saying that God led us into trouble on purpose just to knock us off our feet and show us who the boss is."

"No. That's not what I'm sayin'." The bishop took hold of Morgan's shoulder with one hand, leaned toward him, and looked into his eyes. For the first time, he sounded out of patience when he said, "Morgan, you've got to start seein' something bigger in all this than canals and farms and the price of cotton. The Lord needs you on His side. You're not in a tussle with God, or with Brigham, or with me. We're all together in this. You've got to give over yer heart—yer will—to the Lord and to the cause of Zion. You've got to trust in what we're tryin' to do and quit quibblin' with the details of how we get it done."

Morgan wasn't exactly clear about Bishop's Morrison's logic, but he felt the man's sincerity, felt the Spirit in what he was saying. He even felt some of his own frustration seep away. He let the bishop continue to grip his shoulder, and he kept looking back into his eyes. "All right," he said, "I'll try to understand that. But no one said to me, 'Let's try the sand bench for now and see if it works out—and let's do it together.' What I heard was, 'Do it, even if it makes no sense to you. Your leaders want you to do it, and that means that God does.'"

"I hope we didn't say it quite like that. But I can see where it might have sounded that way."

"What about the Indians who were supposed to attack us if we stayed in West Point? That never turned out to be a problem."

"Someday you'll send a child of yers off on a mission, and

you'll tell him all the things he needs to watch out for. That's what President Young was doing. There were Indian wars going on at that time, and Brigham, in his wisdom, didn't want us to scatter all over the place. How do we know? Maybe if all of you newcomers had stayed there, you would have upset the tribe, and they would've caused trouble for you. For me, it's just wiser to follow the advice we receive from our leaders—and not 'lean unto our own understanding.'"

Bishop Morrison let go of Morgan's shoulder and stepped back a little. Morgan looked about to see that most of the members were gone, having headed back to their houses. Sunday dinner would have to be cooked outside today, with the heat collecting in all the homes. There were good vegetables ready in the gardens, and some families would kill a chicken, but Morgan longed for his mother's roast beef on Sunday, and beef was in very short supply here. He wondered how much he let things like that—the adjustments he had had to make to live here—influence his attitude. He had learned to love the spring blooms on prickly pears, the glowing red bluffs in the sunset, even the soft shades of gray-green in the sage. Maybe a day could come when he could hold up better in the heat and accept the compensating mildness of winter. It was what he wanted: to not be a complainer or a rebel, to give his whole soul to establishing his family here. But what never left him was the feeling that he hadn't made the choice, that he was accepting someone else's idea about what his life should be. And now the bishop was telling him to take that last step: to give his will over to God and commit himself to something bigger than himself. He wanted to understand that, even wanted to find it in his heart to do it, but he wasn't at all sure that he could.

Neither spoke for a time, but finally Morgan asked, "Bishop, don't you ever feel like you're sacrificing *yourself* when you accept what your leaders tell you to do?"

"Maybe I did when I was younger. But the Lord has been good to me, and I have a notion that's because I've learned to listen to the Spirit."

"But that means that you seek your own guidance."

"Of course I do. But I've learned over time, the Lord doesn't send me in one direction and the rest of the Church in another. He speaks with the same voice to all of us."

"But it feels like I'm giving my agency away."

"The Lord takes nothin' away. You offer yer will, and He takes you by the hand and leads you through this life. He lets you know you're not alone."

Morgan wasn't sure. But he did like the way Bishop Morrison expressed the idea. And he had always liked the idea of Zion, of working together with other good people. "Well," he said, "I'll stay. And I'll work as though I'm going to be here all my life. At least for now."

"Test it, Morgan. See what God does to show you that you've made the right choice."

"All right." Morgan thought he had been testing for quite some time, and he even supposed that he had been blessed in some ways. But life in this place was hard, and it was not easy to think that if he were obedient—as always—his reward would be to live through Muddy Valley summers year after year, and maybe eke out a bare living in a place he didn't like.

• • •

Angeline gave birth to her baby just before the end of May, with Sister Ballif there to help her, and with Ruth always close.

Ruth held Angeline's hand as the time came near, telling her, "Squeeze as hard as you want. My hands are hard." Angeline did grip tight, but she didn't scream. She thought that Ruth would be brave at such a moment, and she wanted to show her that she could be strong too. Angeline had once thought of Ruth as a weak little thing, but she was learning there were various kinds of strength. Ruth, above all else, had learned to make the best of her circumstance. She survived. And it wasn't in her to pity herself. Angeline had wanted this baby more than anything, and now she knew she had to accept the pain that came with the birth.

The labor lasted all day, steadily becoming more intense, and then, when Sister Ballif asked for a big push, Angeline exerted herself and finally did let out a loud moan through gritted teeth. She felt the slick surge—and overwhelming relief. She raised her head enough to see a tiny body, slimy with blood, in Sister Ballif's hands. The baby began a croaking little protest that hardly sounded like crying and didn't last very long.

By then, Angeline was looking at Ruth, hoping for her approval. Ruth bent over Angeline and kissed her forehead. They had shared all these hours today, had shared their pregnancies, and Angeline felt an attachment different from any she had ever known. "We're sisters," she said to Ruth.

Ruth looked back at Angeline for a moment, not with surprise, but maybe with wonder that Angeline had said the words. She said, "Yes. Thank you so much, Angie."

And Angeline knew she meant more than thanks for her words. She meant that she wanted this unexpected sisterhood, that she was grateful for it.

"Don't you want to know what you have here?" Sister Ballif was asking.

"Yes, I do," Angeline said.

"Well, you have a boy. A healthy boy. He's as good-looking as that handsome husband of yours." Sister Ballif laughed. "People always say how pretty babies are, and they are before long, but I've seen a lot of new ones, and most of them look like toads—ugly little things with misshapen heads and flat faces, like they've been in a fistfight. But this one I could take home for my own—if you're in a mood to give him away."

Angeline laughed, then said, "Let me see him."

"Just a minute. He's still a mess. Can you give me a little help, Ruth?"

So Ruth brought rags that she had boiled earlier, and she helped Sister Ballif clean the little boy. "Sister Ballif is right," she told Angeline as they worked. "He doesn't look at all like a toad. When my Jefferson was born, he was skinny as these gray lizards that run around outside. This one will be as big as Jefferson in no time at all."

She took the baby to Angeline, who took him in her arms. She held him close and looked into his face. "Hello, my little son," she said. "You're just what I asked for. Your papa is going to be very pleased."

"Yes, he is," Ruth said. "He told me he would welcome a little girl, but I know he was hoping for a boy."

Angeline was unwrapping the baby by then, looking at his arms and legs, his fingers and toes. "He's perfect," she said. "Just perfect. Little Morgan Junior." She was somewhat unprepared for the powerful love she felt so instantly. She couldn't hold back her tears.

Sister Ballif was all business now. "Ruth, you take the baby from Angeline," she said. "We still have to finish up."

So Ruth walked with the baby, held him up to the light from the window, and took a closer look. "He *is* perfect," she said.

But Angeline and Sister Ballif were busy at the moment, and neither replied. Still, Angeline watched Ruth and could see her love for the little one. They had a baby, she told herself—she and Ruth. Soon they would have another, and the two could be raised together.

When the placenta was delivered and Angeline was properly cared for, Sister Ballif said, "Well, it's time we let Papa see his boy, don't you think?"

"He's had a long day," Ruth said. "I think he's right outside." She walked to the door and called him in.

Morgan came in looking curious, maybe even anxious.

"You have a handsome son," Angeline said.

He nodded, looking pleased, but before he took the baby in his arms, he said, "Angie, are you all right?"

It was the right question, and Angeline was very happy to tell him that she was fine.

• • •

In July, Ruth delivered a tiny little girl. Angeline was the one there this time to help Sister Ballif. And Morgan waited outside again. Before the door was opened to him, Angeline asked Ruth, "Have you decided on a name for her?"

"Not really." Angeline's son had always been Morgan Junior, and there hadn't been much discussion about it. But Ruth had hoped for another boy and had thought only of male names. She worried a little that Morgan might love a son more than a daughter, even though he had told her many times that that wouldn't be the case.

"What's your mother's name?" Angeline asked.

"Genevieve."

"What about that?"

Ruth was holding her new baby, but the house was so hot that Sister Ballif hadn't wrapped her in a blanket. The little one wore only a bit of rag pinned around her for a diaper. She was nestled against Ruth, seemingly happy to sleep against her mother's chest. "No," Ruth said. "My mother didn't like that name herself. She wouldn't want to pass it on to her grandbaby. What about *your* mother's name? Isn't it Ella?"

"Yes."

"I like that. But you might want to keep her name for your own first daughter."

"No. I do hope I have lots more children, but I've never thought of using Mother's name. Still, it would be nice to name this little one after her. When I wrote her and told her that Morgan had taken a second wife, I know she wasn't pleased. She didn't say that, but I read it between the lines when she wrote back to me. Maybe, if she heard that you named your baby after her, she would feel that we're not so divided as she and her sister wife have always been."

"Then Ella it is. I like that name. I had a good friend named Ella when I was a little girl." Then Ruth laughed. "I suppose I ought to ask Morgan what he thinks before we make a decision."

"Don't worry about that. We can outvote him two to one. We'll let him name oxen and cows. We'll do the children."

So Ella it was. And, as it turned out, Morgan was fine with the choice.

What Ruth was feeling, more than any time since she had left her parents' home, was that she was surrounded by people who loved her: Morgan and Angeline and Jefferson, and now, these two lovely babies.

DEAN HUGHES

• • •

The summer passed away slowly, and still none of the Saints knew whether they were staying in the mission or leaving. Morgan and the other men often speculated about the future, but Brigham had made no official announcement, and local leaders only said they were waiting to hear from Salt Lake City. Most men wanted to withhold judgment until the prophet took a stand, but several families took Brigham's words as clear proof that they were no longer expected to stay. The number of settlers was dwindling again, and that put in doubt the capacity of the remaining Saints to keep the settlements going.

Morgan had inherited a newly planted orchard in St. Thomas, and he nursed those young trees along, kept them alive, but he did it out of stubbornness as much as anything. He wanted to leave, no question about it, but he had promised to stay, and no matter how much doubt he held onto about directions from the President, he took some pride in being one who had enough grit in him to farm the desert. And actually, his crops were better this year. He was finally in a better place, and more water was now reaching St. Thomas, with the settlement on the bench mostly abandoned and much of the canal water no longer diverted. If anyone could make a go of this valley, he liked to think, he was the man who could do it. When he heard plans for new canals to be dug, able to distribute the water more efficiently, he convinced himself that there may yet be answers to making this valley prosperous. If the decision was for the Saints to stay, he would set the example and work as hard as anyone.

Little "Morgy" was growing so fast he promised to be a strapping, strong boy before long. Ella was a wiry little thing; she wasn't putting on much weight, but she weathered the summer. She didn't

312

cry much, and when she did, it was only a plaintive little whimper that seemed to say, *"Sorry to bother you, but I do have some needs."* Morgan Junior, on the other hand, put up a great howl when he wanted attention, and he wanted it often.

Morgan was amazed to discover how much he could love these two little ones. He enjoyed holding them both, one in each arm, and he loved how they responded to him. They both seemed to like his voice, and he was sure that he was making them laugh. By the end of the summer they were taking on personalities. Ella liked to look around, her eyes jumping back and forth, as though she were surveying everything around her, and she squirmed if Morgan held her too tightly, as though she valued her independence already. Morgy seemed more satisfied with life—as long as he was fed and kept dry—and he seemed a little above it all, as though he were giving serious thought to his own future but hadn't decided on a plan quite yet. Papa didn't tell anyone, but he saw himself in both babies—something around Ella's mouth, and certainly in Morgy's blue eyes. He wasn't surprised at all when everyone told him how beautiful they were.

What also pleased Morgan was the way Ruth and Angeline mothered the babies in turns or together. Both Morgy and Ella seemed to belong to both, and either mother stepped in to give care when care was needed. They were both up at night a great deal, and when one was overly tired, the other would say, "Let me get that burp up. You go back to bed."

All this pleased Morgan. A year ago—less than that—he had doubted that his wives would ever become united. It was a great relief, even a joy, and Morgan settled in with his life. He tried not to think about leaving the valley. It was easier just to work as though he would always be there.

And then word came that the Muddy River Valley was not in

Utah, not even in Arizona, as many had thought. Federal surveyors had come and gone, and in the fall, the announcement came that the changes in borders that the government had made during the last few years had placed the entire valley in the state of Nevada. But that was not the worst. Nevada officials had announced, just as Brigham Young had predicted, that back taxes on the land must be paid, and that only hard currency—gold or silver—would be accepted.

Bishop Morrison explained the situation at a town meeting held after church on a Sunday. He started out the meeting by saying that he finally had some news. "I guess it's bad news, but some of you may not think so." And then he explained about the government ruling.

Lyman Hunt stood up, hat in hand, and asked the bishop, "So where are we supposed to get silver or gold?" Morgan heard the question, but he also heard Lyman's tone of voice. In an indirect way, he was saying that it was time to leave. His scorched face, his ragged beard, and his threadbare shirt spoke even louder. He was worn down, like everyone in the room.

"Most of the settlers in this state are miners," the bishop answered. "Gold and silver are the currencies they deal in here. I don't think the governor cares about farmers—especially about Mormons. If we don't pay, he'll have marshals in here takin' away our property. But they can't get blood from a turnip, and he knows it. I think, if anythin', he just wants us to leave. It's the same old story we've faced wherever we've lived."

"So do we go back to Utah, Bishop?" a brother named Horace Wells asked.

The little church building where the Saints had gathered was stuffed with people, and even now, in October, the room was stifling. Morgan could feel what was happening. This was the last straw. "I can't say that we're pullin' out," Bishop Morrison said. "Brigham knows about all this. I guess we wait to hear his recommendation."

There was silence for a time, and then a low, hard voice rumbled in the room. "I've listened long enough. I'm going." It was Wilfred Shupe. The man had only grown more unpleasant since Polly had left him. She had taken her one little son with her, but she had left him with his own children, and Brother Shupe could be heard at times, all through the settlement, shouting curses at his older boys. He had told some people in town that he was heading north before long to bring back another of his wives, but the mystery to Morgan was why he had stayed here if he hated the place so much. Another brother from Nephi, Utah, where Shupe had once lived, had told Morgan, "He hates every place he lives, and people can hardly stand to be around him. I think he'd rather stay with all of us because we put up with him. To him, that's almost like being liked."

"Please, brothers and sisters, let's allow our leaders to guide us," the bishop was saying. "We've not been released from our missions. Let's not jump to conclusions on our own."

Eb, sitting next to Morgan, turned and whispered, "Here we go again. Brigham already made it clear, he doesn't see any future in this place. Let's get out before snow flies up north."

Morgan knew that Eb was still worried about his family, and this was finally his chance to escape and take his wife home. But Morgan worried that quick, impulsive decisions might result in confusion. He had gradually become accustomed to voicing his opinion in meetings like this, and, at the moment, he felt that a balanced, thoughtful voice was needed. "Bishop," he said, "could I say something?"

The bishop nodded. "Yes. Morgan."

Morgan stood. He was conscious that many people agreed with Brother Shupe, but he said, "We came down here talking about Zion, and I've done a lot of thinking about that lately. Maybe the hardships we've gone through have caused us to work together better than we ever would have in any other place. Personally, I don't want to lose that. I don't want to leave until we all leave together. And I feel like we all ought to go on together to a place where we can use what we've learned. I still want to live in a Zion city, and I feel like this group might be able to create something like that."

Morgan saw people looking at him, some of them nodding. The tension that had started to build was now fading away. Even Brother Shupe was looking away now. He may not have liked what Morgan had said, but at least he didn't argue.

"That's right, brothers and sisters," the bishop said. "We'll get some guidance soon, I'm sure, but let's wait for that before we make a decision. And then let's make that decision together."

What surprised Morgan was that all these thoughts about Zion had been rolling through his brain lately, but he had never put them together into an opinion. Sitting in this crowded church, however, he had looked around at the people he had lived among these last few years, and he knew he didn't want to leave them. The fact was, he wanted to get away from the Muddy as much as anyone, but if most people wanted to stay, he would rather stay than lose his friends.

• • •

Another month passed, and no word came from President Young or from Apostle Snow. However, virtually everyone was expressing the same feeling: they needed to leave and needed to leave soon. What worried Angeline was the anxiety the sisters were sharing with one another. No one wanted to head north in the winter. With a fairly good harvest in, enough food for the winter, and temperatures everyone could live with, the best time to leave would be in the spring.

Angeline talked with Sister Cullimore one afternoon. They had once again become neighbors, and not by accident. The two had been outside in their gardens and had waved to one another, and then Angeline had walked over to say hello. They had talked a little about the good squash and pumpkins they had grown this season, about the river running a little high for this time of year, and about Sister Robinson having her baby the night before. But then the conversation had gone where it usually did these days. Sister Cullimore said, "Henry thinks the Brethren will tell us to leave before long. I'd rather wait until spring, but he says he wants to be somewhere where he can be ready to plant as soon as spring comes on—not off trekking through the mountains."

"I understand that," Angeline said. "But I agree with you. I don't want to move in winter."

"Men think of crops before they think of anything else. What about all the children—and all the little babies—out in wagons in the snow again, just the way most of us were when we came down here?"

And that, of course, was what Angeline feared. She hated to think of Morgy and Ella out in the cold. She had a son now—and a daughter—and they had changed her life. Nothing compared in importance to keeping her children safe.

CHAPTER 17

Morgan had planted his winter wheat. He had no idea whether he would still be living in the valley when it was time for the harvest, but he told himself every day that he would go forward as though he would stay on the Muddy the rest of his life. This was the only attitude he could live with. Still, every day he heard the talk. Most everyone seemed to think that all the settlements would be abandoned soon, and some people were already using the good fall weather as a chance to get out before winter hit hard in Utah Territory.

The worst part for Morgan was that he felt better about staying than he ever had before. St. Thomas offered promise. He was close to some of the families he loved most, and he was having better farming success than he had experienced before. He had never known anything about vineyards, and not much about orchards. But Warren Foote, a man whose judgment he greatly respected, had advised him that he could do better with grapes and fruit than he could with cotton. His fruit trees were growing fast—apples, cherries, apricots, peaches—and he had begun to terrace a hilly part of his two-and-a-half-acre orchard plot for grapevines. Now, however, the terracing was far from completed, and it was hard to do all the digging and excavating when he knew he might have to walk away from all this work. Still, he did it. He worked at the project every day, and part of what drove him, as always, was his need to work. It was work that gave him a way to use his time and his muscles, and it kept his mind busy.

So Morgan continued his terracing. Angeline and Ruth watched over the children, shared the cooking and cleaning chores, and looked after the garden and the chickens. Their days were full, and when Morgan returned to the house each afternoon, he usually found them chatting as they worked. Each of them, when she was alone with Morgan, dropped hints that all was not perfect between them, no matter how placid their sister relationship seemed. Clearly, Angeline liked to be in control, and she sometimes overruled Ruth, apparently not even aware she was doing it. It actually bothered Morgan more than it bothered Ruth. Morgan told Ruth to assert herself a little more, but she would say, "It's all right. She likes to think things out and plan what we do, and it's easier for me to go along with her idea. I really don't mind all that much."

And yet Morgan sensed that Ruth did mind, at least a little. She would sometimes admit that she liked to work at things but take time now and then to rest, to play with the children, not to block out every hour of the day for specific jobs. Still, she told Morgan, "But the two of us get a lot more done together than we would if we did things my way."

And Angeline would say, "I know I boss Ruth more than I should, but she won't give me her own opinion so I just go ahead with mine. I really do wish she would speak up. I know very well that she doesn't agree with me all the time."

"Maybe you need to ask her more often," Morgan suggested.

"Don't misunderstand, Morgan. I'm not mean to her. We get along very well. I'm just saying, I need to understand her ways a little better. We probably *should* slow down at times, but I've never known how to do that." Angeline touched Morgan's arm and waited for him to look at her. "But I do love Ruth. I hope you know that."

And Ruth would say, "I love Angeline. She's been so good to me. This life is so much better than the one I had when I was alone."

Morgan liked hearing that, but sometimes he wished that he had kept the households separate. Most of his time at home was spent with everyone in the main room together, and the babies received most of the attention. He had little chance to share his thoughts with either wife, and he especially missed having time with Angeline. She still liked to have him in her bed when it was their week to be together, and they would talk a little then, but both were so tired, they rarely enjoyed each other as much as they once had—physically or emotionally. Morgan supposed it was the way of life. A honeymoon surely couldn't last forever, but sometimes he remembered that first year of their marriage and longed to have it back. He doubted it was very manly to think that way. Most of the men he knew talked about farming, about religion, about the future; they never hinted that anything was missing from their lives. Of course, Morgan would never express his emotions to any of those men either, but he suspected that others didn't think about some of the things he did, didn't worry about them. Over and over, he told himself that he thought too much. Work was better.

One morning, as Morgan was about to walk to his vineyard terraces just outside the settlement, Ruth said to him, "Morgan, I'm a little worried about Jefferson."

"What are you worried about?" Morgan asked. He had just finished his breakfast and was gathering his tools, which he had left outside the door. Ruth had nursed Ella, who had fallen back to sleep. Angeline was inside cleaning up after breakfast. He could hear her talking baby talk to little Morgy, who was sitting on a quilt close to her. Morgan had noticed Jefferson still sitting at the table. He had been holding his little wooden horse, the only toy he had, but he hadn't been doing anything with it. He was merely sitting, seemingly watching Angeline, but looking a little lost.

"He's with women all his life," Ruth said. "You're gone most of the day, and all he hears is the two of us chatting or fussing over the babies. He's five now, but he seems younger. He doesn't know how to do the things boys do."

"Could he start to play with some of the boys in the settlement?"

"Maybe. But he's always been so timid. I think his father made him scared of life. He doesn't know how to run and play. I've tried to get him outside more, but he doesn't do well out there, especially when it's hot."

"He's still so thin," Morgan said. "Why doesn't he ever put any meat on his bones? We have enough food for him."

"He never eats very much. If he tastes something and he doesn't like it, he simply won't eat it. I've tried to teach him to take at least a few bites of things, but he only cries if I try to force him. He's supposed to start school next year, and I'm afraid other boys are going to think he's a mama's boy."

Morgan was nodding. He knew all this was true, but Jefferson had always seemed very young. Morgan had simply assumed he would start growing up soon, behaving more the way Morgan had when he was a child.

"I was just thinking, could you take him with you today? The weather is so nice, and he needs to see what you do, see what a man's life is like."

"I'll just be digging most of the day." Morgan laughed. "I doubt that will make him want to be a man."

"Maybe he could dig just a little. He needs to get out of the house, exercise, be around you more."

"That's kind of hard with . . ." Morgan was going to say that it was hard to get much work done when he had to supervise a little boy's play, but he saw Ruth's immediate capitulation, the look in her eyes that said, *I knew you wouldn't do it.* When he saw that, he admitted to himself that he was doing the work at the vineyard fully expecting to leave it behind. It didn't really matter how much he accomplished. "Well, all right," he said. "Let's give it a try. If he wears out after a while, I'll bring him back, but you're right. He needs to get out of the house." He raised his fists and flexed his muscles. "I'll make him into a powerful man like me."

"Morgan, you don't have to take him. I just thought—"

"No. You're right. I'll try to teach him a few things."

So Ruth got Jefferson ready, and he did seem happy to go with his papa. He only had one decent set of clothes, but he had some old trousers and an old, patched shirt he could wear today. He did have some worn-out boots that only fit him because he continued to stay so small.

Morgan walked to the shed and brought back a little hand hoe that Angeline sometimes used. He handed it to Jefferson, and then he grabbed a pick and shovel and put them over his own shoulder. "All right, partner," he said. "You and me, we're going to work. Are you ready to do some digging?"

Jefferson smiled just a little and nodded his head.

"Then you have to take big steps because we have a long walk ahead of us."

Jefferson nodded again, and the two set out. But Morgan didn't walk fast. Jefferson never would have been able to keep up with him. Still, the little fellow didn't complain, and he worked very hard to keep up his pace. Morgan's only worry was that when they reached the terraces, Jefferson already looked tired.

"All right, Jeff, my good man. You sit down right there and watch me dig for a few minutes. Then you can try it."

But Jefferson didn't sit down. "I can dig now," he said, and he sounded more sure of himself than Morgan had expected.

"All right. That's good. I'm going to dig with this big shovel, and you dig with that . . . smaller shovel. Come over here and—"

"I want to use the big shovel." Jefferson was standing tall in his ragged clothes and one of Morgan's old hats. Ruth had managed to remodel it enough to fit, more or less, but it slouched over his forehead, almost to his eyes.

"Well, fine," Morgan said. "A big guy like you needs a big shovel. You've got that right." He handed the shovel to Jefferson, who could only reach halfway up the handle to take it. And then Morgan explained how they were going to continue to build levels, like steps, into the side of the hill.

Jefferson kept nodding, as though he understood, but Morgan wasn't sure that he did, and he certainly knew that the boy couldn't use such a big shovel. He worried that that might discourage him, but he hated to tell him from the start that he couldn't do it.

"So here's what I'm going to do," Morgan said. "I'm going to use my pick and loosen up some dirt, and then you can shovel it away. All right?"

Jefferson never seemed to talk more than he needed to. He was nodding once again.

Morgan broke up some of the dirt, and then he asked Jeff, "Can you shovel some of that?"

Jeff nodded, and then he tried to wield the shovel, but he was holding the handle just above the blade, and he couldn't manage to drive it into the dirt more than a couple of inches. When he tried to lift the blade, most of the dirt fell off.

"Here, let me show you. I'll help you." Morgan leaned over the boy and held the handle above Jefferson's hands, and the two together, so to speak, pushed the blade deeper into the earth and tossed a decent shovelful off to the side. Morgan was surprised when Jefferson laughed with apparent delight at his accomplishment. "Good work, partner. You'll grow up to be a common laborer, something every boy should hope to become."

Jefferson, of course, didn't understand Morgan's irony, but he liked the digging—for a time. Maybe he sensed eventually that he wasn't actually doing much, or maybe he simply found the repetition less than exciting. "You dig now," he finally said.

"All right. Do you want to use that little shovel and dig next to me?"

Jeff nodded again, but he soon lost interest in using the hand hoe. He began to play in the dirt, stacking it up with no apparent purpose. That was fine with Morgan for the present. He pushed forward with his work for maybe half an hour. But by then, Jefferson, bored with the dirt, had started wandering about looking for something else to do.

"I'll tell you what I liked to do when I was a boy," Morgan said.

Jefferson looked up, his eyes peering out from under the wide brim of his black hat.

"Have you ever caught a lizard?"

Jefferson shook his head.

"Do you want to?"

He shook his head again, and he actually looked concerned, if Morgan understood what his face was saying. Maybe the boy was afraid of lizards. They got into the house quite often, and Angeline had walloped a few of them with a broom. Maybe Jefferson thought they were dangerous.

"It's fun. And they won't hurt you. Come on, let's see if we can find one." Morgan took Jefferson's hand and helped him up the hillside. It didn't take them long to spot a skinny lizard, gray with clay-brown sides, darting in and out of the sagebrush. As Morgan and Jefferson approached, it stopped on a flat rock and held still.

"Go get him. He's right there," Morgan whispered. But Jefferson didn't move. So Morgan grabbed his hand again, and he hurried in the direction of the lizard. The lizard, of course, was gone in a flash. "We made too much noise," Morgan said. "We have to sneak up and then grab 'em up before they can run."

So they tried. Sneaking about, they didn't really see many lizards, but they did spot a couple, and they managed to get quite close before watching them shoot away. Jefferson laughed each time, and Morgan thought maybe he was starting to have fun.

"I'll tell you what," Morgan said. "I'm too big and noisy. You keep looking around up here, and I'll go dig. Just remember to get close and then snatch him fast." He suddenly grabbed at Jefferson's shoulder, as though a lizard were sitting on it, and Jefferson giggled.

Morgan went back to his digging, and this time he hoped he had found something that little Jefferson could do for himself and enjoy. He knew that the boy wouldn't catch any lizards. It wasn't an easy thing to do. But if he liked trying, that gave him a reason to be outside and moving about—the very thing Ruth wanted.

What pleased Morgan was that every time he looked up, Jefferson was working his way through the sagebrush, looking around, fully intent on finding prey. And now and then, Morgan would hear the boy laugh.

"Are you finding any lizards?" Morgan finally called out.

"Yes. Four. But they all got away."

This was more than Jefferson usually said, and there was delight in the boy's voice.

And then Morgan heard the rattle.

He looked up and saw Jefferson, frozen, staring. Morgan knew what he had found in the sagebrush.

"Jeff, step back. Slowly," Morgan said as calmly as he could.

But the boy didn't move. By then, Morgan was climbing the hill, trying not to make too much noise while still moving fast. When he got to Jefferson, he saw the rattler, curled up, head raised, tongue probing the air, tail shaking. Morgan took a quick step in front of the boy and swung the shovel, slicing the snake open. But he hadn't cut it through, and the diamondback was still squirming. Morgan struck at it again, this time slashing its head off. But Morgan didn't stop. He slammed it again and again, until he felt Jefferson grasping his leg, heard a little sob break from him.

"It's all right," Morgan said. "He's dead now. He can't hurt you."

"Why did you cut it?" Jeff said.

"It's a rattlesnake, Jeff. It's a dangerous snake."

"It was pretty."

"I know. I know." Morgan tossed his shovel aside and then picked the boy up. He walked far enough away that Jefferson couldn't see the snake any longer. "But weren't you scared?"

"Yes," Jeff said. "But you didn't have to hurt him."

"Well, yes, I did. He could have bit you, and he has poison inside him."

"I know."

"It's just the way things are, Jeff. There are things that can hurt us, so we have to protect ourselves. Do you understand that?"

"No." Jefferson squirmed to get loose, so Morgan set him down. Then Jefferson walked back and looked at the snake again. But he didn't say anything.

Morgan wondered what he had taught the boy. Jefferson needed to understand the danger. He couldn't live here and be careless about such things. "Let's walk back to the house now," he said.

Morgan left his tools, since he planned to return. He offered to carry the boy when he could see that he was getting tired, but Jefferson said, "No. I can walk."

"I'm sorry, Jeff. I didn't want anything to happen to you."

"You coulda scared him away."

"Not really. You were very close to him. Rattlers can strike. It's almost like jumping. They can bite you so fast, you hardly know what's happened."

"You didn't have to be mad at him."

Morgan felt a sting in the words almost as though the rattlesnake had struck him. He wondered at himself—why he had attacked so violently, why he had continued to beat on the snake. Jefferson hadn't needed to see that.

As they reached their house, Morgan said, "Jeff, you're right. I didn't have to be so mad. I don't like snakes. But snakes just do what snakes do. They can't help it. I was worried it would hurt you, and I don't ever want anything bad to happen to you." He stopped and took hold of Jefferson's shoulders, turned him. "Don't tell your mama what happened. She'll be too worried, and then she won't want you to go with me to dig. Do you want to go with me again?"

"Yes."

"And chase lizards?

"Yes."

"All right. That's what we'll do."

It was also what Morgan wanted to do. He needed to be closer to Jefferson; he needed to understand the boy's gentle spirit.

• • •

Ruth wondered about Jefferson when he came home from his morning with Morgan. On the one hand, he seemed a little more lively than usual, as though, just under the surface, he was quite excited. But he wouldn't say why, wouldn't even talk much. When she asked him what he had done, he said, "Me and Papa digged," and when she asked more about that, he added, "I catched lizards."

"Really. You caught some?"

"No."

"But you tried to catch lizards?"

"Yes."

"Was it fun?"

"They're too fast. I couldn't catch 'em."

"But you tried and it was fun?"

"Yes."

It was not unusual for Jefferson to keep his feelings to himself, but Ruth was surprised that he wouldn't say a little more. "Do you want to go again?"

"Yes. Papa said he would take me."

"That's good. I'm glad to hear that."

And that was good. But later in the day, when she had a chance to talk to Morgan, he gave her about as much detail as Jefferson had been willing to give. "He tried to dig with the big shovel,"

Morgan said. "You can imagine how that went. Then he played in the dirt for a while, and he chased lizards. He liked that."

"But what if he catches one? Will it bite him?"

"Nah. They don't bite. They're more scared of us than we are of them."

"Thank you so much for taking him," Ruth said. "He wants to go again. Is that all right?"

"Sure it is. He's a good boy. I learned more than he did today."

"What do you mean?"

"Oh, just that he cares about creatures, likes to look at them. He's got a softer heart than I do. That's something I could use."

"You're the tenderest man I've ever known, Morgan."

He took her in his arms.

But Ruth pulled away. "You shouldn't do that. Angeline could walk in at any moment."

"You mean I have to hide from one wife to kiss another one?"

"Yes. You know you do. But next week you'll be with me—and that's different."

Morgan knew that was true, but he had only wanted to hold her for a moment. Sometimes he grew weary of thinking how everything he did might cause pain for one or the other of his wives.

• • •

The following day, Jefferson went with his father to the orchard once again. Angeline thought that was a good thing, but she missed having Jeffy close by. He didn't say much—he puttered around mostly in his own little world—but she felt part of a family when Ella or Morgy laughed or cried or when Jeffy wanted to hear a story.

Midmorning, as the sun was warming the house quite pleasantly, Sister Cullimore called through the open door, "Angeline, are you home?"

"Yes, Sister Cullimore, I'm here. Come in."

Flora Cullimore was a stout little woman, round in every part of her, though Angeline could never figure out why. She kept herself busy day and night, cleaning her house, gardening, and walking about in the settlement, talking to friends or helping out a new mother or a sick family. She also shared all she knew from one house to another, and everyone knew that about her. "If you want to spread the word in this place," Morgan had told Angeline, "just tell Sister Cullimore, and the sun won't set before everyone knows."

Ruth was at the dry sink. She turned and said, "Hello, Flora. Nice morning, isn't it?"

"I can tell you two haven't heard the news," she said.

"What news?"

"There's a meeting called for next Tuesday. Joseph Young is coming down from St. George, and so is Brother Bentley. So I guess we'll finally know what's going to happen to us."

"Maybe they're just paying a visit," Ruth said. "They do that sometimes."

"No. They want everyone to gather—every person in the settlement. They have things they want to talk about."

"Where did you hear this?"

"Bishop Morrison told Brother Fitzmorris, and he told his wife, and his wife told Gladys Wright, and Gladys told—"

"So, anyway, it's an official meeting of some sort," Angeline said. "That's good. But what if they tell us we have to leave right away? I'm not too excited about heading for Utah in December."

"Now, that's just exactly what I've been saying," Sister

Cullimore said. "Would you mind if I sit down? I've walked around this whole settlement this morning."

Angeline glanced at Ruth, and they both allowed themselves a little smile. "Of course you can sit down," Angeline said. "If you like, we have some Brigham tea. I know you like that."

"Oh, yes, that would be wonderful."

Brigham tea was an herbal tea that Angeline didn't really like much. But in recent years, Brigham Young and other leaders had been stressing the Word of Wisdom more than they had when Angeline was young. The truth was, Angeline loved coffee, and she liked black tea, but both were far too expensive to ship all the way to the Muddy. Brigham tea was cheap, even if the ephedra bush was not available in the valley. Those who came south to visit often brought a supply.

Angeline had already boiled some water that morning. She checked it now with her finger and decided it was still warm enough, even though it wasn't as hot as she preferred. Since coming to the Muddy, she had had to make an adjustment. Most of the year, a hot drink was the last thing she wanted. But water from the Muddy was thick with minerals and only tolerable after it had been boiled. So most mornings she boiled water, then let it cool enough to drink.

"So what do you think? How soon will we leave?" Sister Cullimore asked.

"I have no idea. What's everyone saying?" Angeline asked.

"Some say spring, and some say we have to get out before marshals come and confiscate our stock to pay our taxes."

"Which do you think will happen?" Ruth asked.

Angeline had spooned out the herb in three cups, and now she was pouring the water. "You'll have to stir this a good deal," she said. "The water's not very hot."

"I say spring," Sister Cullimore said. "I think we'll leave before the river runs high but after the snows have let up in the north."

"That sounds reasonable," Angeline said. "And where do you think we'll go?"

"Now, that's the interesting question. Ever since Morgan stood up and said that we all ought to leave together and stay together, most of the people—not all, but most—seem to think that's right."

"Well, it's not very often we agree on anything," Angeline said.

"True. But it's not so much that way as it used to be. Those that stuck it out, they all respect each other. I think we figure we're the strong ones. And I don't know how much you notice it, but we look out for one another a lot more than when we started out."

"We started at different times," Ruth said. "But I agree with that. No one goes hungry. No one gets sick without someone stopping by to offer help. I don't think we're a Zion city yet, but we're closer than we used to be."

"Maybe we'll all get taken up," Sister Cullimore said. "Maybe we're so righteous, we'll be like the city of Enoch—just raised straight up to celestial glory."

Ruth and Angeline laughed, but Flora Cullimore seemed about half serious. Angeline stirred her tea, took a sip of the nasty stuff, and thought to herself that one thing everyone shared was the ability to get by with the little they had. The three of them were sitting around the table, all wearing dresses that they wouldn't have dared to be seen in back in northern Utah—threadbare, frayed. She liked that. She didn't like her dress, but she liked that she wasn't embarrassed—since no woman in town was any better off.

More than anything, Angeline thought how much she loved Sister Cullimore, with all her little faults. Angeline was not sure she liked every single person in town. Certainly, she clung to some hard feelings against Wilfred Shupe. But she had seen him at his worst and best, and she had come to pity a man who had so little love to give. So she didn't like everyone equally well, but it occurred to her that she loved them all. She did want to stay with these people, wherever they ended up.

CHAPTER 18

Joseph W. Young visited the Muddy Valley the following week. Richard Bentley, his assistant, traveled with him. The two began meeting with the settlers in each of the towns. The St. Thomas meeting was held on Tuesday, December 20. Virtually everyone was there, and the little church building was more than filled, with many standing along the walls, unable to find seats in the pews.

The meeting began like a church service, with a hymn and an opening prayer by Warren Foote. After another hymn, Joseph Young stood at the podium. He was nephew to Brigham, and appeared to Morgan to be maybe forty or so. His hair was dark, as was his beard. He wore no mustache, so his beard and hair seemed to draw a circle around his serious face. He was known and admired for his leadership in bringing converts across the plains, but his manner was businesslike, with little emotion in his voice—quite different from the personality of his uncle.

Brother Young announced that he had with him a letter from Brigham Young that he would now read to the members. The letter was dated December 14, 1870, and was addressed to "Brother Ewan Morrison and the Brethren and Sisters residing on the Muddy." It explained at first what the Saints already knew: a federal government survey had placed the Muddy Valley in Nevada, and the state government was demanding back taxes. Then Brother Brigham offered his assessment: "Your isolation from market, the high rate at which property is assessed in Nevada, with the unscrupulous character of many of the officers of newly organized regions, all combine to render your continuance in developing the resources of the Muddy, a matter of grave consideration."

Morgan wondered at the words *grave consideration*. That didn't sound so much like a final decision as perhaps a warning. He glanced at Angeline, who was looking at him, and he knew she was thinking the same thing. Would they still not get an answer?

Joseph Young continued to read, slowly and carefully:

"You are occupying soil, climate, and water which are capable of producing a most desirable country, but when you consider the drawbacks with which you are surrounded, you may think them too great to overcome, in view of the advantages to be obtained thereby. You have done a noble work in making and sustaining that outpost of Zion against many difficulties, and exposures, and toil."

Joseph Young hesitated, then added, "Brothers and sisters, you certainly have labored against many difficulties here, as the President has stated. I honor you for your strength and tenacity."

Morgan did appreciate the praise, but he felt some relief as he realized what must be coming next. The important paragraph followed:

"We now advise that you gather together in your several settlements, and take into consideration your future course, and if a majority, after fairly canvassing the subject, conclude to remain and continue to develop the resources which abound with you, all abide by the result. But if the majority of the Saints in counsel determine that it is better to leave the State, whose laws and burdens are so oppressive, let it be so done, but it will not be prudent to reduce your numerical strength much and attempt to remain. May the blessings of Israel's God rest upon you and guide you in your decision."

The letter also offered some strategies. Brigham suggested that, whether the Saints chose to leave or not, they could petition Nevada for an abatement of back taxes. Loose stock could be removed from the jurisdiction to avoid seizure for tax payments. The Saints could also ask, if they decided to stay, for the establishment of a new county. He recommended that local leaders thoroughly investigate all these matters. The letter was signed not only by Brigham Young but by George A. Smith and Erastus Snow.

Joseph Young looked up from the letter, surveyed the room carefully, as if to judge the reaction, and then said, "So the matter is up to you. I think some of you hate to give up what you've worked so hard to establish here. Others, I know very well, have felt for some time that there was no future in this valley. I will say that I think this could be a good place to live, in time, just as the President has suggested, but I suspect the problems with the state of Nevada will continue, and that would add a trial that may well make staying here untenable. Nonetheless, as the President said, it's your decision. What I ask of you now is that you brethren—all who wish to—stand and state your opinion as to whether you wish, as a body, to stand firm and remain here, or whether you wish, as a body, to seek a new place to settle."

Silence fell across the crowded room. Morgan looked around to see who might voice an opinion first. Finally, Art Brooks rose to his full height, towering above everyone, and said, "I say we leave. We've put everything we have into this place, and I've long doubted whether it was worth it. But I see no way we can pay back taxes, especially in gold."

"That's right," people were saying, and Morgan thought maybe that was the end of it. He patted Angeline's hand—his way of saying, *"We'll be fine. We'll find another place. A better place."*

But after a pause of half a minute or so, Henry Cullimore stood up, looking stubby after everyone had seen Art rise so high. "There's just one thing I feel like saying. I don't understand why Brigham and the other folks are telling us what a fine climate and soil we've got here. Brigham came down here and told a lot of people he didn't think much of the place. Now he sounds like he wants to make excuses for sending us here. It's not just high taxes in Nevada that's killed us off. We been roasting in this heat, some of us for years, and what have we got for it? By the time I feed my family, I've got nothing left over. Just look at all of us. We're wearing clothes that is damn near fallin' off us. Maybe Brigham ought to jist admit it: he made a bad decision in the first place when he called us to serve here."

A few people laughed, and others agreed with him, but Warren Foote, who was always level-headed, stood behind Brother Young and walked to the podium. "Let's be just a little careful," he said. "Personally, I could stay if that's what we all decided to do. I've got a vineyard going now and fruit trees coming along. And the cottonwoods we've planted along our streets are getting big enough to provide a little shade. I'll admit, I've lost my shirt down here." He laughed and grasped the front of his faded shirt, pulling at it as though he were about to tear it off. "I've worn out most of my animals, or lost them to Indians, and I've struggled just to live, the same as the rest of you. But I've had a decent harvest this year, and I've done all right at my mill. I've also made my houses quite comfortable. Just when my farm is doing well, it's not easy for me to pick up and leave everything behind. If it were up to me—"

"You put in your years here in St. Thomas, Brother Foote,"

Henry said. "You didn't try to farm that sand bench where a lot of us were. We got nothing out of that."

"Well, I know," Brother Foote said. "I was always against farming there, as you well know, but now you can—"

"We were told by leaders both here and in St. George that the bench was damn near the Garden of Eden, and look what come of it."

"I know that, Henry. But you're here in St. Thomas now. I've been here almost six years, and things are finally coming around for me. I'm just saying that if we stay, in time, things might turn out all right for all of us. We call those Nevada taxes high, but they aren't that much more than in other places."

"And I guess you've got plenty of gold in your pocket."

"No. Of course not. But I've thought about that. There's work I could do in some of the mining towns. It wouldn't take long to earn enough to pay those taxes in hard currency." He held up both hands, as if to say, *"Now wait a minute,"* and then he added, "All I'm saying is that we don't have to hurry to a judgment. There's arguments for staying, just like the letter said. And the other thing is, Brigham knew that cotton would grow here, and he was right. He had some good reasons for trying this place. We don't have to start complaining that he made a bad decision."

"I'll just say this," Henry Cullimore said. "I'm pretty sure the devil invented the Muddy Valley, not the Lord, and Brigham shoulda known he was sending us to the nether part of hell."

At that point, Joseph Young stepped back to the podium. "I'm afraid I can't let that comment go by without a response." He took a long, serious look at Brother Cullimore, and the rest of the congregation quieted. "We had no choice but to leave Nauvoo, back in 1846, and it took a strong leader to hold us all together and keep us moving forward. A lot of Saints complained about President

Young then, just the way you're doing now. But without him, where would we be? Look how we've prospered here in the West. Someone has to direct the affairs of the Church—not just in spiritual matters, but in temporal things, too. We need a leader who has a vision of what we're trying to become and one who's not afraid to make decisions, not afraid to try things that might not always work out. We need to work together, and the only way we can do that is to be organized. That means that someone has to give us direction. We can't just go off on our own, each taking a different path. When a decision is made, we need to support it. Brigham will never take away your right to think for yourself, but I've learned, when we follow his leadership, we all come out better."

Brother Cullimore sat down. Morgan felt a little sorry for him—mostly because he had only expressed what many others, including himself, had said before.

Warren Foote seemed to be thinking the same thing. "I know what you mean, Henry," he said. "We've all struggled with this place. But those of us who are still here, we stayed because we promised to do all we could to build the kingdom in this valley, and we're better people for having done it. If you all want to leave, I'm going with you. But let's think this through, not just get all excited to get away. Wherever any of us go, we'll have to start over again, and I've done a lot of that in my life. I could buck the summer heat all my life if I had to—and on a December day as mild as this, I don't relish going back to the mountains. Every place has its drawbacks. Brigham sent us to a hard place, that's for sure, but I don't regret what I've experienced here with all of you."

Brother Foote walked back and sat down. Morgan had always listened to the man's wisdom. In fact, Morgan found himself wishing that he had moved straight to St. Thomas when he had first arrived. Maybe, by now, he would be set up pretty well. At the same time, he longed for a place that was green, that had trees that could be cut for lumber. A place where crickets chirped at night. If he stayed, he knew he would always be a stranger in this land.

Several more men stood after that. Each one said that he would rather leave, but their voices had become more measured. Bishop Morrison added his assessment, and he agreed that he thought it was time to seek out a better place.

Joseph Young finally said, "You've had your say. Now it's time to think this over, talk and pray with your families, and then we'll meet again at 6:30 this evening. At that meeting we'll take a vote. We'll be holding meetings and taking votes in each settlement in the next day or two."

Morgan felt good about the meeting. Although Henry had said some things that were rather harsh, perhaps they needed to be said, and the general mood was friendly and even spiritual. It was quite clear which way the vote would go. People seemed relieved to receive a release from the promise they had made to build up towns in a place that had always fought so hard against them.

• • •

When Angeline left the meeting with Morgan and Ruth and the children, she found herself wishing she were happier than she actually was. She felt certain that everyone would choose to leave now—or in the spring—but she had given so much to this valley that it was hard not to feel a bit of disappointment at just giving up on it. It seemed as though all their effort had been for nothing. She also worried about Morgy and Ella. Being on the trail, maybe in mud or even snow, would be hard on such little ones.

She was carrying Morgy, who had fallen asleep in the meeting. Ruth was carrying Ella. Morgan, who was walking between them, was holding Jefferson's hand. "There was one thing I wanted to say in there," Angeline said.

"Why didn't you say it?" Morgan asked her.

"You heard what Brother Young said. He invited 'the brethren' to give their opinions."

"That's just a way of speaking—because men do most of the talking at a meeting like that. But he wouldn't have ignored you if you had stood up."

"Maybe not. But I know how people think about me already. I have too much to say. I'm supposed to listen to the priesthood brethren and not have any opinions of my own."

"Maybe women don't speak in meetings like that—at least not very often—but right now, on their way back to their houses, they're telling 'the priesthood brethren' exactly what they think. And we'll hear some of that tonight."

"Why?" Angeline asked.

"Why what?"

"Why does it have to be like that? Why do women feel like they have to work in the background and figure out ways to get their husbands to be their voices? Men think we're like Eve—the one who listened to Satan and brought the curse on the world."

"Well, yes. That's true." But Morgan was laughing, and he quickly added, "Most of the troubles in this world come from men. I wish all the women in the settlement had said what they think. Men don't think enough about the effects of a decision on our families."

Angeline didn't quite trust this. Morgan liked to say the right things to her, but she was quite sure that, deep down, he thought females would only whine about leaving furniture behind and disrupting their children's lives.

"So what was it you wanted to say?" Ruth asked.

Angeline looked around Morgan and nodded to Ruth. "I'm glad you asked. Morgan already forgot that I had something to say."

"Not at all," Morgan said. "Tell us what you were thinking?"

But this was also irritating. "Never mind. It wasn't important."

"Oh, brother," Morgan said, and he let out a sigh. That was his sign that he didn't know how to deal with an emotional female.

But Ruth said, "No, really, Angeline. What did you want to say?"

By now, Angeline would have preferred to let the whole thing go. She did love these warm winter days in St. Thomas. She found herself looking about, enjoying the rusty, wild colors of the desert in a way she never had when she first arrived. What she felt now was that this was a kind of home. She had given up her Farmington home, and she had made the hard trade for this place. It wasn't easy to think of making a home again in some new place, starting over one more time. "It was nothing very important," she finally said. "I was only thinking about the people who have been longing to go back to the places they left behind. We make it seem like they would be doing something wrong if they didn't stay with the rest of us. But I understand how they feel. I feel some of that myself."

"Are you saying you want to go back to Farmington?" Morgan asked.

"No. Not really. But you read the letter my mother wrote a few weeks ago. She talked about missing me, and how much she would like to have us nearer to her—and to be able to see our babies. I suppose a little piece of me wishes I could go back."

"Maybe we'd better consider it, then," Morgan said.

She recognized this as his "I can be reasonable and considerate" manner of dealing with her. He wasn't about to go home, even though he liked Farmington even more than she did. The idea of

staying together with their friends was something he had owned—
and expressed—to everyone, and Angeline knew that he would feel
like a fool if he took his family and went in some other direction.

"I didn't say that, Morgan. I want to stay with these people.
You know that. And my mother would spend her life crying on
my shoulder if we went back to Farmington. I'm just saying that
I understand people who are homesick. We shouldn't shame them
into a decision they don't like." She looked at Ruth again. "Don't
you think that's right?"

"I do," Ruth said. "Maybe you should say that at the next
meeting—just so the ones wanting to separate from the rest won't
feel bad about it."

"Oh, no. It's too sweet and emotional. 'The brethren' don't
want to hear such silliness."

"That's not true. I'll say it tonight, if you don't," Morgan said.

"Oh, thank you. Do my speaking for me."

Angeline knew she was being difficult, but she sort of liked to
see Morgan's eyes roll and hear the breath go out of him.

Morgan let some time pass, then said, "Ruth, tell me what you
think about all this. Would you rather go back to Beaver?"

"By myself?"

"No. I don't mean that. But if we're choosing a place to go, do
you want us to consider Beaver?"

"No, not at all. I'm Ruth: 'Whither thou goest, I will go.' But
I like our neighbors, and I'd like to be with them, too. 'Thy people
shall be my people, and thy God my God.'"

So all that was settled, until Jefferson asked, "Are we going
somewhere, Mama?"

"I think so," Ruth told him. "Maybe somewhere that isn't so
hot in the summer."

"It isn't hot now."

"No. But it will be again. And you don't like hot weather very much."

Jefferson was still clinging to his papa's hand, working hard to keep up with everyone. "Will there be lizards where we go?"

Ruth looked to Morgan for an answer.

"Oh, I think so," he said. "Lizards are pretty much everywhere."

"I almost caught one yesterday."

"He did," Morgan said. "He had one by the tail, but it got away."

"What will you do with one if you catch it?" Ruth asked.

"Have it for a pet."

"And where will you keep it?"

Now it was Jefferson who was looking to Morgan. "I told him we could build a little box of some sort," Morgan answered for him. He laughed. "But I didn't think he would ever catch one. Now I think he just might."

Angeline looked down at Jefferson. "Tell me this, Jeffy. Do you think lizards like to live in a box, or do they like to run around in the desert?"

Clearly, Jefferson needed to think that one over. They were almost home when he finally said, "I think they like to be in the sand, outside."

"So why would you want to put one in a box?" She looked at Morgan and exaggerated a frown. "Oh, I'm sorry. That's a woman's question."

Morgan was shaking his head, but he was smiling. "Actually, it's a very good question. I caught lots of lizards when I was a boy, but then I'd let them go after a while. They just looked so miserable in a little box."

"Did they have sad little faces?" Angeline teased.

"I don't know. Maybe they did. Maybe I just thought they wanted to find a sweetheart. There's nothing better in this life than to have a lovely wife who honors you and respects your opinions."

Now it was Angeline who was rolling her eyes.

Jefferson said, "Maybe I'll just watch them and not catch them."

Angeline had never cared at all about lizards, and she had mostly just been joking with Jeffy, but she was touched by his answer. She hoped men, in time, wouldn't make him feel stupid for being so sweet.

What Angeline also knew was that Morgan was far sweeter than anyone knew. She wondered why men thought they had to hide that part of themselves. She also decided she could be sweeter herself—and not test Morgan's patience quite so often.

• • •

At 6:30 that night, with the sun already down, members assembled for a second meeting at the church. It began again with hymns and a prayer, and then Brother Young asked the people to give their opinions now that they had had time to think things over. The opinions expressed sounded like the ones offered in the earlier session, and the agreement was obvious among the members until Daniel Bonelli stood. "I've listened to all this talk and haven't said anything," he told the congregation. "But I'll tell you this. My wife and I are staying right where we are, no matter what the rest of you do. All this talk of taxes is nonsense. Any one of us could pay our taxes from what we'd earn from two square rods of grapevine. And gold coin can be acquired by selling grapes—or any of our crops."

"Yes. Selling to Gentiles," someone behind Morgan said. "But that's not what we come here to do."

"That's more nonsense," Bonelli shot back. "We can't live in this world and pretend we're the only ones in it. Before long this region will fill up with Gentiles, and we'll just have to accept that. I've taken enough advice from folks in Salt Lake City and St. George. I don't plan to listen to any of that ever again."

"That's fine," Brother Young said. "You go your way and see where you end up. But you're in apostasy, and I hope you recognize that."

"You call it what you want. I'm wore out from listening to people who don't know any more than I do. I can grow good crops here, and I'm going to stay and do just that."

"Does anyone else want to say anything?" Joseph Young asked. He looked around. All was quiet. "All right, then, we'll take a vote."

He asked the men to raise their hands if they favored leaving the Muddy Valley. And then he asked for those who preferred to stay. A count was taken, and then announced. Forty-six had voted to leave, and one was opposed—Brother Bonelli, of course. Brother Young then asked for the women to vote, and only one woman was opposed—Sister Bonelli. No one, however, counted the female votes. Morgan knew what Angeline thought of that, but he couldn't change the way these things were done. Women had recently received the right to vote in Utah elections, and that was something very new. Maybe that was why Brother Young, perhaps as an afterthought, had asked for the women's vote.

The meeting was soon dismissed, but the following day another meeting was convened in St. Thomas. At this session, petitions were presented to the congregations and approved. One petition was directed toward the Nevada government and contended that back taxes were unfair. A long series of arguments posed that the Saints had done much to establish an agricultural base in the state and that their struggles to do that had been overwhelming. In spite of that, they had paid taxes where they thought the money was owed. A second petition asked for a new county to be established in the Muddy Valley, and a third asked the federal government to cede back to Utah the areas taken away in recent years.

One reason for all this was to keep Nevada from putting pressure on the Muddy settlers, to buy them some time so they could leave when they preferred. The petitions were approved, but no one held out hope that the proposals would be honored either in Nevada or in Washington, D.C.

Bishop Morrison reported the vote in each of the settlements. In both St. Joseph and the new settlement, Overton, only one male vote had opposed the decision to leave the valley. So the mission would end; the settlers would move on. The only question that remained was when the exodus would begin.

Brother Young spoke to the congregation again. "You may want to consider leaving a small group—maybe ten men—to continue to grow cotton. It's a commodity we still need, and one that grows well here."

Morgan noticed no sign of agreement, and he personally thought it a bad idea—to break up families and probably cause problems with officials from Nevada.

"In any case, it's something to consider," Brother Young said. "The question about leaving has been settled. What remains is our manner of proceeding. We must do this in an orderly way. Some of you have seen your draft animals die, or you no longer have a wagon that will hold up during a long removal. So it's absolutely necessary that you help each other. I can send you some drivers and wagons from St. George, but you will also need to look to one another, help repair wagons, share animals. I doubt you will all want to leave on the same day. That makes for difficulties on the roads, with too many wagons and animals traveling the same route."

Bishop Morrison addressed the crowd and called for a sustaining vote on a resolution to help each other, to cooperate, and, most important, to leave no one behind. He asked for opinions about that before a vote was taken. Morgan looked around. There had been some stirring and commenting during most of the proceedings, but no one seemed to have any questions now.

So Morgan stood, and the bishop called on him. "I said yesterday that I think we should all stay together, and that is still how I feel. But I think those who want to return to their previous homes—or choose some other place to settle—should not be reproved for making their own choices. No one should be forced to join us."

"That's right, Brother Davis," the bishop said. "Let's help each other get as far as St. George. After that, some may choose to separate from the rest. I'll say this, though: I hope, as you say, that we can find another place to build a Zion city and that we can retain the strong feelin's for one another that we've gained here. I do hope that all will join us, but we won't say a word to those who choose another path."

The resolution passed unanimously.

Brother Young made a final suggestion that a delegation be chosen to seek out a new site for settlement. "I've heard talk of settling in Berry Valley—what some people call Long Valley—in southern Utah. An Indian uprising drove the Saints away from there during the Blackhawk War. But that's settled now, and, from what we're told, it's a fine valley for farms: good water, good soil, and moderate temperatures compared to what you've experienced here—or even in St. George. You need to make that decision, but I recommend that some of your people travel north and have a look at that area."

A delegation was chosen by Bishop Morrison to assess Long Valley as a place to settle. The bishop would lead the group himself, he said, and he named Warren Foote and some of the other experienced settlers to travel with him.

"Let me say one last thing," Brother Young said. "Don't destroy your homes as you leave. I've heard men say that they didn't want to leave their houses and farms for Indians or Gentiles to take over. But that's not the right attitude. If someone can use these little adobe lodgings, there's no harm in that. Or who knows? Maybe at some point we can work things out with the government of Nevada, and some will want to return."

Morgan didn't think that was likely, but he had no desire to destroy the little house where he had lived with his family this last year—or the one still standing on the sand bench. He had built three houses on the Muddy, and he had learned some things each time. He thought those experiences would come in handy when he built his next house—in Long Valley or wherever he and his family settled.

The meeting adjourned, and Morgan walked home. His wives had not come this time. Angeline had said she saw no point, since only men's votes were counted, but she was only teasing this time. Morgan was quite sure of that. The real truth was, she never had liked meetings.

• • •

Ruth and Angeline sat at the table together while Morgan was gone. They drank Brigham tea and tried to think what their lives would be like in the coming years. Ruth, as she had said before, didn't care much where she would live. Her worry was that the children would stay healthy. The ague had taken a number of babies and children in the Muddy settlements, and Ruth always knew that it was rare for a family to raise all their children to adulthood.

"If we leave in spring, the Virgin will be running high," Ruth said. "I hate to think of crossing back and forth with the wagon packed full."

"It's impossible," Angeline said. "There's another way to go, out across the desert, but there's no water for miles and miles. That would be even worse."

"Then we'll have to wait until late in the spring. And that means heat again."

Ruth watched Angeline. She clearly had a lot on her mind. "I think we'll leave sooner," Angeline said. "Before the runoff. I don't see any other way. All the women talk about waiting to leave in the spring, but I know what Morgan thinks—and most of the men. They want to reach the new site before spring breaks so they can get seeds in the ground."

"If we leave in winter, it won't be so bad from here to St. George, but from there, we would have to deal with cold and snow," Ruth said.

"We could make it to St. George and then wait for a time. But men don't think that way. We'll push on, I suspect."

"We'll be all right, Angeline. You and I can take care of each other."

Ruth watched Angeline as she nodded and then looked down at the table. She seemed sorrowful, and yet Ruth knew she wasn't sad to leave.

"It's Morgy you're worried about, isn't it?"

"Yes. And Ella."

"The Lord blessed us, Angie. We have beautiful babies. Now

we'll have to help each other—and trust that the Lord will look after us. Maybe we've earned a few blessings, having stuck it out here."

"I wish things always worked that way, Ruth. I've seen too many faithful people lose their children—or die young themselves. It's such a harsh world. Sometimes I wish the Lord would make it just a little easier."

Ruth had thought the same thing many times, but now she said, "I know. But no one can say we didn't pass our test in this valley."

"But if we lose our babies now, I don't think I could bear up under the grief. I think about that every day."

Ruth thought of telling Angie to have faith, not to think of the worst possibilities, but the fact was, she shared the same fears. "We'll watch out for our little ones together," she said instead. "We'll do everything we can to protect them."

Angeline nodded, but Ruth knew what they were both thinking. Hard things happened in this world, and a mother could not be certain that death and heartache would never visit her own family.

CHAPTER 19

Morgan and Angeline were looking down on the Muddy Valley as they stood on the crest of the Mormon Mesa. It would be their last look over this stretching desert before they pushed on to the north through the Virgin River Valley once again. The plan was to continue on to Long Valley, which was beyond the mountains east of St. George. The delegation that had gone to assess the area reported that the canyon was narrow, but there were good areas for farming, with rich soil. Morgan had asked the men, jokingly, if they had heard any birds singing. "Well, it was winter, so we didn't see an awful lot of birds," Bishop Morrison said, "but we'll have spring there. Real spring, an' I'm sure birds will abound. There are trees, too, tall pines for lumber, and large, open meadows ready to be plowed and planted. The east fork of the Virgin River is a nice stream, clear and cold, not anythin' like the Muddy. Best of all, from what we learned, the summers are warm, with cool nights, but the sun won't burn the hide off a fellah."

That sounded good. But now, as Morgan and Angeline were looking back at the desert where they had lived for three years, Morgan was trying to decide how he felt about the place. For a time, after the December meetings, the discussion—even arguments— had been about when to begin the exodus.

Then the decision had been taken away from them.

A Lincoln County sheriff had shown up in the valley and had met with leaders, demanding that back taxes be paid before March 1. If the people failed to pay, the state government would begin to seize property: animals, wagons, tools. Once the sheriff was gone, Bishop Morrison talked things over with the settlers in each town, and the only path forward was obvious to everyone. All who were leaving—and that turned out to be everyone but the Bonellis— would leave in February, before the sheriff's deadline. If Nevada officials wanted to come after them in Utah Territory, they could try, but it seemed unlikely that they would bother to do that.

The bishop called men to herd most of the cattle out of the valley first, and then wagon trains began to move out early in the month. Now, on February 18, the St. Thomas citizens were the last to leave. Some of them had been in the valley for six years, and Morgan heard in their voices, saw in their faces, that they were resolute in their decision. They clearly knew that it was best to leave, but, at the same time, they were a little sad to give up all they had worked so hard to establish: their houses and sheds, corrals and plowed fields. They were tired, but worse, their exhaustion and suffering seemed buried in the desert sand, there to stay forever. Brother Rintlesbacher, a man who had come to the valley with his fiddle and a good deal of hope, had told Morgan, "I'm wore out, Brother Davis. Bone tired. And what do I have to show for it? I come down here with a good wagon and some young mules, and after three years the wagon is so rickety it won't carry much of a load, and my mules is so used up, they can't pull much weight anyway. I'm leavin' with less than I come with, and, if you want to know the truth, I feel old. It may have been three years, but I feel like I aged twenty."

Morgan knew the feeling.

And now Morgan was watching a waning plume of smoke, the last of a fire from one of the St. Thomas houses. Joseph Young had asked the people not to burn their property, to leave their houses for anyone who wanted them, but the Murdock boy, Alva, had torched his own house. Morgan had asked him why, and he had said, "I want to go someplace where there are schools, and where Mother won't have to work so hard. We're never coming back here!" What Morgan knew was that Alva's mother was a polygamous wife—one wife of four—and there was no question that she had worked harder than a woman with a full-time husband would have done.

But even the boy had sounded sad more than bitter. He had given up a large share of his life for this place, and his family had nothing to show for it, the same as the rest. There had been short-term attempts to give the children a little schooling, but all the moving and rebuilding had worked against a consistent schedule. Children had also worked hard alongside their parents, and they had gotten by far too long in clothing so shabby that they looked like waifs: sunburned, chapped, unkempt. But Morgan admired the children—and their parents—for their resilience and their hopeful attitudes, in spite of everything they had been through.

Angeline took hold of Morgan's arm. "What's on your mind?" she asked.

"I'm just thinking back on our time here," Morgan said. "I feel like a dog running off with his tail between his legs. We took on this valley, and it whupped us, and you know me—I never have liked to quit anything I set out to do."

"But once they slapped those taxes on us—"

"Is that really why we left?"

"It's the reason Brigham gave," Angeline said.

"I know. But after he came down here and saw what this area

was really like, I think he offered us an excuse we could grab onto. It gave us an honorable way to end our mission."

"Sister Cullimore told me that Brigham saw how ragged our children looked, and he got tears in his eyes. I think maybe he was sorry he ever sent us here."

"I understand that. But what I'm wondering is whether it was worth it for you and me."

"And Ruth?"

"We didn't come here with Ruth. She was part of what happened to us. What I remember is the two of us heading down here. I wasn't excited about farming in a desert, but I was floating in air, just thinking about life with you."

"And you're not anymore?"

Morgan laughed softly. "I didn't mean it that way."

Angeline turned him toward her. "We were newlyweds, Morgan. Of course we were excited. Those days and nights in the wagon were the happiest of my life. But no marriage can stay like that forever."

"Maybe not. But didn't you feel like it could?"

"Of course I did. That's part of being young, just starting out."

Morgan knew it was not like him to seek consolation this way, but he needed these few minutes to indulge himself a little. "It was just the two of us then," he said, "and we promised each other that was how it would always be."

"Are you sorry that we took Ruth into our family?"

Morgan smiled. "Is that what we did?"

"Yes. I told you I thought she should join us. You didn't just go off on your own and marry her."

Morgan knew Ruth wasn't very far away, back at their wagon with Jefferson and both the babies. She may well walk over at any time. Still, he said what he really felt. "I guess, if I had it to do over again, I would keep that promise to you. I would tell Bishop Morrison that some other man would have to marry Ruth."

"Why? It's turned out all right, hasn't it?"

"Yes. It's much better than I thought it would be. But it will never seem normal to me. I feel like I have to swim a wide river just to get near you once in a while."

"I know." And now it was Angeline who seemed to need time to consider. They stood, arms linked, and neither spoke for a minute or so. But then she said, "Maybe we would be more like newlyweds now if we hadn't taken Ruth in. I wonder about that all the time. It's the hardest thing I've done in my life, Morgan."

"I know."

"Maybe you feel pushed away, but just think how much I lost."

"All that is part of what we gave up, in my mind," Morgan said. "We came down here as two young people, found each other in that wagon, and then faced a reality so harsh that it broke us at times. I never thought I would speak ill of the prophet, but I've done it at times, and I never thought I'd question all the things I've been taught all my life, but I've done that, too. And one thing I've questioned as much as anything is the very idea of plural marriage. If it comes from God, it's like Abraham's requirement to sacrifice Isaac. But God rescinded that requirement, and we have to live with ours forever."

"But you love Ruth. And so do I."

Morgan had actually never said that to Angeline. He had told Ruth that he loved Angeline and always would, but he had never wanted to hurt Angie by admitting his love for a second wife. "We love people we know well, Angeline. People we care about. Ruth is good, really good, and she loves me. She asks for very little, and she gives all her effort to us and the children. But it's bad to switch back and forth and try to equalize what I feel toward the two of you. It's just more than I know how to do."

"And every time you go back to her bedroom, I cry myself to sleep that first night. But I have to say, Morgan, there have been times when I don't know how I could've survived without Ruth. You're gone all day every day, and she carries half my load—usually more than half. She loves me and believes in me. She brings the best out of me. And you may not understand this, but she's given me Jeffy and Ella to love as much as Morgy."

"I understand all that. But you will have more children, and when I think of the two of us, with children, that just seems so much simpler."

"I feel that way too. But we do have Ruth, and we have her children. We can't ever let them feel that we don't want them."

"I know. That's exactly right. We'll make the best of our lives, all of us together. Just don't hold me away."

"I'll try not to." Morgan glanced to see that tears were now running down her cheeks. "I love you so much, Morgan. And I think maybe this time has been good for us. We're stronger than we were."

"It's what I keep telling myself, but I still long to have life on our own terms."

• • •

Ruth was at the wagon. She had finished nursing Ella, and she wanted to go have a look off the mesa, the same as Morgan and Angeline. But she saw how busily they were conversing, and she knew they needed some time alone. All too often, the three of them were together, along with Jefferson and the babies.

What Ruth understood, and would always know, was that she

had come between them. She loved them both, and she appreciated their goodness to her, but she saw their sacrifice every day. She
still felt disappointment that her life had worked out the way it
had, that she had been forced to look to another woman's husband
as her provider and protector. Morgan was the best man she had
known in her life, but she always knew that however kind he was
toward her, he could never feel as much love for her as he did for
his "real" wife.

What she also knew was that there was nothing she could do
about the situation, and nothing that she actually wanted to do.
She was blessed to be with Morgan and Angeline; she doubted that
any other couple would have accepted her with such good will. It
was wrong for her to complain, even to herself.

She finally did get down from the wagon and walk to the edge
of the mesa with Ella in her arms and Jefferson walking at her side.
Morgy was asleep in the wagon, and she felt all right about leaving
him there, not far off, for a few minutes.

Ruth walked to some women she knew, not to Morgan and
Angeline, and she listened to the sisters talk about the trials they
had faced during their time on the Muddy. They complained
about the heat and the flies and the illnesses; the adobe shacks
they had lived in; the scorpions and snakes and tarantulas; the
sandstorms and dirty water to drink. They said they were glad to
leave and would never miss this place. Still, she heard solemnity in
the tone of their voices, and she understood. It did seem a somber
day.

Sister Cullimore had been silent through all the talk—unusual
for her—but then she said, "It seems hard that God would ask so
much of us and then send us on to start again, worse off than when
we came."

Ruth didn't say it, but she thought to herself that she was better off. She had lost a husband who had turned out to be a disappointment, and she had gained a husband who was a much better man. She also had a lovely new daughter. And she had learned more about love and work and faith than she had a right to hope for. She had almost nothing to take with her from this valley, but she had some things she could carry along with her into the next life.

"I will say this," Sister Cullimore continued. "I doubt I'll ever feel deprived again in my life. We done without here—done without almost everything. If Long Valley offers *anything* more, I'll feel rich."

Everyone agreed with that.

• • •

When Angeline heard a horse approaching, she turned to see who the rider was. It was Bishop Morrison. "Morgan," he said, "I need to talk to you."

"You two talk," Angeline said. "I want to see how Ruth and the children are doing."

Angeline had noticed Ruth and some of the sisters gathered in a little pack, gazing down on the valley. As she approached them, she said, "Anyone thinking about going back?"

"Laws, no," Sister Cullimore said.

And Lizzie Bachelor laughed as she said, "I was just feeling sorry for all the mosquitos that will be comin' out this spring. They'll be looking for me, since they like to suck on me so much, and I fear they'll die of thirst."

"Maybe we've done the wrong thing, then," Angeline said. "Mosquitos and flies and grasshoppers have to live too, you know."

"I'm not so sure about that," Lizzie said. "When God was

creatin' 'all creeping things,' I think He got carried away. We could get by without so many bugs."

"Life is supposed to test us," Angeline said. "Maybe the test wouldn't be great enough without mosquitos and rattlesnakes."

"Maybe not. But I think I've had my fill of the bad stuff for a while. It's about time the Lord let me experience a decent house, cool nights for sleeping, and maybe even one new dress before I die."

• • •

Bishop Morrison swung down off his horse. "Morgan," he said, "we need to move on as soon as our animals have rested just a little more. No one knows better than you do how to get these wagons down that steep grade on the other side of the mesa. So I want you to lead out in that operation."

"Well, I do have a pretty good idea about doing that. But it shouldn't be too bad if we all work together."

"Some of our people are scared to death of that downhill road. I've had three or four of the men tell me this mornin' that they want you up front, showing them how to get them off this mountain."

"Well, sure," Morgan said. "I can do that."

"All right. Do you want to take my horse, or—"

"No. I'd rather be on foot. We'll just take one wagon down at a time, and I'll show the men how to block wheels and use the chains."

Bishop Morrison nodded, then slapped Morgan on the shoulder. "I'm the one called to lead these people, but if a man wants to build a house, grub sagebrush, sharpen a plow—or get off this mesa—he doesn't turn to me. He turns to you."

"Well, I'd rather grub sagebrush than give a sermon any day. You do better at that than I ever could."

"Oh, you'll give sermons, Brother Davis. You've shown us many times that you do think about spiritual matters as much as practical ones. That's why people listen to you when you speak your mind."

But Morgan knew his own heart, knew the things he had thought and even expressed at times. "You're building me up way too much," he said. "I don't have the faith I ought to have. You know what we've talked about before. And you know how angry I was when you and Erastus Snow told us to farm that sand bench."

"But you did it," the bishop said. "And you gave it your full effort."

"Yes, I did. But you told me yourself, you agree with me now—it was a bad decision."

"I know what you're sayin'. But let me tell you how I see it." He waited until Morgan looked back at him, straight on. "You learned more from workin' with your brothers and sisters than you would have learned from stayin' at West Point. That's what you can take with you as we leave—and even into the next life: the man you're becoming."

"Bishop, I'm sorry, but that's a little hard for me to swallow. I know what we've talked about before, but I still say, a man has to use his own good sense."

The bishop smiled. He took hold of the lapels of his waistcoat, reaching under his long beard, and he stood with his feet rather far apart. He looked steady and sure of himself. "Morgan, we've gone around this whole circle of talk a few times afore. But I don't think you've ever caught on to what I've tried to tell you."

"You keep telling me to give up my will, to let God take over my life. And I guess that's right. I also understand what Joseph

Young told us about following our leaders. But it's one thing to listen to the Lord, and it's another to listen to someone who says that an angel is sitting on his shoulder, telling *him* what *I* ought to be doing. The way I look at it, I can pray too. I can get my own answers."

The bishop was nodding now, still smiling. "That's right. Exactly right," he said. "But there's more to it than that. Zion keeps goin' right on into the next life. If we give up this thing we call *self* and pitch in with the Lord—and with our brothers and sisters— we stop worryin' so much about things that don't matter. Brigham thought this valley might be a good place to grow cotton, and he was right. Still, things didn't work out. But that doesn't mean that God had nothin' to do with the decision. He sent us to this earth to do hard things and come back to Him humbled—and stronger. So how can you say that it wasn't worth comin' here?"

"Yes, I understand that. I know I learned from being here. But—"

"But you want to make your own mistakes—not live the ones other people make."

Morgan smiled and nodded. "I guess I do."

"Son, let go. Stop fightin' everythin'. Trust. Let the Lord lead you to the experiences you need to have."

Morgan took a deep breath. He wanted to trust. He wanted to give up his pridefulness. He wanted to accept the Lord's grand scheme for His children. His problem was how to explain all this to himself. When he tried, he could only think of digging out that canal, over and over.

"Do you know about the flood, Morgan?" the bishop asked.

"What flood?"

"In West Point."

"Yes, I do. Last fall."

"Maybe Brigham knew something," the bishop pointed out.

"I know. I've thought about that. Maybe it wasn't Indians we needed to worry about. Maybe President Young just knew something would happen there."

"Maybe so. And I'm glad to hear you say that. It shows me you're trying to trust."

Morgan wasn't sure about that. He couldn't really say that Bishop Morrison's arguments made sense to him—entirely—and yet he knew he felt better when he stopped fighting everything the man said. He liked the bishop. And he felt his goodness and faith, which he liked better than his own anger and contentiousness.

"Morgan, much is goin' to be asked of you in the days ahead. The Lord knows yer heart, and He knows that no matter how much you resist, you hear His voice, and when it comes right down to it, you do obey."

Morgan knew that obedience didn't stop the battles he fought with himself. Still, he felt an affirmation, a sense of peace, as he tried to accept Bishop Morrison's words.

"Well," the bishop said, "let's get set up to lead these people off this mountain, and then let's go see if we can't come a little closer to makin' oursel's a real Zion this next time."

"All right." Morgan looked into Bishop Morrison's good eyes. "I'll do all I can to make it happen. I do feel happier when I forget my own concerns and just concentrate on what I can do to build Zion."

"That's right. That's what counts for all of us."

• • •

Angeline was thinking about the way her life was going to change now. There would be so much to do—a new house to build, new land to open, a new town to establish. James and Lydia Wilcox had decided to return to Salt Lake City, mostly because Lydia's mother wasn't well. Angeline understood that, but she already felt the loss of a good friend. Their other close friends—even Eb and Mary Ann—were going on to Long Valley, at least for now. But life was changing for all of them. Lyman and Alice Hunt had a new baby girl, and Susan Brooks was expecting again. Each couple was looking more to their own family concerns and found less time for socializing. What was becoming obvious was that each part of life, each era, would change her, make her a new person. Something in her resisted that idea, made her feel nostalgic for the girl she had been, but she also knew there was nothing she could do about such things. It was the nature of life.

What had changed Angeline more than anything was knowing that she could bear a child. She hoped that many more would come. Now, as she thought of Morgy, it occurred to her that she wanted to be with him when he woke up. So she walked to the wagon and looked in. Morgy was still asleep, with a quilt tucked around him. He looked lovely, as he always did when he slept. But then she saw something—or heard something—that she didn't like. His breathing seemed heavy, and his face was flushed. She instantly picked him up and felt his head. He was hot. He had a fever.

• • •

Morgan walked to the wagon, but by then Angeline was already coming toward him, carrying Morgy. He saw in her face that something was wrong. "He has a fever," she said. "He's limp as a rag. I don't know what's wrong with him."

"It's not the ague. It wouldn't start this time of year. He's probably just caught cold."

"He's not coughing. But he's breathing hard, like maybe he's sick in his lungs. Have you seen Sister Ballif?"

"No, but I'll find her," Morgan said. "Cool him off, if you can. Use the water in our barrel and just wash it over him."

"I know. I can do that. But find Sister Ballif."

"All right. But don't worry too much. Every child gets sick now and then." But he knew what Angie was thinking, knew how deep her fears ran. He trotted away, and when he found Sister Ballif, he hurried her over to his wagon.

Sister Ballif took little Morgy in her arms, felt his head. He was nine months old now, and he was usually lively, up and looking about, but he looked half asleep now, not really aware of what was going on around him.

Morgan stood behind the wagon as the two women leaned in and continued to wash Morgy, talking to him. "Babies get fevers like this—and they come on fast," Sister Ballif said. "But they usually get better fast, too." She looked back at Morgan. "My husband says that you're going to help take the wagons off the mesa. You go do that, and we'll be fine here. I don't think Morgy is all that sick."

Morgan looked at Angeline. "Yes, you go ahead," she said. "Sister Ballif knows what to do."

Morgan wasn't sure he wanted to leave; he was more worried about Angeline than Morgy. Still, she had put her trust in Sister Ballif, so he accepted the advice and walked across the mesa and over to the spot where wagons were already lining up.

Before long he was thinking almost entirely about the task ahead. He helped some men set the chains, and then he lined up a crew of workers to be ready to block the wheels of the wagons when needed. Most of the men had made the ascent here before, but this descent was something new for them.

The work was engaging, and slow, and the day stretched on as men lowered one wagon after another over the steep cliff at the top of the mesa and then used chains to slowly let them down the upper, steep part of the hill. Late in the afternoon, there were only two wagons left to take down—three, counting Morgan's own. Eb Crawford had been helping him direct the operation. He would take his family—Mary Ann, Eliza, and their new little boy, Alvin—down the hill second to last. Morgan was calling out directions to the men chaining the wagons when he heard Eb behind him, his voice full of alarm. "Morgan, your wife just sent word, you have to get back to your wagon, *right now.*"

"What's happened?"

"I don't know. But hurry back. I'll take over for you here."

Morgan was already running. He could tell that Eb knew something he wasn't saying. And Morgan didn't know what he would do if Morgy . . . but he didn't say the words to himself. He merely ran harder, until his chest was pulsing with pain. His legs gradually slowed even though he didn't let up, and the distance seemed twice as long as it had been when he had walked over.

When he approached the wagon, he could see Angeline holding the baby, looking wild, her hair loose and blowing in the wind, and her face blotched red. "Morgan, you have to do something," she was screaming. "He's *dying.*"

Morgan was still drawing in air, his chest pounding. He took Morgy from her arms, looked into his face, and felt his arms. The boy's skin was white, his lips blue, his breathing seemingly stopped. Morgan could only think that the boy was already dead. "How long has he been like this?"

"I don't know. Maybe . . ."

Morgan was still breathing hard from his run. He wanted to do something, but his head was full of confusion. Nothing seemed possible now.

"He's been getting worse," Sister Ballif said. "His breathing got very bad—and then, just before you got here, it stopped."

Morgan felt helpless. Why were the women looking at him?

"Bring him back," Angeline said. "Morgan, please, bring him back."

She was asking him to bless the baby. He understood that. But something else was filling Morgan's head—a powerful impression. He didn't decide. He simply did it. He pushed his mouth against the baby's open mouth and blew breath into his lungs.

"Stop that!" Sister Ballif shouted. "You'll choke him."

But Morgan breathed into Morgy's mouth again. This time, he thought maybe he felt a change in his little body. And then, without knowing he was going to do it, he held Morgy up, raised him toward the Lord, and shouted, "In the name of Jesus Christ, I command you, Morgan Davis Junior, to come back to us. *Now.*"

But nothing happened. Morgan waited and wondered. He lowered Morgy to his chest, held him against his heart. He tried to tell himself that he would have to accept this. He would have to trust. He whispered, "Oh, Lord, let him live," but he knew he was powerless to change anything. He looked at Angeline, whose eyes were crazy with fear and, already, with grief.

A few seconds passed, and Morgan accepted that one more test had just begun for him and for Angie. It seemed more than they could live through. But they would have to live through it. So he said the words in his head—the words he knew he would have to tell Angeline he had said: "Thy will be done."

Morgy gasped.

Morgan heard a gurgle in the little one's throat, and then the baby coughed, sputtered, and began to cry.

Angeline grabbed him, turned him over, and thumped his back. Morgy expelled some phlegm, coughed again, then cried again. "You're all right, Morgy," Angeline told him. "You're all right." She was crying now, but she whispered between sobs, "Thank you." She was looking at Morgan.

"I didn't do it," Morgan said, and then he gave his own thanks. "Thank you, Lord, thank you."

Angeline held Morgy close, and Sister Ballif put her hand on his head and then touched his face. "I don't feel the fever now," she said.

Angeline kept saying, "Thank you, thank you."

Morgan finally broke down. He dropped to his knees on the ground. He was still breathing hard, but he was also crying. It had all happened so fast, he was still trying to comprehend what was going on inside him.

Sister Ballif took the baby, and she and Angeline walked to the back of the wagon. Morgan didn't know what they were doing, but he needed this time to think. He needed to sort out what he was feeling. He had the impression that he was changed, that he knew something, but he had no words to describe what it was.

He got up. People had begun to gather, and he didn't want them to see him that way—on his knees, crying. But he also didn't want to talk to anyone. He was still trying to find words that explained what had just happened. So he got up and walked away from everyone, stood and looked at the horizon, at the red sun that was penetrating a bank of clouds, turning the whole earth shades of orange. And after a time he found some words—just not all that he was looking for.

He walked back to his wagon and pulled Angeline by the arm, taking her away from the baby and Sister Ballif and all the others.

"This was real," Morgan told her.

"What?"

"What happened was real."

Angeline shrugged, still not understanding. She was disheveled, her face still red, but Morgan saw the relief she was experiencing. He could see that she was changed too.

"I worry too much about things that don't matter," Morgan said.

"I know that. It's what I was just thinking. We both do."

"We talk like truth floats somewhere in the air, and we can never quite grab hold of it. But this was real."

She nodded, and tears filled her eyes again. He could see that she understood.

"I accepted, and the Lord knew I did," Morgan said.

"Yes. I saw that."

They went back to Morgy. Sister Ballif was holding him, stroking his head. He was sleeping, his breath easy now. Morgan took him and touched his cheek to Morgy's. Then he held out one arm and pulled Angeline to him, with Morgy in the middle.

"I love you, Angie," Morgan said.

"I love you too."

And then Morgan felt an arm around his back. Ruth had come to them, embracing Morgan but also Angeline. "I was so scared," she said. "I thought he was gone."

Morgan hadn't known that Ruth had been there, that she had seen all this. But now he was glad she was with them. "I love you, Ruth," Morgan said. "I love both of you. We're going to be all right."

AUTHOR'S NOTE

Muddy is historical fiction. The general events I describe did happen, but most of the characters in the novel are fictional. There was no Davis family among the missionaries called to the Muddy River Mission. I sometimes use names that are common among members of The Church of Jesus Christ of Latter-day Saints in order to add a note of authenticity, but readers should not, on the basis of the names, assume a connection to actual people.

Some names—Brigham Young, Erastus Snow, Joseph Young, Anson Call, Warren Foote, Jacob Hamblin, George A. Smith, and Bathsheba Smith—are obviously names of actual leaders during the time. When these characters speak, I am careful to find a source that verifies that they actually held the opinions they express. I create dialogue for them, but I try not to misrepresent their thinking. I also use accurate descriptions of their appearances, and I try to offer a sense of each person's personality and style of speaking.

I do write about some of the actual Muddy River missionaries, especially local leaders, but when I could not find adequate information about them, I chose to fictionalize their names and imagine their characteristics. I didn't want their relatives to write to me and say, "That's not at all what my great-grandfather was like." Simply recognize that I used certain characters to play known roles, such as the bishops, but the characters in the novel may differ considerably from the historical individuals.

I have not used footnotes, but for those who would like to read more about the early settlement of Moapa Valley in southern Nevada, let me mention some of the sources I used.

An important document was the *Autobiography and Journal of Warren Foote, 1817–1903*. It provided me with details of history as well as a sense of the challenges in settling such a formidable desert. A typescript is available at the Harold B. Lee Library at Brigham Young University, or in the archives of the Church History Library operated by The Church of Jesus Christ of Latter-day Saints. The text can also be accessed electronically on the internet.

Two useful books are *Zion on the Muddy: The Story of the Saints of the Moapa (Logandale Nevada) Stake,* written and compiled by G. Lynn Bowler, Logandale Nevada Stake Historian (Springville, Utah: Art City Publishing, 2004); and *100 Years on The Muddy,* compiled by Arabell Lee Hafner (Springville, Utah: Art City Publishing, 1967).

Many articles have appeared in newspapers, magazines, and journals, but the most thorough and informative I found was: "New St. Joseph, Nevada: The Muddy Mission Experience Revisited," by Carolyn Grattan-Ariello, published by the *Nevada Historical Society Quarterly* (Spring 1986), 31–52.

A helpful unpublished thesis is: *A Matter of Faith: A Study of the Muddy River Mission,* by Monique Elaine Kimball (University of Nevada, Las Vegas, 1988). This work can also be accessed online.

Some biographies relate the Muddy River experience through the perceptions of individual participants. The best of these is the chapter on that period in *Samuel Claridge, Pioneering the Outposts of Zion* by S. George Ellsworth (Logan, Utah: Howe Brothers, 1987), 83–112.

AUTHOR'S NOTE

One last suggestion: Anyone who wants to experience the personality and ideas (and speculations) of Brigham Young should study his sermons in the *Journal of Discourses*. At the beginning of this book, in my "Note to the Reader," I suggested that comprehending the people of another century is like entering a time machine. As you step into another time, expect surprising differences. Reading Brother Brigham's conference talks is educational, spiritual, shocking at times, and, above all, grandly entertaining.

The full story of the Muddy River missionaries does not end with their exodus. Most of those who departed in 1871 continued on to Long Valley, and eventually they were the nucleus of the group that settled Orderville and established the United Order there. A sequel to *Muddy* will follow, and will be titled *River*. So don't say good-bye to these characters quite yet. There's more to the story.